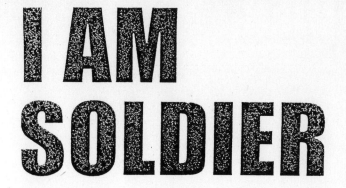

I AM SOLDIER

WAR STORIES FROM THE
ANCIENT WORLD TO THE 20TH CENTURY

OSPREY
PUBLISHING

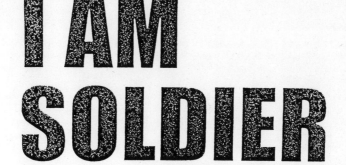

I AM SOLDIER

WAR STORIES FROM THE
ANCIENT WORLD TO THE 20TH CENTURY

EDITOR
PROFESSOR ROBERT O'NEILL

INTRODUCTION BY
RICHARD HOLMES

First published in Great Britain in 2009 by Osprey Publishing, Midland House, West Way, Botley, Oxford OX2 0PH, United Kingdom

443 Park Avenue South, New York, NY 10016, USA.

Email: info@ospreypublishing.com

A CIP catalogue record for this book is available from the British Library.

ISBN: 978 1 84603 515 9

Previously published in the Essential Histories series, Osprey Publishing Ltd:

David Nicolle, ESS 1, *The Crusades*; John Sweetman, ESS 2, *Crimean War 1854–56*; Robert K. Krick, ESS 5, *American Civil War (3)*; Daniel Marston, ESS 6, *Seven Years' War 1756–1763*; Gregory Fremont-Barnes, ESS 7, *The French Revolutionary Wars 1792–1802*; Carter Malkasian, ESS 8, *The Korean War 1950–53*; Todd Fisher, ESS 9, *The Napoleonic Wars (2)*; Stephen D. Engle, ESS 10, *The American Civil War (2)*; Matthew Bennett, ESS 12: *Campaigns of the Norman Conquest*; Geoffrey Jukes, ESS 13, *The First World War (1): The Eastern Front*; Duncan Anderson, ESS 15, *The Falklands War 1982*; Gregory Fremont-Barnes, ESS 17, *The Napoleonic Wars (3)*; David Horner, ESS 18, *The Second World War (1): Pacific*; Anne Curry, ESS 19, *Hundred Years' War 1337–1453*; Efraim Karsh, ESS 20, *The Iran-Iraq War 1980–1988*; Michael Whitby, ESS 21, *Rome at War AD 293–696*; Peter Simkins, ESS 22, *The First World War (3): The Western Front*; Michael Hickey, ESS 23, *The First World War (4): The Mediterranean Front*; Geoffrey Jukes, ESS 24, *The Second World War (5): Eastern Front*; Douglas V. Meed, ESS 25, *The Mexican War 1846–1848*; Waldemar Heckel, ESS 26, *The Wars of Alexander the Great: 336–323 BC*; Richard Bonney, ESS 29, *The Thirty Years' War 1618–1648*; Russell & Stephen Hart, ESS 32, *The Second World War (6): Northwest Europe*; John Haldon, ESS 33, *Byzantium at War AD 600–1453*; John A. Lynn, ESS 34, *The French Wars 1667–1714*; Robin Havers, ESS 35, *The Second World War (2): Europe*; Philip de Souza, ESS 36, *The Greek and the Persian Wars 499–386 BC*; Frances Lannon, ESS 37, *The Spanish Civil War 1936–1939*; Andrew Wiest, ESS 38, *The Vietnam War 1956–1975*; Gregory Fremont-Barnes, ESS 39, *The Napoleonic Wars (4)*; Carl Benn, ESS 41, *The War of 1812*; Kate Gilliver, ESS 43, *Caeser's Gallic Wars 58–50 BC*; Daniel Marston, ESS 44, *The French-Indian War 1754–1760*; Daniel Marston, ESS 45, *The American Revolution 1774–1783*; Stephen Turnbull, ESS 46, *War in Japan 1467–1615*; Robert J. Knecht, ESS 47, *The French Religious Wars 1562–1598*; Paul Collier, ESS 48, *The Second World War (4): Mediterranean*; Alan C. Huffines, ESS 50, *The Texas War of Independence 1835–1836*; Stephen Badsey, ESS 51, *The Franco-Prussian War 1870–1871*; Gregory Fremont-Barnes, ESS 52, *The Boer War 1899–1902*; Michael Hicks, ESS 54, *The Wars of the Roses 1455–1485*; Alastair Finlan, ESS 55, *The Gulf War 1991*, this extract by permission of Kent State Univ. Press; Ian Knight, ESS 56, *The Zulu War 1879*; Stephen Turnbull, ESS 57, *Genghis Khan and the Mongol Conquests 1190–1400*; Peter Gaunt, ESS 58, *The English Civil Wars 1642–1651*; Charles M. Robinson III, ESS 59, *The Plains Wars 1757–1900*; Stephen Tunbull, ESS 62, *The Ottoman Empire 1326–1699*; Alastair Finlan, ESS 63, *The Collapse of Yugoslavia 1991–1999*; Peter Cottrell, ESS 65, *The Anglo-Irish War 1913–1922*; Gregory Fremont-Barnes, ESS 66, *The Wars of the Barbary Pirates*; Brad E Kelle, ESS 67, *Ancient Israel at War 853–586 BC*; Gregory Fremont-Barnes, ESS 68, *The Indian Mutiny 1857–1858*; Peter Cottrell, ESS 70, *Irish Civil War 1922–23*.

The book and author are listed under each chapter heading.

Page layout by Myriam Bell
Index by Alan Thatcher
Typeset in Bembo and Quay Sans ITC
Originated by PPS Grasmere, Leeds, UK
Printed in China through Worldprint Ltd

09 10 11 12 13   10 9 8 7 6 5 4 3 2 1

For a catalogue of all books published by Osprey please contact

NORTH AMERICA

Osprey Direct, c/o Random House Distribution Center 400 Hahn Road Westminster MD 21157 USA

E-mail: uscustomerservice@ospreypublishing.com

ALL OTHER REGIONS

Osprey Direct, The Book Service Ltd, Distribution Centre, Colchester Road Frating Green, Colchester, Essex, CO7 7DW

E-mail: customerservice@ospreypublishing.com

www.ospreypublishing.com

Front Cover: Marines engaged in street fighting during the battle for Seoul during the Korean War. American incendiary bombs, artillery shells and tanks reduced the city to rubble. (US Army)

CONTENTS

INTRODUCTION

'Every man thinks meanly of himself for not having been a soldier,' said the lexicographer Dr Samuel Johnson to his biographer James Boswell. Across the two millennia covered by this book all sorts and conditions of men have found themselves in uniform. Some, like the Spartan Aristodemos, killed fighting the Persians at Plataea in 479 BC, had been brought up in a society that valued military virtues and expected its young men to demonstrate them. Indeed, the 17th-century Japanese warrior Kato Kiyomasa opined that 'a samurai who practices dancing … should be ordered to commit hara kiri.' Others, like Sergeant Charles Windolph of the US 7th Cavalry, who fought at the battle of Little Bighorn, became a successful soldier in one army only after dodging conscription into another. The military career of the Serb Konstantin Mihailovic was even more unpredictable: captured by the Turks, he fought for them as a janissary, but at last gratefully returned to his own people.

Young men often found war appealing for all the wrong reasons. 'It was like a game for us,' thought an Iranian child soldier of the 1980s, 'I was a little boy who wanted to play with guns.' Edward Costello joined the British 95th Rifles because he 'was highly delighted with the smart appearance of the men, and with their green uniform.' Many of history's soldiers were not ashamed to do battle for money. Sydnam Poyntz, who fought in both the Thirty Years' War and the English Civil War, changed sides when it suited him. He reported ruefully that he 'sent home often tymes Mony to my Wife, who it seems spent at home what I got abroad.' In contrast, there were soldiers who fought for firmly held convictions. Nehemiah Wharton, London apprentice turned Parliamentarian sergeant, had strong Puritan beliefs, which encouraged him and his comrades to plunder houses they thought owned by 'Papists' and to 'purify' parish churches by smashing stained glass windows and burning altar rails.

Whatever a man's reasons for enlisting, his first experience of battle often came as a shock. US Lieutenant Alex Vernon, preparing for action in the Gulf, admitted: 'I cannot handle this. I am not cut out for it. All I want to do is cry.' However, once the action had started he coped well. Faced with an Iraqi bunker that was too close for his tank's main armament and too well-protected for its machine gun, he told his driver: '"Hit the bunker, Reynolds. Crush it." We barely noticed the bump.' Deneys Reitz, a Boer commando in South Africa, was struck by the emptiness of his first battlefield, and then horrified by the 'ashen faces and staring eyeballs' of the first dead he saw. This 'came as a great shock, for I had pictured the dignity of death in battle, but I now saw that it was horrible to look upon.'

Most soldiers found that the strain of prolonged action eventually wore them down. In March 1918, with the British Army reeling under the impact of the German spring offensive, Private 'Fen' Noakes experienced the fatalism of sheer exhaustion.

'I ran for some distance with the rest,' he admitted, 'and then, with a feeling of disgust for the whole job, I slowed down to a walk. I really didn't care which way things went.' 'The losses get to you sooner or later,' wrote John Young, an American Squad Leader in Vietnam. 'Sooner or later you realise that the only objective is simple survival. War burns away the veneer of what we call civilisation, and shows you that the last 10,000 years have not made much difference in what we are.'

However, in war, there were those who thrived. Tom Derrick, an Australian infantry officer who won the Victoria Cross in 1943, was a natural fighter, both on the battlefield and off it. Faced with a strong Japanese position, he told his company commander, who wanted to refer the problem to the commanding officer: 'Bugger the CO. Just give me twenty minutes and we'll have the place.' Later, hit by a burst of machine-gun fire, he faced death with equanimity: 'I've been hit. I think it's curtains. I've copped it in the fruit and nuts [guts].' He insisted that other wounded should be evacuated first, and died the next day.

Sometimes soldiers hated their enemy. Blaise de Monluc, who fought in the French Wars of Religion, boasted that his path could be charted by bodies hanging from trees. His contemporary François de La Noue, abhorred war, suggesting that chivalrous acts should be remembered because 'those who follow the profession of arms may learn to imitate them and avoid the cruelties and base acts which many of them perpetrate because they do not know or do not wish to know how to curb their hatred.' Sauk war chief Black Hawk 'had a good opinion' of a brave and skilled opponent, and declared that 'it would give me pleasure to shake him by the hand.'

A Second World War Russian soldier admitted that he had doubted tales of German atrocities until he reached recaptured Russian territory and discovered that they were true. Later, 'some of us vented our hatred on German civilians, even on some who claimed to be Communists, in ways I shudder to think of.' Charles Upham, one of the only three men to win the Victoria Cross twice, acknowledged that hatred of Germany and her allies has played its part in his success: 'I hated Germans,' he said. Donald Burgett, serving in an American parachute infantry regiment during the Battle of the Bulge in the winter of 1944–45, saw his enemies as abstract objects: it was a case of kill or be killed. Yet when he encountered a badly wounded German who was immediately shot by another American, Burgett threatened to blow the man's brains out if he ever did such a thing again, and the German's imploring face frequently returned to haunt him.

There were moments of euphoria. Charles Windolph recalled that: 'You felt that you were somebody when you were on a good horse… You were part of a proud outfit that had a fighting reputation, and you were ready for a fight or a frolic.' Captain Cavalié Mercer, commanding a Royal Horse Artillery battery at Waterloo, described the sheer euphoria of driving off a French attack: 'Intoxicated with success, I was singing out, "Beautiful! – Beautiful."' Yet he was profoundly upset when one of his men was hit by a cannon ball. 'I shall never forget the scream the poor lad gave when struck... That scream went to my very soul. For I accused myself of having caused his misfortune.'

The threat of sudden death often proved less alarming than the prospect of painful wounds. Edward Costello was shot in the knee in 1810 and evacuated to a hospital in Portugal. 'The heat of the weather was intense and affected our wounds dreadfully,' he wrote. 'Doctors were scarce ... maggots were engendered in the sores, and the bandages, when withdrawn, brought away lumps of putrid flesh and maggots.' He eventually cured himself by 'syringing sweet oil into my wounds.' Just outside Bastogne in 1944 one of Donald Burgett's comrades was hit in the stomach. The paratroopers piled the protruding entrails on a tattered raincoat, washed them as best they could, and then bound the man's abdomen with strips of coat while they waited for him to be evacuated.

Happily not all soldiers' memories are of battle. Food looms large in their recollections, and there are striking similarities in the military diet across the ages. An 18th-century soldier of the British 68th Foot Regiment remembered good rations of bread, cheese, beef and pork, but far more common were things like the 'double baked hard-tack' which formed the staple of the Byzantine Army, the 'corn dodgers' – corn-meal cooked with water – of the American Civil War, the cabbage soup and buckwheat porridge of the Russian Army, and the 'stodgy, lumpy and tasteless' K-Rations of the US Army.

Soldiers could be extraordinarily sentimental. John Beatty, a Union infantry officer in the American Civil War, mused on how his thoughts tuned 'to the cottage home, to wife and children,' and he found comfort in 'those sweet old church songs, familiar from earliest childhood.' A First World War British soldier described the excellent food available in Egypt, but added: 'I would rather have come to dear old Blighty and as cold as it is to stand in the food queues all day just to get amongst a little bit of civilisation to hear the Old English language spoken once more.'

War affected its participants in a variety of ways. 'I returned from the war selfish,' thought Alex Vernon, 'the world had robbed me, and now it owed me.' Charles Upham went back to farming, and shunned fame's spotlight. 'I don't want to be treated differently from any other bastard,' he declared. Some veterans came to feel that they were closer to other soldiers – even the very men that they had fought against – than to civilians who had not shared the experience. Fen Noakes argued that should 'the fighting men ... of both sides come together there can be no doubt that complete unanimity would result.' Military service often combined the best of times and the worst of times, events which were painful to remember but were never quite forgettable, catalogued, in these pages, in words which demand our attention.

Richard Holmes, 2009

THE ANCIENT WORLD

He who loses his life falling in the front ranks,
brings glory to his father, his comrades and his city...
Never do the name and glory of his bravery die out,
but he is immortal even as he lies in his grave.

(Tyrtaios fragment 12)

PEKAH, SON OF REMALIAH

Ancient Israel at War 853–586 BC

Brad Kelle

Pekah, son of Remaliah, was arguably the most significant figure in Israel's history during the 8th century BC, and is known to us from both the Hebrew Bible/Old Testament and Assyrian inscriptions. He affected the reigns of five different Israelite kings, and dramatically altered the course of Israelite policy in relation to Aram-Damascus, Judah, and Assyria. Although all reconstructions of ancient persons remain tentative, it seems that during the course of his military career Pekah progressed from being a common soldier, to a rebel leader, to a royal officer, to the sole ruler of the northern kingdom of Israel. The Hebrew Bible/Old Testament records a few specific pieces of biographical information for him: firstly, before he became king he served as a military officer to the preceding king; secondly, he reigned for 20 years in Israel; thirdly, while he was king, he joined King Rezin of Damascus in an attack on Jerusalem. Pekah's life also provides a glimpse of the experiences of being a soldier in ancient Israel.

The significant part of Pekah's career began around 750 BC when Rezin, who had recently usurped the throne, launched his effort to throw off Assyrian control of the west, and to re-establish Aramean dominance in Syria-Palestine. Probably due to his desire to replace Assyrian control, Rezin immediately initiated hostilities against Israel, where the central administration in Samaria had been pro-Assyrian in its foreign policy since the time of Jehu (*c.* 841). While Rezin tried to gain control over the Israelite territories that most directly bordered his own, namely Gilead in the northern Transjordan and Galilee north of Samaria and west of the Jordan River, he was probably already working to form a coalition to oppose Assyrian dominance and to reassert the level of regional control that Damascus had possessed under Hazael in the 9th century.

Pekah was an Israelite soldier from Gilead, who evidently came to sympathize with the anti-Assyrian sentiments of his Aramean neighbour to the north. In this context, we can imagine what experiences he and his fellow soldiers underwent. As a 'regular' soldier in the standing army, Pekah may have been a member of a division of 50 or 100 infantrymen under the command of one ranking officer. At times joining with similar divisions and at times operating independently, Pekah's division was probably a mobile infantry group, not stationed in any one town but moving from camp to camp throughout the region, yet having strong ties to its men's ancestral home towns in the area. As an infantry group, its members almost certainly operated as foot soldiers, carrying a spear or javelin, personal shield, and perhaps a sword at their side. Standard dress was probably a short tunic and boots, while battle gear was likely to include scale armour, a breastplate, and perhaps a helmet. In a tumultuous border region like the Transjordan area of Gilead, a soldier like Pekah was probably involved in continual deployments and redeployments designed to counter Aramean moves into Israelite territory. At times, soldier divisions probably formed reaction forces and mobilized to besiege and retake towns that had fallen under Aramean occupation and plunder.

On other occasions, Pekah perhaps found himself temporarily garrisoned in a town in order to fortify it against Aramean advancement. It is not difficult to imagine that a border-region native like Pekah would have grown weary of the constant warfare within and destruction of his ancestral territory. To a soldier hailing from and serving in a territory so heavily influenced by the anti-Assyrian efforts of Damascus, the stubborn loyalty of the central Israelite government in Samaria to an Assyrian Empire without any strong presence in the region and the resulting hostilities with Aram-Damascus may have been difficult to support.

Perhaps for this reason, the presentations in later biblical and extra-biblical texts imply that when Rezin finally gained control of Gilead and Galilee, Pekah emerged from the Israelite ranks and was installed as ruler of these areas under Aramean oversight. Thus, Pekah emerged as a rival claimant to the throne in the Kingdom of Israel near the end of the reign of Jeroboam II, and both Assyrian and biblical texts present him as the primary ally of Rezin for the next two decades. He probably represented a significant faction of the Israelite population that saw the Damascus-led anti-Assyrian policy as the proper course for the kingdom at the time.

For the next 15 years after 750 BC, Pekah continued his presence as a rival ruler and fostered further division among the people of Israel over which foreign policy to follow. Because of this division within the kingdom, these years also saw a steady loss of territory and control by the central government in Samaria. Rezin and Pekah even jointly harassed Judah as early as the time of King Jotham (c. 750 BC): 'In those days, the Lord began to send King Rezin of Aram and Pekah son of Remaliah against Judah.' By the time of Jeroboam's successors, Menahem (746–37 BC) and his son Pekahiah (736–35 BC), the king who sat in Samaria probably had firm control of only the capital city and its immediate vicinity, with Pekah holding Galilee and Gilead.

We cannot be certain about what happened next, but when Pekahiah succeeded his father Menahem to the Israelite throne in 736 BC, Pekah's status may have changed. It was possibly at this point that King Pekahiah established Pekah as a shalish ('officer' or 'captain') within his military administration, which is how the Hebrew Bible/Old Testament remembers Pekah. This move would appear to have been an attempt to reunify the government and regain lost territory that was under Pekah's rule or influence.

At times, the rank of shalish designated a personal assistant to the king, but Pekah's experience as a 'captain' was more likely as a member of a group of commanding officers or elite warriors within the military organization.

However, given the long-standing history of Pekah's rebellious activity, it is likely that he served only as one member among Pekahiah's group of 'captains' rather than as a personal attendant of the king. A possible representation of Pekah in this capacity appears on an 8th-century seal found in the Samaria region. The seal, which was used to affix personal identifications to correspondence, bears the Hebrew name Pekah and pictures a striding figure with a wig, a short tunic, and a javelin in an upraised right hand. If the representation is Pekah, it shows him without a crown and is similar to the seals of other officers but not those of kings.

Pekah did not last in the role of Pekahiah's captain, however. Around 735 BC, when the Assyrians withdrew from the west after having conquered Hamath in northern Syria, and Rezin's coalition entered into open rebellion against Assyria, Pekah made his move on the throne in Samaria. As the Hebrew Bible/Old Testament indicates, sometime between September and November 734 BC, Pekah led a contingent of 50 men from Gilead into Samaria, assassinated Pekahiah in the palace citadel, and usurped control of the entire northern kingdom.

> Pekah son of Remaliah, his [Pekahiah's] captain, conspired against him with fifty of the Gileadites, and attacked him in Samaria, in the citadel of the palace along with Argob and Arieh; he killed him, and reigned in place of him.

His coup was both an internal palace revolt by a royal officer, and the product of rebel groups in particular areas that were sympathetic to Rezin's anti-Assyrian movement. For over a century, Pekah's royal predecessors in Samaria had successfully maintained at least powerful influence if not control over the southern kingdom. But, upon Pekah's usurpation the Judean king, Ahaz, asserted his independence. He refused to join the anti-Assyrian coalition, so Rezin and Pekah led a coalition force south from Samaria and laid siege to Jerusalem shortly after Pekah's coup: 'Then King Rezin of Aram and King Pekah son of Remaliah of Israel came up to wage war on Jerusalem; they besieged Ahaz but could not conquer him.' Seen more specifically from Pekah's perspective, this siege was not simply about establishing a unified front against Assyria, but was an attempt to resubjugate Judah and gain a level of authority equal to those who had gone before him. When Tiglath-pileser III led the Assyrian Army down the Mediterranean coast in late 734 BC, Pekah withdrew from Jerusalem, separated from Rezin, and retreated into his capital at Samaria. He would never again leave the city. As the Assyrians systematically subdued the members of the coalition and killed Rezin, a pro-Assyrian overthrow movement apparently formed within Israel. Prophets began to describe Pekah and his capital as a promiscuous woman and sickening wound and to declare that it was God's will to bring destruction upon them:

Plead with your mother [Samaria?], plead … that she put away her whoring from her face, and her adultery from between her breasts… When Ephraim saw his sickness, and Judah his wound, then Ephraim went to Assyria, and sent to the great king.

In this atmosphere, Tiglath-pileser did not need to attack Samaria. While Pekah remained barricaded in his capital, Tiglath-pileser designated Hoshea, a previously unknown figure who was perhaps the leader of the overthrow movement, as the new ruler of Israel, probably returning Judah to Israel's control, and departed the region in early summer 731 BC: '[They killed] Pekah, their king, and I installed Hoshea [as king] over them.'

Exactly when and how Pekah met his end is unknown. He was probably able to hold out in Samaria until around October or November 731 BC, but was eventually deposed and killed by Hoshea: 'Then Hoshea son of Elah made a conspiracy against Pekah son of Remaliah, attacked him, and killed him.' Pekah had succeeded, however, in introducing the sentiments of rebellion against, and freedom from, Assyria that would surface repeatedly throughout the reign of his assassin Hoshea and ultimately result in Israel's destruction by 720 BC.

ARISTODEMOS THE SPARTAN

The Greek and Persian Wars 499–386 BC

Philip de Souza

One of the many individuals whom we encounter in the course of Herodotus' *Histories* is the Spartan citizen Aristodemos, who died at the battle of Plataea. Aristodemos was born to a Spartan couple in one of the five villages that comprised the 'city' of Sparta, probably some time between 520 and 515 BC. He was named after the mythical father of the first two Spartan kings. A Spartan father did not automatically have the right to raise his own sons. As soon as they were born he was obliged to show them to a group of older citizens who would inspect the infant and decide whether he was physically normal and likely to be a healthy child. Any children who failed this inspection were placed in an isolated gorge and left to die. The boys who passed the inspection were deliberately toughened from an early age by bathing them in wine, feeding them with plain food and getting them accustomed to enduring harsh conditions. On reaching the age of five, a boy was removed from his parental home and placed with other boys of the same age in a barracks. He stayed in this group until he reached manhood, around the age of 19 or 20, and was only then admitted to the ranks of Spartan citizens as one of the Equals, or citizens with full rights.

The upbringing of Spartan boys was organized as a formal training called the *agoge*, aimed at preparing them for their future role as citizen soldiers. It therefore concentrated on skills and attributes thought appropriate to a hoplite. Discipline, conformity and group values were emphasized, as were physical and mental toughness. Singing and dancing were compulsory, with a focus on keeping in time and learning to recite by heart the choral poems of the poet Tyrtaios. From the age of ten athletic training, singing and dancing were also competitive, with regular prizes for the best boys and tests to determine if they were strong enough to proceed from one stage to the next. The young boys went barefoot and wore very little clothing, being allowed only a single cloak for protection against the weather. They often exercised naked, as did the Spartan girls, who were not put through the *agoge*, but were raised to be fit and tough, so that they would produce strong healthy children. Food was simple and scarce, both to encourage a slim physique and to accustom the boys to function properly while hungry. This also encouraged them to steal additional food, which was not disapproved of because it promoted stealth and resourcefulness, but they were severely punished if they were so careless as to be caught. A famous story was told of the Spartan boy who was caught by one of his elders and tried to hide a fox that he was carrying in his cloak. The fox gnawed through his stomach, but the boy did not cry out for fear of revealing it, so he died rather than be discovered. All stages of the *agoge* were supervised by older men, some of whom became close friends of individual boys. This practice often led to pederasty, but it was encouraged as a way of integrating the boys with the older men whom they would eventually join on a permanent basis as members of a *syssition*, or citizens' barracks.

Aristodemos passed all the tests and was elected to one of the *syssitia*. He was now a full Spartan citizen and had to be ready to be called up into action as part of the Spartan Army, which usually comprised men aged between 20 and 40. When he reached his mid-20s he was required to take a wife. His choice of partner would to some extent have been his own, but it may have required the approval of the senior men of his village, and the girl's father would have had to approve of him as a husband. Men normally married women five or so years younger than them. The purpose of marriage was to produce more children for the Spartan state, so that the numbers of Spartans were maintained. A close emotional bond between husband and wife was not considered necessary. Until the age of 30 Aristodemos did not live with his wife, but stayed in the barracks with his *syssition* comrades. His visits to his wife were supposed to be carried out only in darkness and not too frequently. They were, however, expected to result in pregnancy. If they did not, he would not have been expected to keep his wife, but to repudiate her as barren and find another. Aristodemos did father at least one child, a son, and may have had more.

Once he turned 30 Aristodemos was considered a full Spartan citizen. He could now live in a house with his wife and family. He would join in the supervision of boys and young men and train with his messmates for war. The older Spartans were expected to be role models for the younger ones, examples of *andragathia*, meaning 'manly virtue.' A fine opportunity for Aristodemos to put his training into practice and demonstrate his manliness arrived in 480 BC when he marched off to face the Persians at Thermopylae. Aristodemos would normally have expected to go to war with the other mature men of his village, grouped in a regiment of up to 1,000 men, which was called a *lochos*. For Thermopylae, however, special arrangements had to be made, because there was an important religious festival going on and it was considered insulting to the gods for the Spartan Army to leave before it was completed. King Leonidas was chosen to command the Greek Army and he obtained a special religious dispensation to take 300 men, as a bodyguard. He would normally have been assigned young men in their 20s, but in view of the likelihood that they might be defeated by the huge Persian Army he decided to choose older men who had already produced at least one son to maintain the ranks of the Spartans. Aristodemos was among those chosen and doubtless considered it a great honour to be singled out in this way.

At the pass of Thermopylae, while the Spartans were waiting for the Persians to make their move, they had plenty of time to contemplate the enormous size of Xerxes' army. It was probably at this time that one of the local Trachinian men remarked that when the Persians finally got round to shooting their arrows there would be so many of them that they would blot out the sun. One of the Spartans, called Dienekes, said to his comrades, 'What our friend from Trachis says is good news, for if the Medes hide the sun then we shall be fighting in the shade.' It is also likely that, as they waited, the Spartans recited some of the more inspiring of Tyrtaios' verses. King Leonidas is said to have particularly approved of Tyrtaios' poems as suitable for firing up the spirits of the younger men so that they would be brave and daring in battle.

What happened next to the 300 Spartans with Leonidas at the pass of Thermopylae is famous; they were all slaughtered by the Persians whilst bravely defending Greece and Sparta. All, that is, except for two. Aristodemos and another Spartan called Eurytos had picked up eye infections, which became so acute that they were told by the king to remove themselves from the ranks as they were incapable of fighting. They were taken to the nearby village of Alpenos by their helot (slave) attendants to recuperate. As the majority of the Greek Army retreated past them, sent away by Leonidas before the Persians could surround them, the two Spartans argued over whether it was their duty to go back and die with their comrades, even though they could not see, or stay out of the battle as ordered. Eventually Eurytos forced his helot to lead him back to the battle and was promptly slain, though the helot managed to escape. Aristodemos obeyed orders and stayed put, thereby surviving the battle. One other Spartan, called Pantites, also survived because he had been sent off to Thessaly as a messenger before the battle started and by the time he got back it was over.

While Leonidas and his 298 dead Spartans were praised as great heroes, Aristodemos and Pantites found themselves despised when they returned to Sparta. It was generally felt that if they were true Spartans they would have died with their comrades. They were assumed to have been too afraid to fight, a slur on his manly virtue that Aristodemos felt very strongly. His sense of hurt would only have been compounded by the epitaph that was composed for the Spartans who died with Leonidas at Thermopylai. It was inscribed on a monument erected at the place where they made their final stand:

Stranger, tell the Spartans that we lie here in obedience to their words.

Yet Aristodemos had been ordered by Leonidas to retire from the battlefield and he obeyed the king's orders. It was only the difference of opinion with Eurytos, who had disobeyed orders and returned to Thermopylae, which had caused the other Spartans to criticise Aristodemos for not doing likewise. Some people even suggested that he and Pantites had both been sent as messengers and had deliberately delayed their return to avoid the battle. In short, they were both labelled cowards. The accusation of cowardice was the most damning that could be made against a true Spartan. Men who had run away from the enemy or refused to fight alongside their comrades were called *tresantes*, meaning 'tremblers.' They were despised because they were the very opposite of the Spartan hoplite ideal. 'Tremblers' were required to wear coloured patches on their red cloaks to distinguish them and they were shunned by the rest of the Equals. Their own messmates from the *syssition* would have nothing to do with them, even to the point of refusing to speak to them. They could not hold any of the public offices and were unable to gain justice for insults or injuries, nor could they make legal agreements with other Spartans. No Spartan would allow his daughter to marry a 'trembler' and Aristodemos must have been concerned for the future of his own offspring, for no one would want to marry their children to the sons or daughters of a 'trembler.' Pantites found it all too much to bear and hanged himself, but Aristodemos endured the shame, hoping for an opportunity to restore his reputation.

That opportunity came the following year. In spite of the accusations of cowardice and his isolation from the rest of the Equals, Aristodemos was among those men who were called by the ephors (officials in charge of Spartan daily adminstration) to join the army that the regent Pausanias took to the battle of Plataea. The Spartans were anxious to have as large an army as possible so they probably sent almost all the citizens aged under 40, keeping only the oldest men back to guard Sparta against a possible Messenian helot uprising. Aristodemos marched with the men of his *lochos*, but he would still have been cold-shouldered by them. His only company would have been his personal helot attendant, carrying his equipment and cooking for him. As he approached the plain of Boiotia where the Persians were camped, his one aim would have been to show that he was not a coward, but a true Spartan. By an act of conspicuous bravery he could earn public honour and restore his reputation; even if it should cost him his life it would be worth it for the sake of his family. Pausanias positioned his army on a ridge of hills near Plataea, but several days of cavalry attacks forced him to retreat by night. The Persians attacked the Spartans at dawn, first with cavalry and then infantry, who halted within bowshot of the Spartans and fired arrows at them from behind a wall of wicker shields. Pausanias needed to charge the Persians, but he delayed, waiting for reinforcements and good omens. It was usual for the commander, accompanied by two ephors and his official diviners, to sacrifice a goat and to inspect its entrails just before the ranks of the Spartans charged forward to engage with the enemy to see if the gods were sending a good omen for the success of the battle. When the ephors and the diviners pronounced the omens favourable then the army could charge. The first time that Pausanias did this the omens were unfavourable, so he ordered the Spartans to wait. The men grew increasingly impatient as the Persians poured more arrows into their ranks, so Pausanias sacrificed again, and again, but still he did not give the order to charge. Eventually Aristodemos could take no more and, without waiting for the command, he broke out of the ranks of his *lochos* and charged at the Persians. To his left the Tegeans, allies of the Spartans, also rushed forward. Pausanias chose this moment to order the Spartans forward as well, as apparently the omens were now good. Aristodemos probably killed several Persians before he was cut down himself. The Spartans and Tegeans drove the Persians back, killed their commander Mardonios and won the battle.

Aristodemos certainly showed courage with his charge at the Persian ranks, and Herodotus felt that he was the bravest man on that day, but the Spartans did not agree. They refused to honour him as a hero of the state because they felt he had deliberately chosen to get himself killed. He had shown that he had the courage of a true Spartan, but he had failed to meet their high standards of discipline and obedience. Although he did not have a tomb, thanks to the enquiries of Herodotus and Spartan legend, he has achieved lasting fame.

TWO GENERALS AND A SATRAP

The Wars of Alexander the Great 336–323 BC

Waldemar Heckel

PARMENION AND PHILOTAS, GENERALS

When Alexander ascended the Macedonian throne in 336 BC, two powerful generals of Philip II exercised considerable influence at the court and in the army. Only one, Antipater, was in Macedonia at the time. The other, Parmenion, had been sent by Philip to command the advance force in Asia Minor. He was an experienced and well-loved leader of men. In the year of Alexander's birth, 356 BC, Parmenion had defeated the Illyrian ruler Grabus, while Philip himself was besieging Potidaea. Twenty years later, he was the senior officer in the army and his sons, Philotas and Nicanor, commanded the Companion Cavalry and the hypaspists respectively. These were amongst the finest troops in the Macedonian Army.

Parmenion's contributions were, however, a source of embarrassment to the young king, who believed that the success of others detracted somehow from his own glory. He was particularly annoyed when he learned that in Egypt Parmenion's son, Philotas, was boasting that all the king's successes were due to his father's generalship.

The information had come to Alexander in an unusual way. Amongst the spoils taken at Damascus was a woman named Antigone. This woman was of Macedonian origin, from the town of Pydna, but had been captured by the Persian admiral Autophradates while travelling by sea. Antigone had thus become the mistress or concubine of a Persian notable and had been deposited at Damascus before the battle of Issus in 333 BC. When Parmenion captured the city and the spoils were divided, Antigone became Philotas' mistress. What he told her, by way of bragging about his own family's achievements or disparaging those of the king, she repeated to others, until the talk was reported to Craterus, a faithful friend and officer of Alexander. Craterus disliked Philotas personally – and in this he was not alone, for Philotas had many enemies who were at the same time close friends of the king. Craterus therefore gathered incriminating evidence from Antigone and brought this to Alexander's attention. However, at that time, with the outcome of the war against Darius of Persia still undecided, the king chose to overlook the indiscretion.

Things changed, however, when Alexander found himself master of the Persian capitals. Parmenion had suddenly become expendable, and he was left at Ecbatana when Alexander pushed on in pursuit of Darius and Bessus. At first, it was to be a temporary measure, but Darius' murder altered the complexion of the campaign. Craterus, who had been groomed as Parmenion's replacement – at both the battles of Issus and Gaugamela he was the old general's second-in-command – had proved himself more than capable; furthermore, he was younger, more energetic and, more importantly, unswervingly loyal to the king. These circumstances, and the fact that Parmenion's elimination required justification, gave rise to stories that Parmenion's advice was timid or unsound and that his performance at Gaugamela was substandard. Separated from his influential father, Philotas became more vulnerable to the intrigues of his enemies. This vulnerability was increased when, during the march through Aria, Philotas' brother Nicanor died of illness. Indeed, not only was the family itself weakened, but also many who had served with Parmenion were no longer with the army. Hence, when Philotas was implicated in a conspiracy at Phrada (modern Farah) in what is now Afghanistan in late 330 BC, there were few to defend or protect him.

The crime itself was one of negligence rather than overt treason. A young Macedonian – he is described as one of the *hetairoi*, and hence not insignificant – by the name of Dimnus had divulged the details of a conspiracy to which he was a party (though he was clearly not its instigator), to his lover, Nicomachus. The latter, fearing for his life if the conspiracy should fail and he be implicated, told everything he knew to his brother, Cebalinus, who promptly went to report the matter to Alexander.

Unable to gain access to the king, Cebalinus informed Philotas and urged him to deal with the matter. But on the following day, when he approached Philotas again, Cebalinus discovered that the latter had not spoken to the king concerning the conspiracy because, as he claimed, it had not seemed to him a matter of great importance. Cebalinus therefore devised other means of revealing the plot, mentioning Philotas' suspicious behaviour. Alexander called a meeting of his advisers – excluding Philotas, who might otherwise have been summoned – and asked for their candid opinions. These were freely given and unanimous: Philotas would not have suppressed the information unless he were either party to the plot or at least favoured it. Such negligence could not be excused when it involved the life and safety of the king, so Atarrhias with a detachment of *hypaspists* – in effect, these were the Macedonian military police – was sent to arrest Philotas.

Confronted with the facts, Philotas confessed that he had indeed learned of the conspiracy, but that he had not taken it seriously. If this was the truth – we shall never know what went through Philotas' mind – he may have reflected on an earlier episode, when his father had sent an urgent letter to Alexander, alleging that Philip of Acarnania, the king's personal physician, had been bribed to poison him in Cilicia. In the event, the report proved false and Parmenion's reputation was tarnished.

On the other hand, in the shadowy world of the Macedonian court, where kings had often been murdered for merely slighting a man's honour, anything was possible and everything potentially dangerous. Philotas' trustworthiness was called into question: had he not been guilty of disloyal talk in the past? As a young man, he had been raised at the court of Philip as a companion of Amyntas, son of Perdiccas, whom Alexander had executed on suspicion of aspiring to regain his throne. Furthermore, his sister had been married briefly to the king's bitter enemy Attalus. When questioned under torture, Philotas admitted also that another adherent of Attalus, a certain squadron commander named Hegelochus, had suggested to Parmenion and his sons that they murder the king, but the plan was rejected as too dangerous. At any rate, it seems that the topic of Alexander's removal from power had certainly come up.

The younger commanders urged the king not to forgive Philotas a second time, for he would continue to be a danger to him. Their professed concern for Alexander's safety masked, only slightly, their hatred for Philotas and their desire for military advancement; this could best be achieved by eliminating him and members of his faction. For Alexander, although he concurred with their opinion, it was nevertheless a difficult decision. How would Parmenion react to his son's execution? He remained in Ecbatana, astride the lines of communication and at the head of a substantial army. If Philotas were to be executed for treason, then the charge must be extended to include his father. The army, which tried Philotas and found him guilty, accepted also the guilt of his father. The Macedonians were realists and recognized that expediency must triumph over legal niceties. Philotas was publicly executed; his father in Ecbatana was presented with a letter outlining the charges against him and struck down as he read them.

MAZAEUS, A SATRAP

Servant of three kings, Mazaeus is known from both historical sources and coin legends to have been satrap of Cilicia, and later of Syria and Mesopotamia (Abarnahara, 'the land beyond the river') in the time of King Artaxerxes III. Under Darius III he had doubtless fought at Issus, although there is no mention of him. In 331 BC, he had been ordered to prevent Alexander's crossing of the Euphrates at Thapsacus, but had insufficient numbers to do more than harass the bridge-builders. Upon Alexander's arrival, Mazaeus withdrew and rejoined Darius, who was now following the course of the Tigris northward.

At Gaugamela Mazaeus commanded the Persian cavalry on the right wing and led a charge of dense squadrons together with the scythe-chariots, inflicting heavy casualties. He then sent a squadron of Scythian horsemen to capture the Macedonian camp, while he exerted pressure on Parmenion and the Thessalian cavalry on the Macedonian left. In turn, Parmenion was forced to send riders to recall Alexander, who had gone in pursuit of Darius. Eventually Mazaeus was overcome by the tenacity of the Thessalians and the demoralizing news of Darius' flight.

It is highly likely that the great battle-scene on the so-called Alexander Sarcophagus from Sidon – now in the Istanbul Museum – depicts Mazaeus' valour. Mazaeus fled from the battlefield to Babylon, which he promptly surrendered to the Macedonians. In return he was installed as its satrap, the first Persian to be so honoured by Alexander. The Alexander Sarcophagus also depicts a notable Persian engaged in a lion hunt together with Alexander and other Macedonians – one of the Macedonian riders may be Hephaestion. If this depicts a historical event, then it could not have occurred before late 331 BC, and the most likely Persian with whom Alexander hunted is once again Mazaeus.

When Alexander pursued Darius in his final days, Mazaeus' son, Brochubelus or Antibelus, defected to him. Mazaeus himself remained in office and served his new master loyally until his death in late 328 BC.

CP. SEXTUS BACULUS, ROMAN CENTURION

Caesar's Gallic Wars 58–50 BC

Kate Gilliver

Centurions are often considered to be the backbone of the Roman legions, and rightly so. It may seem odd, but at the time of Caesar's campaigns the legion had no official commander; thus the centurions (and the six military tribunes attached to the legion) had a vital role in providing the leadership, experience and stability that the legion needed to operate effectively. Centurions were the highest echelon of professional soldiers in the legion and their senior officers and commanders were politicians whose military experience and skill could vary considerably. The 60 or so centurions in each legion were appointed by the army commander – the provincial governor. While some may have been appointed because of their social status, the majority gained promotion through experience, leadership and conspicuous courage. This must have encouraged ambitious private soldiers to prove their worth on the battlefield to gain promotion to the rank of centurion. It also drove centurions to continue to prove themselves to their peers and to the soldiers under their command, so they led from the front, and often suffered disproportionately high casualty rates because of this. In the reverse at Gergovia, for example, 46 of the 700 killed were centurions. These high casualty rates may have been exacerbated not just by centurions seeking to engage the enemy, but by the enemy deliberately targeting them. Centurions could have made themselves highly visible in battle, and probably did, through their armour, equipment, and particularly their helmets, which had distinctive transverse crests, as well as by wearing their decorations as a clear marker of their courage.

Sensible commanders recognized the value of their centurions not only in leading men into battle, but also in providing valuable advice based on their experience of war. Caesar regularly invited the senior centurions of his legions to the briefings and councils of war he held with his senior officers; he would have listened to their advice and used them to pass on information and orders to the rank and file. Their understanding of an intended battle plan was vital for success simply because they were the ones leading the men on the ground. The value Caesar placed on his centurions is also reflected in the good press he generally gives them in his account of the campaign in Gaul.

The XII Legion had been raised by Caesar in 58 BC in preparation for the campaign against the Helvetii, a tribe originally from what is now Switzerland, and although it consisted largely of new recruits, it had a core of experienced centurions, who would have had to train their new soldiers on the job. The Chief Centurion (Primus Pilus) of the XII was Publius Sextus Baculus, a man renowned for his bravery, but he would also have been an experienced and trustworthy leader for such an appointment. He was probably transferred from another legion, and would have been appointed by Caesar himself. During its second year in existence this legion suffered in the battle against the Nervii in 57 BC; most of the centurions were killed or injured, including all those from the legion's IV cohort. Baculus was seriously injured in the battle, but was able to remain with his legion or rejoin it later, after treatment in a camp hospital. Towards winter in the same year, Caesar sent the legion into the Alps with Galba. The legion was already under-strength and was probably still short of experienced officers following the battle with the Nervii when it came under attack in the village of Octodurus and was pinned down by Alpine tribesmen. Baculus and a fellow officer, a military tribune, together advised Galba that the situation was too desperate to hold and they should break out. Galba listened to the advice of his juniors and in the ensuing break-out the XII Legion managed to turn the tables on the enemy and put them to flight with heavy casualties.

We hear nothing more of Baculus for the next three years, but he probably remained with his legion for the campaigns in northern and western Gaul. He reappears briefly in 53 BC during a German raid on a Roman camp garrisoned by the inexperienced XIV Legion, 200 cavalry and 300 legionaries from other legions who were on the sick list and recovering in camp. Baculus was presumably one of the sick, but we do not know if this was because he had been injured in battle again. A group of soldiers and camp servants out foraging was attacked by the German cavalry and some of them tried to make it back to camp. Baculus rose from his sick-bed and helped to hold the gates of the camp, allowing the rest of the garrison time to man the fortifications. Already weakened through illness, Baculus was seriously injured and fainted, but was dragged back to safety by his companions. He probably recovered from this injury (Caesar would almost certainly have reported it had he died), but nothing further is known of him.

Centurions were promoted for their courage, but they were expected to continue to show bravery to justify their position, and to push for further advancement to the ranks of the senior centurions in the legion. Titus Pullo and Lucius Vorenus were two centurions in Quintus Cicero's legion who were in competition with each other for promotion to senior centurion. The attacks on Cicero's camp during the winter of 54 BC gave the two an opportunity to compete with each other to see who was the bravest. Both took part in a sortie, Pullo charging first with a spear but getting into trouble when his sword got stuck in its scabbard due to a javelin which had pierced his shield and hit his sword belt. Vorenus came to his aid and forced the Gauls to retreat, but then tripped and became surrounded. Pullo rescued his rival and the two of them made it back within the fortifications after killing a few Gauls. Despite their rivalry they had saved each other's lives and had shown themselves to be equal in bravery. Caesar says nothing more about them, like Baculus, so unfortunately we do not know if they were promoted.

At the end of their service, Caesar's centurions who had survived the wars in Gaul and the Civil War were probably wealthy men from the booty they had acquired and the bonuses they had been paid. Many of the soldiers of these wars were settled with land in military colonies in Provence or in northern Italy. The centurions were given larger allotments than the ordinary soldiers and often held public office in their local towns.

ABBINAEUS, ALARIC, THEORIC AND NARSES

Rome at War AD 293-696

Michael Whitby

ABBINAEUS, COMMANDER OF A PROVINCIAL GARRISON

Flavius Abbinaeus joined the army in AD 304/5 and served for 33 years in the contingent of Parthian Archers based in middle Egypt. This was a mounted unit whose name indicates that it was originally raised for service on the eastern frontier, or from captives taken on that frontier, but which was later recruited in the normal way from Roman provincials. In 337/8 Abbinaeus, now a non-commissioned officer, escorted an embassy of Blemmyes (tribesmen from the southern Egyptian border) to Constantinople, where he was promoted to protector by Constantius, a step that included the honour of being allowed to kiss the purple imperial robe. Protectors operated as a group of junior staff officers who undertook a variety of imperial business, and Abbinaeus was detailed to escort the embassy home; after three years among the Blemmyes, Abbinaeus returned to Constantius, who was then in Syria, and received promotion to command the cavalry squadron at Dionysias. Back in Egypt Abbinaeus faced competition for this position since others also had secured letters of appointment through patronage. Abbinaeus appealed to Constantius and had his post confirmed, but in 344 he was dismissed by the local count; his position was ratified on appeal. He then remained in office until after 351. The desirability of Abbinaeus' command is revealed by a collection of papyri that illustrate the vicissitudes of his career, the interaction of his troops with the local population, his soldiers' close involvement in the maintenance of law and order, and the extraction of imperial revenues from their district.

ALARIC, ROMAN OFFICER AND TRIBAL WARLORD

Alaric was born in about AD 370 into the Balthi, a leading family among the Gothic Tervingi who lived on the Danube Plains. As a youth he probably participated in the Danube crossing of 376 and observed the subsequent encounters with imperial forces; at some stage he became an Arian Christian, the standard creed among the

Goths. By the early 390s he had emerged as leader of a warband in the Balkans who opposed Emperor Theodosius, but in 394 he commanded tribal allies in Theodosius' expedition against the western usurper Eugenius. Disenchanted by inadequate recompense for his contribution to victory at the Frigidus River and the heavy casualties suffered by his followers, he proceeded to ravage the central and southern Balkans, taking advantage of tensions between Rome and Constantinople. By 399 he had secured one major wish, the senior Roman command of general of Illyricum, which provided him with salaries and provisions for his followers.

In 401 he invaded Italy and besieged the western emperor Honorius in Milan, but was defeated by the western generalissimo Stilicho; he was forced to withdraw to the Balkans as his men suffered from heat and poor food. He remained in the north-eastern Balkans, attempting to secure a permanent territory, until 407 when he was appointed general by Honorius as part of a western attempt to annex the Balkans. However, the planned campaign was cancelled, relations between Alaric and Honorius deteriorated, and Alaric invaded Italy again to secure payment for his contracted services. While negotiating with Honorius at Ravenna about territory, alliance, and payments of gold and corn, Alaric besieged Rome. Honorius procrastinated, but in 409 the threat of starvation forced the Senate at Rome to agree terms; Alaric had the senator Attalus proclaimed emperor and Attalus appointed Alaric as senior Roman general.

Tensions between Attalus and Alaric, plus further unsuccessful negotiations with Honorius, resulted in Alaric returning to Rome, which was easily captured on 24 August 410. Occupation of the city for three days may have relieved Alaric's frustrations, but did not satisfy his followers' needs for territory. Thereafter he led his forces south, with North Africa as his probable goal, but was thwarted while trying to cross to Sicily; as he withdrew northwards he became ill and died. His brother-in-law Athaulf took over the army, which he led into southern Gaul in 412 where the Visigothic kingdom was established in Aquitania.

THEODERIC, OSTROGOTHIC KING

Theoderic was born in the mid-fifth century into the Amal family, which led one of the Gothic groups in the northern Balkans. In AD 461/2 he was sent as hostage to Constantinople, where he remained for ten years, receiving his education. After succeeding his father in 474, he spent 15 years attempting to establish a base for his people in the Balkans, either through negotiation with or intimidation of the eastern emperor Zeno. Theoderic's successes were marked by appointments as Roman general in 476–78 and again in 483–87, when Zeno employed him against other tribesmen in the Balkans as well as Isaurian rebels in the east. Rebuffs resulted in the sacking of cities, such as Stobi in 479, or the ravaging of provinces, for example Macedonia and Thessaly in 482. The death of his main Gothic rival,

Theoderic Strabo, in 481 allowed Theoderic to unite most Balkan Goths under Amal leadership, but he was still unable to achieve his main goal of acquiring a secure and productive territory. In 488 Zeno agreed that Theoderic should move to Italy to attack Odoacer (who had ruled since deposing the last western emperor in 476): if successful, Theoderic could rule on behalf of Zeno. Theoderic forced Odoacer back into Ravenna; after three years of blockade the rivals agreed to share power, but Theoderic soon accused Odoacer of treachery and had him killed. Zeno's death in 491 complicated Theoderic's position, but in 497 Emperor Anastasius recognized him as ruler of Italy; to his Gothic followers Theoderic was king, even sometimes Augustus (emperor), the status to which he clearly aspired, although he was careful to protest his subservience in dealings with Constantinople.

Theoderic's 33-year reign (493–526) came to be regarded as a golden age in Italy, especially in contrast to the fighting of the 540s, and his first two decades were highly successful. Marital diplomacy built links with the main tribal groups in the west, and from 507 brought the Visigothic kingdom in Spain under his control. The Senate and pope at Rome were courted by special treatment and the carefully crafted Roman image of the new regime; religious divisions between Rome and Constantinople facilitated this rapprochement. For Goths, Theoderic remained the war leader, but this was now only one facet of his complex public image. Theoderic's last decade was less rosy. The absence of a son, and the early death of his son-in-law, raised the issue of succession, while Anastasius' death in 518 brought religious reconciliation between Rome and Constantinople and so made Theoderic more suspicious of leading Romans. Theoderic's death in 526 rapidly brought the tensions within his kingdom to the surface.

NARSES, IMPERIAL EUNUCH AND TRUSTED GENERAL

The eunuch Narses originated from the Persian part of Armenia but was brought up in the palace at Constantinople in the late fifth century. He advanced through the grades of servants of the bedchamber, reaching the position of treasurer and senior official in AD 530; in this capacity he provided money to Persarmenian deserters, and travelled to the east to secure valuable booty. In 531/2 he became imperial sword-bearer, and on 18 January 532 his distribution of bribes was crucial in undermining the cohesion of rioters in Constantinople whose violence was threatening to topple Emperor Justinian. In 535 he undertook another delicate mission, this time for Empress Theodora, to reinstate Bishop Theodosius at Alexandria and exile his opponents; for over a year Narses remained in Alexandria, conducting a virtual civil war against Theodosius' opponents.

In 538, at nearly 60 years old, Narses embarked on what was to prove a highly successful military career by leading reinforcements to General Flavius Belisarius, who was on campaign in Italy. Narses criticised Belisarius' conduct, and their rivalry led to the loss of Milan. Narses was recalled to Constantinople, to be followed by the allied contingent of Heruls, a nomadic Germanic tribe, who refused to remain without him. In 541/2 Narses was again employed on sensitive business, first to spy on an alleged plot that involved Justinian's senior financial minister and then to investigate unrest in Constantinople. In 545 his contacts among the Heruls were exploited to persuade their leaders to enrol for service in Italy.

Narses' big chance came in 551, after Belisarius had failed to stabilise the military position in Italy and Justinian's first choice as replacement (his nephew Germanus) had died. Narses was now appointed supreme commander in Italy, a post he accepted on condition that he was provided with the men and money needed to finish the war. Assembly of troops and other preparations detained Narses in the Balkans, and he did not arrive in Ravenna until 6 June 552 after outmanoeuvring Gothic contingents blocking the main routes. Later that month Narses marched against the Goths' leader Totila, whose various attempts at deception he outwitted and whom he then crushed in battle through intelligent tactics. In July Narses rapidly recaptured Rome before confronting the Goths near Naples. Clever planning again secured victory, although contemporaries also gave credit to Narses' devotion to the Virgin Mary.

For the next decade, Narses was occupied in reducing Gothic strongholds in central and northern Italy and defeating Frankish invasions. Meanwhile he was entrusted by Justinian with the massive task of returning Italy to civilian rule, as well as ensuring adherence to the emperor's preferred religious doctrines. By 559 he had received the title of patrician, the Empire's highest honour, and by 565 he had also become honorary consul, a demonstration of his place in the traditional Roman hierarchy. Justinian's death in 565 complicated Narses' last decade, as his relations with Justin II were less close. The migration of Lombards into the Po valley from 568 posed new military challenges, but he remained in post until his death in 573/4, at the age of almost 95.

WAR IN
THE EAST

One should rise at four in the morning, practise sword techniques, eat one's breakfast and train with the bow, the gun and the horse.

(Kato Kiyomasa)

THEODORE, CAVALRY TROOPER

Byzantium at War AD 600–1453

John Haldon

Life as a soldier in the Byzantine Army must have varied enormously from century to century as the empire's fortunes changed, and depending on the commanding officers, so too did the type of unit, and so forth. We have very little evidence about individual soldiers, but we can build up a picture of some events in the life of a hypothetical soldier from several sources, so that in the account below, all the things that happened to him, the actions ascribed to him or to others, the duties he carried out and the fighting in which he was involved, can be found in medieval sources of the period from the 7th to the 12th centuries, and are all perfectly compatible with the actual historical context. We will follow the daily routine of a typical cavalry trooper on campaign under the general Bardas Skleros in the Balkans in AD 971. The soldier's name was Theodore, a fairly common and popular name, and one shared by one of the most famous soldier saints of the eastern Christian world, St Theodore the recruit, one of the four patron saints of soldiers along with saints Demetrios, Merkourios and George. Theodore came from the village of Krithokomi near the fortress town of Tzouroullon in Thrace. Theodore was the son of a soldier himself, and the family's land was subject to the *strateia*, the military service due from those enrolled on the thematic military service register. His family was not well off, but their neighbours, who were also liable for military service, were permitted to contribute jointly to arming and equipping a single cavalry soldier. Theodore's skills had brought him into a unit of lancers, medium cavalry armed also with bows and maces, where he held the rank of *dekarchos*, commander of a troop of ten men, in a *bandon* or squadron of 50 soldiers. He served effectively on a full-time rather than a seasonal basis and a campaign offered him the chance of a promotion, perhaps to second-in-command of his squadron.

In the spring of 970 the empire faced an invasion from a large Rus' force deep into imperial territory in Thrace, where it took the local garrisons by surprise and was able to sack the fortress of Philippoupolis (modern Plovdiv), before advancing along the road to Constantinople. Since the Emperor John had most of his effective field units in the east, where they were campaigning near Antioch, he appointed Bardas Skleros, together with the *patrikios* Peter, both experienced commanders, to take a medium-sized force – numbering some 10,000 – and scout the enemy dispositions in the occupied territories. As a secondary objective they were to exercise the troops and prevent enemy raiders committing further depredations. At the same time, spies – disguised in Bulgarian and Rus' costume – were sent into enemy-held territory to learn as much as they could about the Rus' commander

Svyatoslav's movements. Svyatoslav soon learned of the advancing imperial column, and in response dispatched a force of both Rus' and Bulgar troops, with a supporting detachment of Petchenegs, a war-like Turkic people from the Eurasian steppe with whom he was temporarily allied, to drive the Romans off.

The march north followed the established pattern. Bardas needed to move quickly, and so forced the pace somewhat. Within imperial territory he could rely on the co-operation of local officials to supply his troops; once in enemy territory his soldiers and their animals had to live off the land. But regardless of where it was, the army always entrenched for the night. The scouts and surveyors sent ahead to locate an appropriate site had to ensure both an adequate water supply as well as good defensive properties, and preferably in relatively open country to avoid the possibility of surprise attack. On this campaign, the latter was difficult since the army passed through hilly and wooded scrubland for much of its route. Byzantine camps followed a standard pattern. The commander's standard was set up in the centre and each of the subordinate officers – Bardas had divided his force into three divisions of about 3,500 men – were assigned to share the four quarters into which the camp was divided. The various units pitched their tents around the perimeter, in battle order as near as possible in case of a surprise attack. The camp itself consisted of a simple ditch dug by the soldiers themselves, with the earth thrown inside, stamped down and surmounted by the spears and shields of the troops. Where circumstances and manpower permitted, the camp was meant to be at least two and a half bowshots across so that the animals could be quartered safely in the middle sections. The largest camps, which could contain a major field army of over 20,000 men and animals with their baggage, were more than a mile along the side, with a v-shaped trench some six to eight feet in depth.

Theodore's unit, like all units, had to set up its own rotating watch within the camp, but the commanding officer also needed to set up a watch for the camp as a whole. Each unit along the perimeter provided soldiers for this patrol, called the *kerketon*. Other units had to be sent out to forage for supplies and fodder for the horses, accompanied by supporting troops for protection – it was important to pitch camp and secure the immediate area before sunset so that supplies could be got in as quickly as possible. Leaving camp after sunset was usually prohibited, except for the outer line of pickets, groups of four men sent out to cover the major approaches to the camp when it was clear that no enemy was yet in the immediate vicinity. The men were organized in tent-groups of eight, called *kontoubernia*, sharing a hand-mill and basic cooking utensils as well as a small troop of pack animals. Soldiers were issued with two main varieties of bread: simple baked loaves, and double-baked 'hard tack,' referred to in late Roman times as *bucellatum* and by the Byzantines as *paximadion* or *paximation*. Hard tack, more easily preserved and produced, could be baked in field ovens – *klibanoi* – or simply laid in the ashes of camp fires, an advantage when speed was essential, as was the case during this expedition. The ration per diem included two to three pounds of bread and either dried meat or cheese; wine was also issued, but it is not clear how often or in what circumstances. The amount of meat relative to the rest of the diet was often minimal or absent altogether, but would still provide a reasonable amount of nutrition, since ancient strains of wheat and barley had considerably higher protein content than modern strains.

The camp routine was marked by the trumpet signals for the evening meal, lights out and reveille; trumpet signals were also employed to issue commands to the various units and divisions to strike camp, assemble in marching order and begin the march. Leaving camp was always a dangerous time, for as the troops defiled through the main entrances they were for a while exposed to archers or even a rapid hit-and-run charge from enemy horsemen. A particular order for exiting camps was laid down and followed, and once the army was out of the entrenched area it would be drawn up for a while in a defensive formation until the troops fell into the marching order for the day.

The speed at which armies moved varied according to terrain, weather and the number and types of troops. Unaccompanied mounted troops could cover distances of up to 40 or 50 miles per day, provided the horses were regularly rested and well nourished. Small units generally moved more rapidly than large divisions, even up to 30 miles per day for infantry in some contexts. Average marching speeds were much slower: three miles per hour for infantry on even terrain, two and a half on broken/hilly ground. Mixed forces moved at the speed of the slowest element; but speed also depended on the conditions of the roads or tracks followed, the breadth of the column, and its length. Thus a division of 5,000 infantry, which is what Bardas probably had at his disposal, marching at the standard infantry rate of about three miles per hour over good ground, ordered five abreast and with each row occupying a (minimal) two metres, would stretch over a two-kilometre (1.2 mile) distance. There would be a gap of about 20 minutes, at the very least if not more, between the front and rear elements. Theodore's column marched three abreast along the narrow, often wooded tracks followed by the imperial troops on this campaign, and his division of 1,000 cavalry would have extended back nearly six miles (9.5km), and the whole army some 14 miles (22.5km). The rearmost units would be well over one hour behind the van.

Having left the camp, Theodore's unit was placed in the van division, behind a screen of scouts deployed well ahead of the column, and ahead of the main contingent of cavalry and infantry. The baggage train, to which a group of units was assigned on a rotational basis for protection, was placed in the centre, and other units patrolled at some distance, where the terrain allowed, on either flank. On open terrain in enemy country the army would march over a broader front in a formation that could be rapidly deployed into battle order, and for passing through narrow passes or across rivers another formation was employed.

As the march progressed, some of the scouts returned to inform the general that the enemy was not far away, near the fortress town of Arkadioupolis (modern Luleburgaz). The three divisions were given separate tasks: two were concealed in the rough scrub and wooded terrain through which the track led in the direction of the enemy, while Bardas took command of the third section of the army himself. Leaving the two divisions in ambush with clear instructions, he himself led a fierce and unsuspected charge against the foremost enemy units, made up of Petcheneg mounted archers. In spite of the greater numbers in the enemy force, he managed to lure the enemy out of their encampment and withdraw in good order, encouraging more and more of the enemy to pursue without any clear plan of attack or order. It must have seemed as though the outnumbered Byzantine force, which managed to avoid being completely surrounded, was doomed. Yet discipline, training and leadership told, and Skleros finally ordered the prearranged signal to be given for the whole force to fall back. Meanwhile Theodore's unit, one of the two corps that lay in ambush, prepared itself: the order was given to remain absolutely silent, to place all supernumerary baggage animals with their attendants well to the rear, to check their weapons, and to deploy into a battle order appropriate to the terrain. One of the priests who accompanied the force offered up a quick prayer – a standard practice before battle. As the van division approached, drew level with and then withdrew beyond them, a single trumpet-call ordered them to break cover and charge into the flank of the unsuspecting enemy. Caught in the open in close combat, the Petchenegs had no chance to deploy at a distance suitable for the use of their archery and, after being brought to a halt – at which point the van division about-faced and counter-attacked in its turn – they turned and fled. The Rus' and Bulgar troops, meanwhile, who had been hurrying to catch them up, on the assumption that the Romans had been routed, suddenly found themselves caught up in the panic. As the rout became general and the Roman forces pushed home their advantage, heavy casualties were inflicted on the fleeing enemy troops. A contemporary source remarks that the Romans lost some 550 men and many wounded, as well as a large number of horses, a direct result of the fearsome archery of the Petchenegs. The combined enemy force, however, lost several thousand. The short encounter won important breathing space for the Emperor John, furnishing him also with vital information about the composition, fighting abilities and morale of the enemy.

After any encounter with the enemy, the commanding officers held a muster to establish casualties. Specially detailed soldiers were deputed to check the fallen, to carry or help the wounded back to the temporary Roman camp, where the divisional medical attendants and surgeons tried to deal with those wounds that were not likely to be fatal. Far more men died of wounds than in battle itself, of course. In a contemporary treatise instructions are given that the wounded were to be taken back towards imperial territory with a section of the rearguard, transported on the pack animals no longer required for the army's supplies. Occasional references in the chronicles of the period bear this out, as well as describing the problems of extracting arrowheads, with fractured or broken bones, and related injuries.

Theodore was lucky – not only was he not injured, but also his officer had noted how he had dashed in to rescue a comrade from the spear of an attacking Petcheneg, and he was cited for his bravery. He was given a golden arm-ring (taken from one of the dead enemy horsemen), and promoted to *drakonarios* – bearer of the unit banner, a considerable honour, and bringing with it some extra privileges in camp and a small risc in his *roga* (his pay).

The defeat of the enemy force gave the emperor time to organize a major offensive, which was, in the event, far more successful than was originally planned. Theodore's unit was involved too, and fought on the left wing at the second battle of Dorostolon in July 971. Theodore eventually retired to his family holding in Thrace where, with his savings from his salary and his promotions – he eventually reached the rank of *drouggarios*, roughly equivalent to brigadier – he invested in an imperial title, that of *kandidatos*, which brought with it a decent annuity, and expanded his property. He ended his days as an important local notable – and his grandchildren enjoyed his tales of bravery and fierce barbarians.

SUBADAI BA'ADUR, MONGOL GENERAL

The Mongol Conquests

Stephen Turnbull

In most accounts of the Mongol conquests, Genghis Khan's subordinates come over as two-dimensional characters, mounted automatons moving as stereotypically as the myth of Mongol supremacy would always have us believe. Yet in the service of Genghis Khan were many leaders of great military talent who were personalities in their own right. One of them was Subadai Ba'adur, whose name variously appears as Subedei, Sabatai, or Subodei. He was born in about 1176, the son of a blacksmith of the Uriangqadai clan and joined Genghis Khan's band when he was still a youth in about 1190. Along with his brother, Jelemei, Subadai rose quickly in Mongol service and commanded cavalry at the age of 25. Subadai appears to have been a heavyweight in more ways than one, and had to travel to battles in some form of carriage to spare the backs of the slight Mongol ponies!

Subadai is the exemplar of that remarkable and commendable loyalty shown by subordinate generals of the Mongols towards their ruling khan. 'As felt protects from the wind,' he promised Genghis Khan, 'so I will ward off your enemies.' His first independent command was 1205–06 when he successfully pursued and killed Kutu and Chila'un, sons of the defeated Merki leader, Tokhto'a. Subadai commanded a *tumen* (10,000 men) in the wars against the Xixia, and we read of him being given joint command of the 3,000 Mongols sent in pursuit of the shah of Khwarazm after the Samarkand operation. When the shah died in 1221, Subadai was one of the commanders entrusted with the reconnaissance mission 'to the Western lands' that took the Mongols into Russia for the first time. This operation was a remarkable feat that brings great credit upon Subadai. Having destroyed several towns in Azerbaijan, the Mongols were bribed to spare Tabriz, and Subadai and his men wintered in eastern Armenia. In 1221 Subadai helped to defeat King Giorgi the Brilliant of Georgia near Tbilisi. From there they returned to Azerbaijan and were on the point of marching against Baghdad to destroy the Abbasid caliphate, but instead returned to Georgia, defeating another Georgian army using the tactic of false retreat. They then swung north and advanced into southern Russia and captured Astrakhan. Pushing on across the River Don they penetrated the Crimean peninsula and were in the Ukraine to winter the snows of 1222–23. In 1223 they began to return home, only to be intercepted by an allied enemy force. These were the soldiers Subadai and his colleagues led to their deaths at the battle of the Kalka River.

After the conquest of Azerbaijan and Georgia, they came upon the nomadic Polovtsians, referred to as Kipchaks or Cumans (Kumans). By 1223 the Mongols had completed these operations and regrouped in the southern Russian steppes. At that time what we now know as Russia and the Ukraine were ruled by a number of princes who jealously defended their own territories. These Russian princes would appear to have had no intelligence about the campaigns and conquests of Genghis Khan, and the first information that a new enemy had appeared in the southern steppes was brought to Mstislav Mstislavitch in Galich by his Polovtsian father-in-law, Khan Kotyan, whose nomadic territory lay close to the eastern most bend of the Dnieper. The *Chronicle of Novgorod* tells us:

> He brought them numerous presents: horses, camels, buffaloes and girls. And he presented these gifts to them, and said the following, 'Today the Tartars [Mongols] took away our land and tomorrow they will come and take away yours.'

Mstislav of Galich immediately summoned a council of war in Kiev. The two other southern regional princes attended it, Mstislav Romanovich of Kiev and Mstislav Svyatoslavich of Chernigov. They made the decision that the Russians and Polovtsians should move east to seek out and destroy the Mongols wherever they might be found. When the expeditionary force was on its way, the Mongol envoys met the main body at Pereyaslavl and tried to dissuade them from fighting. But when a second attempt at parley failed, the army crossed the Dnieper and marched eastwards across the steppes for nine days, little knowing that they had been misled by a Mongol false retreat conducted on a grand scale. Here they encountered a Mongol army at the Kalka River and were heavily defeated:

> ... his Kuman warriors failed, and retreated in such haste that they galloped over the Russian camp and trampled it underfoot. And there was not time for the Russian forces to form ranks. And so it came to complete confusion, and a terrible slaughter resulted.

Mstislav of Kiev defended himself inside a hastily erected stockade until he was persuaded to give himself up by Ploskyn, a Cossack leader fighting for the Mongols who swore 'on the holy cross' that Prince Mstislav would be released for ransom, but:

> ... this accursed Ploskyn lied, and he bound the princes hand and foot and turned them over to the Tartars [Mongols]. The princes were taken by the Tartars and crushed beneath platforms placed over their bodies on top of which the Tartars celebrated their victory banquet.

Subadai successfully led the Mongol Army home having covered around 4,000 miles in less than three years.

Subadai may have served in Genghis Khan's last campaign against the Xixia, but the next action for which he is renowned was the successful siege of the Jin's southern capital of Kaifeng in 1232, where Subadai had to contend with thunder crash bombs thrown by catapult. That was the last Subadai was to see of campaigning in China, although in 1257 his son, Uriyangkhadai, led an army into the country now known as Vietnam, and his grandson, Bayan, was to accomplish the destruction of the Southern Song in 1276.

Subadai's last and greatest campaign was the invasion of Russia and eastern Europe. Batu, son of Jochi, was the overall leader, but Subadai was the actual commander in the field, and as such was present in both the northern and southern campaigns against Russia and the Ukraine. He commanded the central column that moved against Hungary. While the northern force of Kaidu, ruler of Eastern Turkestan, won the battle of Liegnitz and his uncle Kadan's army triumphed in Transylvania, Subadai was waiting for them on the Hungarian plain. The newly reunited army then withdrew to the Sajo River, where they inflicted a tremendous defeat on King Bela IV at the battle of Mohi. Subadai masterminded the operation, and it was to prove one of his greatest victories.

The king had summoned a council of war at Gran, an important settlement on the south of the Danube bend upstream from Buda and Pest. As Batu was advancing on Hungary from the north-east, it was decided to concentrate at Pest and then head north-east to confront the Mongol Army. When news of the Hungarians' apparent intentions reached the Mongol commanders they slowly withdrew, drawing their enemies on. The Mongols took a stand near Eger to the east of the River Sajo, on a flat plain bounded to the north by the famous wine-growing area of Tokay. It was a strong position. Woodland prevented their ranks from being reconnoitred, while across the river on the plain of Mohi, the Hungarian Army appeared to be very exposed.

Subadai launched the battle of Mohi during the night of 10–11 April 1241, only one day after his compatriots had won the great battle of Liegnitz. One division crossed the river in secret to advance on the Hungarian camp from the south-east. The main body began to cross the Sajo by the bridge at Mohi. This met with some resistance, so catapults were used to clear the opposite bank. When the crossing was completed the other contingent attacked at the same time. The result was panic, and, to ensure that the Hungarians did not fight desperately to the last man, the Mongols left an obvious gap in their encirclement. As they had planned, the fleeing Hungarians poured through this opened trap, which led to a swampy area. When the Hungarian knights split up, the light Mongol archers picked them off at will and it was later noted that corpses littered the countryside for the space of a two days' journey. Two archbishops and three bishops were killed at the Sajo. By late 1241 Subadai was discussing plans to invade Austria, Italy and Germany, when the news came of the death of Ogodei Khan, and the Mongols withdrew.

With his return to Mongolia Subadai's name disappears from history. Perhaps he retired from active service, because we know he was dead by 1248. He remains one of Genghis Khan's most celebrated generals, and there is a statue of him in Ulan Bator, honouring a fine soldier and a loyal and honourable follower of the Mongol Khans.

KONSTANTIN MIHAILOVIC, SERBIAN JANISSARY

The Ottoman Empire 1326–1615

Stephen Turnbull

Few janissaries ever had the opportunity, or even the inclination, to return to the Christian fold. Far fewer ever thought to record their experiences in writing and for this reason the testimony of Konstantin Mihailovic, the so-called Serbian janissary, is of immense interest and importance. Konstantin Mihailovic was a native of Ostrovica, a town difficult to locate for certain but probably identical to the Ostrovica about 40 miles south of Belgrade. His memoirs tell us nothing of his early life. Instead we are introduced to him at the siege of Constantinople in 1453 at which he claims to have been present, although this may be a fabrication. He implies that he was one among 1,500 cavalrymen supplied by George Brankovic, the despot of Serbia, under the requirements of his vassalage to the Turkish sultan. Konstantin's narrative is somewhat stilted here. He wants to record his involvement in this major historical event, but is also reluctant to admit that he was required to serve on the Turkish side. As Konstantin was only a boy it is unlikely that he took part in any fighting, and none is recorded in his memoirs. Instead we have some vivid eyewitness descriptions of some of the key moments of the siege, such as the dragging of the Turkish ships overland into the Golden Horn.

By the time his story has become more reliable the political problem has disappeared, because the Turks have now invaded his home country and Konstantin is involved in the resistance against them. This was Mehmet the Conqueror's second Serbian campaign of 1455. Starting from Edirne, the Ottoman Army marched via Sofia and laid siege to Novo Brdo, which capitulated on 1 June 1455 after a siege of 40 days. This was the occasion when Konstantin was captured:

> The Emperor [the sultan] himself standing before the small gate sorted out the boys on one side and the females on the other, and the men along the ditch on one side and the women on the other side. All those among the men who were the most important and distinguished he ordered decapitated.

The boys were taken 'into the Janissaries,' and Konstantin was among them:

> … I was also taken in that city with my two brothers, and wherever the Turks to whom we were entrusted drove us in a band, and whenever we came to forests or mountains, there we always thought about killing the Turks and running away by ourselves among the mountains, but our youth did not permit us to do that.

Konstantin's mention of his youth clearly refers to the unlikelihood of them being able to overpower their captors, but flight was still possible:

> for I myself with 19 others ran away from them in the night from a village called Samokovo. Then the whole region pursued us, and having caught and bound us, they beat us and tortured us and dragged us behind horses. It is a wonder that our soul remained in us. Then others vouched for us, and my two brothers, that we would not permit this any more, and so they peacefully led us across the sea.

It is from this time that Konstantin is commonly assumed to have become a janissary. However, we see him in action the following year, 1456, at the siege of Belgrade, which would not have allowed time for the training required. Also he refers to 'the janissaries' in his account in a way that does not imply that he was actually serving in their ranks. We may therefore assume that Konstantin was attached to the janissary corps in some way. His account of the events of the siege of Belgrade is very interesting. For example:

> The highest lord after the Emperor, named Karadiabassa [Karaca Pasha], was standing on a rampart alongside the great cannon observing, and a cannoneer fired from the great cannon into a wall, and the stone, having torn loose from the wall, struck Karadiabassa in the head. He was not alive for long.

The sultan was then advised to send the janissaries into the attack. Konstantin watched them going in:

> … and so they stormed until they got into the city. Four hundred and some Janissaries were listed wounded, but also some, but not many of them, killed. Then, in a short time we saw the Janissaries running back out of the city fleeing and the Hungarians running after them and beating them.

This was the beginning of the rout. Konstantin's next campaign in the sultan's service was against Trebizond (Trabzon), a land he says that is 'mountainous and great, surrounded everywhere by heathens – all Tartars such as the great Khan':

> And also rains fell every day so that the road was churned up as high as the horses' bellies everywhere. And so with great effort we arrived at a mountain in the Trebizond area. The road descending from the mountain was ruined and blocked.

This called for desperate measures, and Konstantin tells us how the sultan was forced to destroy and burn the supply waggons and give the horses away. The baggage was carried on camels instead. The excellent discipline of the janissaries is illustrated by the amusing incident that followed, because one of the camels carrying treasure slid off the mountain path. The chest it was carrying broke open, disgorging 60,000 gold pieces. The janissaries immediately mounted guard with their swords until the owner of the treasure came along, and when the sultan arrived on the scene he demanded to know why the whole convoy had come to a grinding halt:

> … and immediately the Emperor gave the order permitting anyone who could to pick up the gold pieces, and the army moved forward. And it was lucky for those

who were there at that time, for some did well in that accident. I too happened upon it but late, for the gold pieces were already where they belonged and only black earth remained, for whoever could had grabbed them up with mud and grass, and from each other's hands as necessary.

The next time Konstantin is in action we find him in the sultan's advance against the notorious impaler lord, Vlad Dracula of Wallachia. Konstantin's vivid account of the war against this larger than life character is very valuable. He confirms Dracula's use of impalement, and adds the gruesome detail that Dracula cut off the noses from his victims and sent them to Hungary, boasting about how many Turks he had killed.

Konstantin was present at the janissaries' attempt to cross the Danube at Nicopolis:

> Then the Emperor immediately ordered that they be given 80 large and well-rigged boats and other necessities for shooting: guns, mortars, field pieces and pistols. And when it was already night we boarded the boat and shoved off downstream in that river so that oars and men would not be heard. And we reached the other side some furlongs below where the Voivode's army lay, and there we dug in, having emplaced the cannon and having encircled ourselves with shields and having placed stakes around ourselves so that the cavalry could do nothing to us. Then the boats went to the other side until the Janissaries had all crossed to us.

Konstantin records that 250 janissaries were killed by cannon fire as they disembarked, but the Turkish cannon fire and the sheer weight of numbers eventually drove the Wallachians away. The sultan must have been very concerned over the possible outcome, because Konstantin tells us that he distributed 30,000 gold pieces among his troops and assured the janissaries that as a result of their service they would be permitted to leave their property to whomsoever they chose after their deaths. Konstantin then describes the Turkish advance to Tirgoviste and Dracula's surprise attack:

> We were always on the lookout for them and every night surrounded ourselves with stakes. Despite this we couldn't always protect ourselves, for striking us in the night they beat and killed men, horses and camels and cut down tents so that they killed several thousand Turks and did the Emperor great harm. And other Turks fleeing before them towards the Janissaries, the Janissaries also beat back and killed so as not to be trampled by them.

Konstantin spares us a description of the 'forest of the impaled.' Perhaps his lowly rank did not permit him to ride so close to the vanguard and the sultan? In any case, the campaign ended soon, and Konstantin's memoirs go on to tell us about his involvement in the Bosnian campaign of 1463, an action that had fateful personal consequences for him:

> And so we marched to Bosnia and came to the lands of a Bosnian prince named Kovacevic. Not knowing that the Emperor was on the march they surrendered to the Emperor. Then they cut off his head… And from there we marched into the King's land and he [the Sultan] first besieged a fortress called Bobovac. Not having cannon with him he had them cast there below the fortress, and he took the fortress by battering it with these guns.

Bobovac was a small castle in eastern Bosnia. The Bosnian king Tomas fled from his capital of Jajce at the approach of the Turkish Army, hoping to reach Croatia.

Part of the Ottoman Army went in pursuit of him while the Sultan besieged Jajce. The king eventually surrendered at the fortress of Kljuc:

> And Machmutbassa [Mahmut Pasha], having heard this, besieged the fortress, and the next day he negotiated with the king [to come] down from the fortress, swearing on books of soap, of which there was earlier discussion, promising that nothing would happen to his neck.

The curious comments about swearing on 'books of soap' rather than the Koran is a fabrication inserted by Konstantin to show the deceit of Mahmut Pasha, because King Tomas surrendered and was executed. In reality Mahmut Pasha was sincere in his desire to save the Bosnian king's life, but was overruled by the sultan.

At the end of the Bosnian campaign, Konstantin Mihailovic was left with a garrison of janissaries to defend the fortress of Zvecaj. He appears to have had considerable responsibility, because he was given half a year's wages for each janissary and had another 30 Turkish soldiers with him. But their resistance was feeble, because Zvecaj was besieged and captured by King Matthias Corvinus of Hungary. Konstantin was among the prisoners taken, and when his identity became known he was repatriated to the Christian side, rich in experience and memories:

> And King Matthias, having taken Jajce with a treaty immediately marched back to the Hungarians at Zvecaj, and we also had to surrender; and whatever Turks were at Jajce and Zvecaj, few of them returned to the Turks, for King Matthias wished to keep them with him. And I thanked the Lord God that I thus got back among the Christians with honour.

With this event he abruptly concludes his personal reminiscences. The rest of his memoirs, including a large introductory section, are observations and reflections on the Ottoman Army and society. The remarkable document ends with the words: 'Lord God Almighty, help faithful Christians against the ignoble heathens, to wipe them out. Amen.'

KATO KIYOMASA, ONE OF THE SEVEN SPEARS OF SHIZUGATAKE

War in Japan 1467–1615

Stephen Turnbull

One of the most striking features of the Sengoku Period was the way the turbulence and disorder of the age allowed men from relatively obscure backgrounds to achieve great power and influence through the exercise of their military skills. Every foot soldier, it seemed, carried a general's war fan in his knapsack. The greatest example of such a rise to power was, of course, Toyotomi Hideyoshi, who made sure that no one else could follow his lead by the Sword Hunt and Separation Edicts of 1587 and 1591, which disarmed the peasants and made a clear distinction between samurai and farmers. Before the ladder of promotion had been removed, however, at least one other commoner from Hideyoshi's home village made his own rise to martial stardom. His name was Kato Kiyomasa.

Born in the village of Nakamura, which has long since been swallowed up within the modern city of Nagoya, Kato Kiyomasa was called *Toranosuke* (the young tiger) in his childhood. He was the son of a blacksmith who died when the boy was three years old. The young Toranosuke saw the example Toyotomi Hideyoshi set of leaving the peasant life and enlisting as a soldier in the armies of Oda Nobunaga. Through a familial relationship between the two boys' mothers, Toyotomi Hideyoshi took Toranosuke under his wing when his father died. Kato Kiyomasa soon proved to have a considerable aptitude for the military life, and his first opportunity to demonstrate it came at the age of 21 in the battle of Shizugatake, where the absence of a flat battlefield and lines of arquebus troops allowed the individual samurai spirit to be expressed in an unfettered way. Kato Kiyomasa fought on horseback in classic style, with the support of a loyal band of samurai attendants, and wielded his favourite cross-bladed spear to great effect. It was not long before a number of enemy heads had fallen to Kiyomasa, and to intimidate his opponents he had one of his attendants tie the severed heads to a long stalk of green bamboo and carry it into Kato's fresh conflicts like a general's standard. Kato Kiyomasa was named that day as one of the Seven Spears of Shizugatake – the most valiant warriors – and from that time on his fortunes prospered.

In 1585 Kato Kiyomasa received from Hideyoshi the important role of *Kazue no kami*, effectively Hideyoshi's inspector of taxes, and in 1588 he began a long association with the island of Kyushu through the following sequence of events. A *daimyo* called Sasa Narimasa had sided against Hideyoshi at the time of the Komaki campaign of 1584, but had been defeated and forced to submit to Hideyoshi's rule. Following the Kyushu campaign in 1587, Sasa was transferred to captured territory in northern Higo province, but Hideyoshi was so dissatisfied with his behaviour that Sasa was forced to commit suicide.

Kato Kiyomasa was given Sasa's fief, centred around the castle town of Kumamoto, where he was to be based for the rest of his life, and the city still honours the memory of its most famous inhabitant. Statues of Kiyomasa abound, and all show him in full armour with a striking helmet design. It was supposed to represent a courtier's cap, and was made by building up a crown of wood and papier mâché on top of a simple helmet bowl. Several of these helmets still exist. Some portraits of Kiyomasa also show him with an extensive beard, which was quite unusual for a samurai. Another characteristic of Kiyomasa was his fanatical attachment to the Nichiren sect of Buddhism, to the extent of using a saying of Nichiren – *Namu myoho renge kyo* (Hail to the Lotus of the Divine Law) – as his motto and war cry. It was also inscribed on the breastplates of his foot soldiers, and his most treasured possession was a white flag with the same motto, said to have been written by Nichiren himself. This was carried as his battle standard in every encounter he fought. Kato's religious affiliation contrasted markedly with the Christianity espoused by his neighbour in southern Higo, Konishi Yukinaga, and the two men did not enjoy friendly relations.

In 1592 the invasion of Korea was launched, and Kato Kiyomasa was given command of the Second Division of the Japanese Army. Unfortunately his rival, Konishi Yukinaga, was given command of the First Division. So easy was Konishi's landing and so rapid was his progress up Korea that it seemed that there would be little glory left for Kato Kiyomasa's troops. In fact, by the time the Second Division caught up with the First at Ch'ungju, Konishi's men had reaped all the battle honours. A furious row then broke out between the two commanders over who should now lead the final advance on Seoul. A compromise was reached by which the two divisions took separate routes, but again Konishi beat his rival to the glory of being first into battle, because when Kato Kiyomasa arrived at the gates of the capital he found Konishi's men on guard duty, and he had to persuade them to let him in!

Konishi's troops were tired after their 20-day march through Korea, so it was sensibly agreed that Kato's division should now take the lead and pursue the retreating Koreans northwards. Kato Kiyomasa set off in high spirits, only to come to a grinding halt on the southern bank of the wide Imjin River. There he sat for almost a month, and it was only when an unwise Korean raid presented the Japanese with some boats that a crossing was made. By this time the king of Korea had made his escape, and at a council of war held in Seoul, the Japanese high command agreed that Konishi should continue northwards in pursuit of the king, while Kato Kiyomasa headed north-east after the two Korean princes who had taken refuge somewhere near the Tumen River.

Kato Kiyomasa's campaign in Hamgyong province, the wildest area of Korea, was the crowning glory of his military career. He crossed the peninsula from Seoul and made his way along the east coast, meeting his first armed resistance at the battle of Songjin, where a Korean army trapped Kiyomasa's force inside a rice warehouse. The Japanese defended the position so well, with massed arquebus fire from behind barricades of rice bales, that the Korean general withdrew for the night. Without waiting for the next day Kato launched a night raid, and drove the Korean soldiers into a trap. As the Korean general then fled north, creating panic as he went, Kato's subsequent progress was made that much easier. He eventually caught up with the Korean princes at Hoeryong, a Korean penal colony on the Tumen, where he discovered to his surprise and delight that the princes had been taken captive by their own rebellious subjects. With his primary objective attained, Kato Kiyomasa resolved to invade China, or at least a few square miles of it immediately across the border. Here lived the Jurchens, called the Orangai by the Japanese, and with Koreans acting as guides, Kato Kiyomasa became the first, and only, Japanese general to enter China during the Korean campaign. The Jurchens proved to be stubborn fighters, and at one stage Kiyomasa had to take his precious Nichiren flag in his own hands when his standard bearer was killed. Following this excursion, the Second Division followed the Tumen down to the sea, and enjoyed a moment of poetic whimsy on the beach at Sosup'o, where an offshore island looked like Mount Fuji. It was about this time that developments elsewhere in Korea sounded the death knell for the Japanese invasion, and within a few months Kato Kiyomasa was to be found defending his line of forts before abandoning them altogether as the army regrouped at Seoul. A retreat to the coast followed, where Kato Kiyomasa took a prominent part in the last siege of the first invasion at Chinju, and he is credited with the use of reinforced wooden waggons to protect foot soldiers digging away the foundation stones of the wall to create a breach.

Kato's troops garrisoned the fort of Sosaengp'o as his contribution to the limited occupation of Korean territory that was carried out by Japan over the next four years.

Kato Kiyomasa was one of the leading generals put into the field when the Japanese invaded Korea for a second time in 1597. He took part in the capture of Hwangsoksan Castle, but his most important role was in defence of the fortress of Ulsan during a long and bitter winter siege, when soldiers froze to death at their posts. Kiyomasa had come to Ulsan from Sosaengp'o with a small force, and he immediately took charge of the situation, inspiring his men to hold out until a relieving army arrived, in spite of 'human wave' attacks against the walls by thousands of Chinese.

On his return to Japan, Kato Kiyomasa took over his manorial responsibilities at Kumamoto once again, and because of the unpleasant experience of being besieged in Ulsan, he resolved to make Kumamoto Castle impregnable. He planted nut trees within the baileys to provide food, and all the mats within the living quarters were stuffed not with the usual rice straw but with dried vegetable stalks, so that even they could be eaten in an emergency. It would no doubt have given Kiyomasa great satisfaction if he had known that Kumamoto Castle would indeed withstand a siege in 1871.

When the *daimyo* split into the two factions that led to the Sekigahara campaign of 1600, Kiyomasa's remoteness from the scene meant that he could take a more calculated view of the likely outcome than many of his contemporaries. His old rival and neighbour Konishi Yukinaga declared for Ishida Mitsunari and lost his head as a result, so Kiyomasa was quick to seize for himself the other half of Higo province in the name of Tokugawa Ieyasu. Yet there was a less selfish reason for Kato's choice, because Toyotomi Hideyori, Hideyoshi's heir, was still alive, and Kato's loyalty to Hideyoshi's memory led him to believe that Hideyori would be safer if there was peace between him and the Tokugawa. Hideyori was present at a meeting held in Nijo Castle to discuss his future, and it is said that Kiyomasa had a dagger concealed on his person which he intended to use on the shogun if Hideyori's safety was threatened. As it happened, Kato Kiyomasa did not live long enough to witness the death of Hideyori at Osaka Castle, because he died himself in 1611, possibly from the effects of poison, and Tokugawa Ieyasu may have had a hand in his death. Like several other Sengoku *daimyo*, Kato Kiyomasa left writings behind in which he tried to make recommendations for the successful samurai life. His *Precepts* include the following observations:

> One should rise at four in the morning, practise sword techniques, eat one's breakfast and train with the bow, the gun and the horse.
>
> If one should require diversions, one should make them such outdoor pastimes as falconry, deer hunting and wrestling.
>
> The practice of Noh [style] dancing is absolutely forbidden. When one unsheaths one's sword, one has the cutting down of people in mind. As all things are born from what lies in the heart, a samurai who practises dancing, which lies outside the martial arts, should be ordered to commit hara kiri.

Having been born into the house of a warrior, one's intentions should be to take hold of a long and a short sword and die. If a man does not explore the nature of *bushido* everyday, it will be difficult for him to die a brave and manly death.

THE MEDIEVAL WORLD

I entrust to you the care of France. Deliver up to the King of France my sword of tempered steel. Commend me to the King and to all the lords of the land. Pray for me, all of you, for my time has come. Be men of honour. Love each other and serve your crowned king with total loyalty.

(Jean Cuvelier)

His people might not find, in all the way, horse-meat nor man's meat nor so much as drink for their horses, save in one little brook, wherein was full little relief [because] it was so muddied with the carriages that had passed through it.

(The Arrival of Edward IV)

TWO CRUSADERS AND TWO FURSAN

The Crusades

David Nicolle

PAGAN PEVEREL, AN ANGLO-NORMAN CRUSADER

Pagan Peverel was an Anglo-Norman knight who took part in the First Crusade, but like so many other participants this formed only a small part of his career. Pagan was probably the third son of Ranulph Peverel who, according to one story, made his fortune by marrying one of Duke William of Normandy's Saxon concubines. His eldest brother may even have been the duke's illegitimate child. While Pagan's brothers made good marriages and became important men, he became a soldier and accompanied Duke Robert of Normandy on crusade. He probably took over as one of Robert's standard-bearers following the death of Roger de Barnevilla outside Antioch. Pagan may also have participated in the duke's raid on the Fatimid headquarters during the battle of Ascalon.

Pagan then returned to England, where he found favour with King Henry I, though probably more for his loyalty to the Norman ducal family than for his prowess on crusade. According to the *Liber Memorandum Ecclesie de Barnewelle*, Pagan Peverel was 'a member of the King's household, an oustanding soldier … and praiseworthy above all the nobles of the kingdom in matters of warfare.' In 1105 he was granted the manor of Shefford in Berkshire, but five years later had a serious quarrel with Ramsey Abbey over the possession of two villages, Stowe and Gretton. The king ordered a public trial of the two claims. Pagan lost and, according to the somewhat biased *Miracles of St Ivo*, he and his companions subsequently suffered a number of divinely ordained accidents. Pagan Peverel died after 1133, his son William then went on crusade and himself died in Jerusalem in 1147.

OTHON DE GRANDSON, THE SERVANT OF THE KING

Othon de Grandson was from the middle ranks of the feudal elite and his career is unusually well recorded. Born in 1238, the eldest son of Pierre, Lord of Grandson in Savoy in what is now western Switzerland, Othon was considered to be destined for great things. He was probably brought up on stories of the Crusades, since his grandfather had died in the Holy Land. He and his brother went to England to be educated in the royal households around 1247. Othon soon became a valuable man and seems to have been a companion of Prince Edward, the future King Edward I. In fact Othon accompanied Edward on crusade to Tunisia and Palestine in 1270, being credited with saving the prince's life by sucking out the poison from an assassin's dagger. He certainly remained one of Edward's most trusted men.

As King of England, Edward planned to go on crusade again and to that end sent Othon de Grandson to do some diplomatic groundwork in 1290. As a result this Savoyard knight found himself in Acre when the final Mamluk attack came. Some sources say Othon fought bravely until resistance collapsed, while others claim he deserted his post. He certainly escaped with the money that Edward had entrusted to him, while losing his own possessions. Othon de Grandson spent the rest of his career serving the English crown, taking part in wars in Scotland and France and becoming Warden of the Channel Islands. Nevertheless, he died at the age of 90 only 50 miles from his birthplace, and was buried in Lausanne Cathedral.

JUM'AH AL-NUMAYRI, AN ARAB CAVALIER

We only know of Jum'ah al-Numayri because he was the friend and military mentor of Usamah Ibn Munqidh and is frequently mentioned in Usamah's memoirs. These make it clear that Jum'ah was a highly rated and experienced cavalryman in the little garrison-army of Shayzar in central Syria. He was an Arab soldier who, as his name indicates, came from the Banu Numayr tribe. This tribe had played a major military role in Syrian affairs for hundreds of years. In the 10th century their stronghold was the Harran area, and by the end of the 11th century, the Banu Numayr were allies of Usamah's tribe.

Several men with the name al-Numayri served in Shayzar, including Jum'ah's son Mahmud, but Jum'ah was the most senior. Usamah described him as: 'Our leading cavalryman and our most experienced soldier.' Usamah also recalled there was a knight in the neighbouring Crusader garrison at Afamiyah, his name being 'Badrhawa.' This Badrhawa was one of the enemy's most valiant men and used to say: 'Perhaps one day I shall meet Jum'ah in single combat.' Meanwhile Jum'ah used to say: 'Perhaps one day I shall meet Badrhawa in combat.' But they never did meet, because the Frank was killed by a lion while riding to Antioch.

Usamah's memoirs contain numerous accounts of Jum'ah's character and exploits. One in particular sheds a fascinating light on the concern for personal honour and reputation among the elite Muslim cavalry of this period. Jum'ah, it seems, was terribly upset after being wounded by a younger and less experienced Kurdish horseman in the rival army of Hamah. The youngster was named Sarhank Ibn Abi Mansur. Later in the same battle Jum'ah went off on his own, then returned laughing, announcing that he had hit Sarhank while the latter was surrounded by his comrades and had then himself escaped unscathed.

MUZAFFAR AL-DIN GÖKBÖRI, THE LOYAL TURK

Muzaffar al-Din Gökböri, whose name means 'Blue Wolf' in Turkish, came from a powerful Turkish family. His father was a Seljuk governor of Irbil in northern Iraq and became a loyal follower of Zangi, the first Muslim ruler to roll back the Crusader advance. Gökböri served Nur al-Din and supposedly became titular governor of Harran at the age of 14. In 1175 he commanded part of the Aleppo-Mosul army against Saladin at the battle of Hama. But Nur al-Din's inheritance was fragmenting and Gökböri recognised that Saladin was the rising star. He therefore invited Saladin to invade the Zangid lands north-east of the Euphrates river. Saladin attacked in 1182 and a year or so later gave Gökböri the towns of Edesa and Sumaysat as his reward. Gökböri also married one of Saladin's sisters, al-Sitt Rabia Khatun.

In 1185 some of Saladin's advisers accused the Turk of disloyalty and suggested executing him. Instead Saladin confiscated two of Gökböri's towns but allowed him to remain in his service. During Saladin's great victory at Hattin in 1187, Gökböri lived up to his reputation for standing firm while others quailed and so Saladin gave the Turk his father's original governorate around Irbil. There the great warrior showed himself to be an enthusiastic patron of learning and the arts. Gökböri is also said to have been the first Islamic ruler to encourage the previously unofficial Mawlid al-Nabi (Birthday of the Prophet Muhammad) festivities, perhaps in imitation of the Christmas celebrations held by Irbil's large Christian community. At the age of almost 80, Gökböri and his men joined the troops of the caliph of Baghdad to shadow the Mongols who were now ravaging Iran. He fell ill during the campaign and returned home to Irbil, where he died in June 1233.

VIKING LEGEND, ENGLISH PATRIOT AND TWO NORMAN EARLS

Norman Conquest

Matthew Bennett

HARALD HARD-RULER, KING OF NORWAY (1015–1066)

Harald fought his first battle in 1030, aged about 15, at Stikelstad near Trondheim, attempting to restore his uncle Olaf to the throne. Olaf (later St Olaf) was killed and Harald was wounded, fleeing eastward to Sweden and then to Russia. He was welcomed by Grand Prince Jaroslav of Kiev, whose wife was Swedish, and who valued Scandinavian links. Harald served a military apprenticeship, fighting in the Polish campaign of 1031, and then against other enemies of Kiev: the Byzantines, Estonians and steppe nomads. He also made an impact on Jaroslav's daughter, Elizaveta.

In about 1034, Harald moved on to Constantinople to serve in the Byzantine emperor's famous Varangian Guard, made up of Scandinavian and Rus 'axe-bearers.' He campaigned in Asia Minor, expelling the Arabs (by 1035) and even reaching the Euphrates. From 1038 to 1041, he served under George Maniakes in the reconquest of Sicily until the famous general was recalled and imprisoned by a jealous emperor.

Coup and counter-coup saw Harald himself in jail for a while, on charges ranging from withholding booty to rape and murder. Released in mid-1042, he soon returned to Kiev and married Elizaveta. In 1046, he sailed for home as a rich and renowned warrior. On the way he met up with Swein Estrithsson, who was trying to establish his claim to the throne of Denmark against Harald's nephew Magnus, now ruling in Norway. After initially fighting Magnus, Harald bought peace with his enormous fortune. When Magnus conveniently died in 1047, Harald was the natural successor, spending the next two decades consolidating his rule and engaging in a raiding war with Denmark. Defeated in naval battle by Swein in 1049, Harald tried again in 1062. In another naval encounter at Nisa, the ships of both sides were roped together to form a fighting platform, although Harald kept a mobile reserve that sailed around the Danish fleet. Attacked from the rear, the Danes fled, losing many vessels but saving their men, among them the king. A peace treaty followed in 1064, for Harald now had his eyes on a greater prize: England. Harald's resources meant that a bid for the crown was well within his grasp. Fate decided otherwise and he died in battle, remembered for his bravery, ruthlessness, wealth and a talent for poetry, like the sagas that record his own deeds.

HEREWARD 'THE LAST ENGLISH REBEL' (*fl.* 1060S–1070S)

Made famous by the great Victorian novelist Charles Kingsley (amongst others), as 'Hereward the Wake,' legends grew early about this obscure thegn. The 12th-century Latin text *Gesta Herewardi* describes his outlawry as a youth and adventures in Flanders (some of which may actually be true), Cornwall and Ireland (which are not) before returning home. There he discovered that his brother had been murdered in revenge for killing two Frenchmen, so he took up arms against the invaders. After a series of incidents, including a rescue from prison by his men worthy of a Hollywood 'Robin Hood,' King William is represented as being so impressed by the Englishman's chivalry that he pardons him at the end of the poem. This 'happy ending' conceals, though, the reality of the expulsion of the landed gentry of which Hereward was a part.

The Domesday Book records that he held three manors in Lincolnshire worth 40 shillings (£2) each, yet on two occasions states that he did not possess some of his estates because of his 'flight' into outlawry. This may have reflected his involvement in the rebellion of 1069, perhaps prompted by an attempted takeover of his land by the invaders. Ogier, who appears in the *Gesta* as a main opponent, is probably Ogier the Breton, later possessor of two of the manors named. The third manor went to Frederick, who was killed by Hereward in 1070. This made him a powerful enemy, for Frederick's brother-in-law was the Norman noble William de

Warenne, castellan of Lewes in Sussex and close to the king. Hereward held lands of Peterborough Abbey, and was involved in the sacking of the house when the Danes came in the summer of 1070. Since he had such a dangerous reputation, only Ely could give him any refuge, and its defenders did well to hold out against the royal forces for as long as they did. After the island fell in mid-1071, Hereward escaped to the forest of Bruneswald. This can be identified with Leighton Bromswold, the Northamptonshire estate of his companion in arms, Thorkell of Harringworth. His eventual fate is unknown.

ROGER DE MONTGOMERY, EARL OF SHREWSBURY AND ARUNDEL (c. 1093)

Although his birth date is unknown, Roger was a close contemporary of Duke William, his cousin and companion in war since at least the siege of Domfront in c.1048. Marriage into the Bellême family made him one of the richest lords in Normandy, controlling castles and lands along the sensitive southern border, as well as his family estates in the heart of the duchy. As a most important vassal, Roger advised the duke on his invasion plans at Lillebonne, and is one of only a handful of men praised by William of Poitiers for his valour at Hastings.

The Conqueror displayed his trust in Roger by making him earl of Shrewsbury in about 1071, where his task was to contain and subjugate the Welsh. He was responsible for constructing the city's castle, along with many others, including one at Montgomery in southern Shropshire (although the present stone castle is from Henry III's reign). These fortifications both defended the frontier and provided bases for making inroads into Welsh territory, his son Hugh leading raids as far as Ceredigion and Dyfed. Such was the range of his responsibilities that he was twice an earl. He also constructed Arundel Castle in Sussex as part of the south-coast defences, based upon groups of estates known as rapes.

His wife Mabel having been killed in a feud in Normandy in 1082, Roger married Adeliza de Puiset. Together they founded Shrewsbury Abbey, bringing monks from Sées to staff it, and the community, although not the magnificent red sandstone buildings, were complete by 1087. Roger also revived the monastery of St Milburga (an English royal saint) at Much Wenlock, and established a collegiate church at Quatford, also in Shropshire. His sense of piety was matched by his sense of place, and at Arundel he sponsored a priory dedicated to St Nicholas (the Normans' favourite saint). Roger was the archetypical great lord of the Conquest, with nationwide power and cross-Channel authority. His adoption of local saints proved his determination to become an Englishman whilst remaining proud of his Norman inheritance. It seems that he was happy to remain in his adopted country when he died about 1093, at his Quatford castle: he was buried between the two altars of Shrewsbury Abbey rather than being returned to the duchy.

HUGH D'AVRANCHES, EARL OF CHESTER (?–1101)

Hugh came from Danish stock in western Normandy, his grandfather Thurstan Goz having been a rebel against the young Duke William before the region was brought under ducal control in the 1050s. Hugh's father, Richard, made his peace with William, and Hugh inherited the county of Avranches at the western base of the Côtentin Peninsula. He was a substantial supporter of the invasion and received William's gratitude, being given lands in 20 counties. Gerbod, a Fleming, had been made responsible for Chester, but in 1071 he went back to Flanders and Hugh was awarded the territory and an earldom.

By this gift the Conqueror was recognizing Hugh's talents as a warrior and his enormous energy in confronting the Welsh. With the help of his nephew Robert, he made inroads along the north coast, even reaching Anglesey. These territories were lost in 1093, when Hugh was in Normandy supporting William Rufus in the continuing disputes between the Conqueror's sons. On his return, Hugh reconquered the lands and punished the rebels by ravaging and mutilation, establishing a castle at Aberlleiniog in Anglesey. In 1098, Magnus Barelegs, King of Norway, raided the island and defeated Hugh. Overall, though, Hugh was an immensely successful border baron. He was caricatured by the chronicler Orderic Vitalis as a man of gross appetites, both sexually, with many mistresses and bastard offspring, and at the table, becoming so fat that he could hardly walk. Hugh was also known as Lupus (the Wolf) for his severity against the Welsh. For all his brutality, however, Hugh seems to have been genuinely pious. When in 1092 he replaced the secular canons of St Werburgh's, Chester, with monks from Bec, he asked the saintly Archbishop Anselm to consecrate his new church (the present cathedral). The unlikely combination of these two men at the ceremony could have led to many jokes about the strange friendship between the Wolf and the Lamb.

BERTRAND DU GUESCLIN, ANDREW TROLLOPE AND OSBERN MUNDEFORD, COMPANIONS AT ARMS

Hundred Years' War

Anne Curry

BERTRAND DU GUESCLIN

Bertrand du Guesclin (c.1320–80) came from a relatively poor cadet branch of the Breton minor nobility, but rose to be France's great hero. Within seven years of his death, a poem on his life was composed by a Picard, Jean Cuvelier, confirming du Guesclin as a legend in his own time. The poet tells us that mothers in France, when chastising their children, would say 'be quiet, or else du Guesclin will come to get you.' Richard the Lionheart had been similarly invoked by mothers in the past. Du Guesclin was short in stature, ugly and careless about his appearance. According to Cuvelier, even when he was a child, his parents despaired of his violence: he was always ready to fight, and organized his peasant friends into rival groups. He ran away to Rennes in his late teens and began to demonstrate his prowess in tournaments, especially that held in June 1337 to celebrate the marriage of Jeanne de Penthièvre and Charles of Blois. Here, with a borrowed horse, he felled 15 other combatants before revealing his identity, to the amazement of the crowd.

In the early stages of the Breton civil war, du Guesclin led a small group of partisans in the region of Rennes in support of Charles' claim to the duchy. In 1350, he took the English-held stronghold of Fougeray by trickery. He waited until the commander had taken most of the garrison to Vannes to assist Thomas Dagworth, and then disguised 30 of his own soldiers as peasants, and even some as women, so that they could enter the place under the guise of delivering timber. These actions were those of a freelance guerrilla. It was not until the death of his father in 1353, when he inherited the family manor, that he joined the royal army, serving under the marshal of France, Arnoul d'Audrehem, in Lower Normandy.

In 1357, Rennes looked poised to fall to Henry, Duke of Lancaster. Du Guesclin, then in the company of Pierre de Villiers, captain of Pontorson, managed to bring much-needed supplies into the city. He followed this with a sortie against the English, who were thereby forced to raise the siege, bringing the French their first piece of good fortune since the capture of King John. Du Guesclin was rewarded by the Dauphin with a grant of 200 livres tournois, hardly a huge sum, but he had come to the notice of the right people. When de Villiers was called to Paris, du Guesclin took over control of Pontorson, a key garrison on the frontier of Brittany and Normandy, with 120 men under his command. Over the next 23 years he was involved in almost every major theatre, rising through a series of regional commands on behalf of the king and the princes of the blood. He was much relied upon to clear routiers from various areas, and for royal actions against Charles of Navarre. Using the age-old tactic of a feigned retreat, he succeeded in defeating the latter at Cocherel on 16 May 1364.

This led to his being created royal chamberlain and count of Longueville. But he was captured at the battle of Auray on 29 September 1364 when fighting in the cause of Charles of Blois, a reminder that military service for men like du Guesclin was not exclusively for the king. The king assisted in payment of his ransom, and his service thus continued in the later 1360s, leading a 12,000-strong force in support of Henry of Trastamara's ambitions in Castile. Here he was captured again in the Black Prince's victory at Najera on 3 April 1367, by Thomas Cheyne, a man of relatively low rank – a timely reminder that in military action, neither social status nor military reputation rendered combatants less vulnerable. Charles V again assisted in the payment of ransom, which was set by Edward III at 100,000 francs, testimony to du Guesclin's perceived significance.

Du Guesclin served on subsequent campaigns under the king's brother, the duke of Anjou, against the routiers in Languedoc, and under Trastamara in Castile. He was to play a fundamental role in Charles V's battle-avoiding strategy when war reopened in 1369, being appointed constable of France in 1370, and containing the great English chevauchées of 1370 and 1373. He also prevented the English seizing Saint-Malo in 1378, although his willingness to negotiate their withdrawal led to criticism at the French royal court. Although du Guesclin had an excellent reputation as a war leader, his relatively low social origin was never forgotten by some. Warfare did offer opportunities for those who could prove their value, yet armies of both sides remained very class-based in their structures of command. Du Guesclin had made it to the top through his own prowess and bravery. At the assault on Charles of Navarre's stronghold of Melun in 1359, for instance, he fought on despite being hit on the head by a large projectile. He was a firm disciplinarian, but he was also much loved by his soldiers because he lived as they did. He was also full of guile and cunning, and was prepared to take risks. Du Guesclin was thus a quintessential soldier who rose from the ranks, not only to be constable, but also to be buried at the order of Charles V next to the king himself in the royal necropolis of Saint-Denis. Cuvelier's poem ends with a poignant death-bed scene, where the dying constable calls the marshal to his side.

> I entrust to you the care of France. Deliver up to the King of France my sword of tempered steel. Commend me to the King and to all the lords of the land. Pray for me, all of you, for my time has come. Be men of honour. Love each other and serve your crowned king with total loyalty.
>
> (Jean Cuvelier, *The Life of the Valiant Bertrand du Guesclin*)

ANDREW TROLLOPE AND OSBERN MUNDEFORD

Andrew Trollope came from Thornley, a village in south-east Durham, and was related to cloth dyers. We find him in 1427 as a mounted man-at-arms at the garrison of Fresnay-le-Vicomte on the southern frontier of Normandy, serving under the captaincy of Sir John Fastolf. Amongst his colleagues was Osbern Mundeford of Hockwold in Norfolk, whose father had served in the Agincourt campaign and who was of low gentry status.

In 1428 Trollope moved to Tombelaine, a particularly uninviting sand-bank location established against French-held Mont-Saint-Michel, but he and Mundeford found themselves together again in Fresnay in the early 1430s. Mundeford was soon specializing in military administration as marshal of the garrison, responsible for discipline and the provision of victuals. Trollope was often deployed in field detachments. In 1433 he was in Fastolf's company reinforcing Caen, and in 1440 Trollope served on a raid into Picardy under Matthew Gough, a soldier whose own renown gave him a place in Welsh poetry. Trollope must have distinguished himself with the overall commander, John Beaufort, Earl of Somerset, since he then joined the latter's personal retinue, but by 1442 he was back in Fresnay as lieutenant to the then captain, Sir Richard Woodville. Mundeford also participated in some field actions in the 1430s, but by 1445 was combining military and civil command as bailli and captain of Le Mans and captain of Beaumont-sur-Sarthe. His commander was now Edmund Beaufort, who had succeeded his brother John as earl of Somerset in 1444. Mundeford found himself in a difficult position when asked to implement the royal decision of December 1445 to surrender Maine to the French, but he had to obey orders, even if at first he questioned them. Once Edmund Beaufort had arrived as lieutenant-general of Normandy in 1448, Mundeford was made treasurer of the duchy, attempting an overhaul of tax collection in 1449. He was also made captain of Pont-l'Evêque and of Fresnay.

In 1449 Trollope was Mundeford's lieutenant at Fresnay. The men were by now brothers-in-law, for Andrew had married Osbern's sister, Elizabeth. When Charles VII reopened the war in July, Mundeford was collecting revenues and foodstuffs for English garrisons between Vernon and Mantes, and on 12 August he was amongst those captured at Pont-Audemer. Ten days later he was a prisoner at Chateaudun, where he was interrogated about the fall of Pont-Audemer.

> He told us on oath that at 11 or 12 at night he was lying in his bed when he heard a noise in the town and the alarm was raised. He got up but only had time to put on his shirt with his brigandine over the top … he soon found where the French had broken ten or twelve of the palisades and was able with the help of three or four other English to drive them back … but two days later, in the middle of the afternoon, he was told that the town was on fire and the French had launched an assault … as the fire spread, the English took refuge in a stronghold.
>
> (Deposition of Mundeford, Bibliothèque Nationale, MS fr. 4054, f. 147)

Trollope as lieutenant surrendered Fresnay to the French in March 1450, but he had not forgotten his companion and brother-in-law: one of the terms of the surrender was that Mundeford should be released. The story is made all the more interesting by the fact that both men continued their military careers after the loss of Normandy. In the early 1450s Mundeford was marshal of Calais and Trollope master porter under Edmund Beaufort. As the Wars of the Roses escalated, they found themselves 'by the sword divided.' Mundeford was back in England supporting the Lancastrians, but Trollope, still at Calais, was chosen by the earl of Warwick to take troops to England to assist Richard, Duke of York. Yet old Beaufort loyalties, based on experiences in France, died hard. On the eve of the battle of Ludford Bridge (12 October 1459), Trollope was persuaded to defect to the Lancastrians, plunging the Yorkists into disarray when he disclosed their intended plan of action. He then joined Edmund Beaufort's son, Henry, in an attempt to take Calais from the Yorkists, and was installed as captain of nearby Guînes.

The lives of Mundeford and Trollope were again entwined. In June 1460, Mundeford assembled troops at Sandwich to reinforce Guînes, but Yorkists from Calais fell upon him. Taken across the Channel, he was summarily executed on the sands below the Tour de Rysback. Trollope was forced to surrender Guînes. He made his way back to England where he gained prominence in the Lancastrian victory at Wakefield on 31 December 1460, using subterfuge to entice the Yorkists from their stronghold at Sandal. He also participated in the Lancastrian victory at St Albans (17 February 1461), during which he was wounded in the foot by a calletrappe (a device for damaging horses' hooves). He was knighted after the battle.

When the Yorkists seized London, Trollope had a price put on his head. He met his end at the battle of Towton (29 March 1461), sharing command of the Lancastrian vanguard with the earl of Northumberland. Thus, both Trollope and Mundeford fought and died for their king in France and in England, and, no doubt like many, forged friendships and relationships as they did so.

NICHOLAS HARPSFIELD, YORKIST

Wars of the Roses

Michael Hicks

Like most of the combatants of the Wars of the Roses, Nicholas Harpsfield was not a professional soldier but a civilian who became embroiled in the conflict. Of Harpsfield Hall in Hertfordshire, he was the son of an English soldier in Normandy, where he was probably brought up bilingual. He was with York in Ireland in 1460 and thereafter became a clerk of the signet, a career civil servant in the king's own secretariat, an educated man fluent both in Latin and French, and a married man with children.

In October 1470 Harpsfield was presumably with King Edward when the Lancastrians invaded and the king himself was almost captured, fleeing via King's Lynn to Burgundy, where Harpsfield was certainly in Edward's company. Presumably he returned in March 1471 and shared in Edward's victories, since on 29 May he wrote in French to Duke Charles the Bold on the king's behalf. There were two enclosures: a copy of the alliance between Henry VI and Louis XI of France against Burgundy, a clear breach of the treaty of Péronne, and a brief *Mémoire* on paper. The *Mémoire* is a short factual account in French of the Barnet and Tewkesbury campaign that Harpsfield had almost certainly penned himself. Many copies were made, some incorporated into French and Flemish chronicles. The *Mémoire* is also the core of a much longer English history, *The Arrival of Edward IV*, probably also written by Harpsfield. *The Arrival* is a precise day-to-day account of events between 2 March and 16 May 1471 which sets out how, with God's help, Edward had overcome almost overwhelming odds and which looks forward to future peace and tranquillity. Although known only through one copy, it was a propaganda piece and sought to impose an official Yorkist interpretation on what had occurred. No matter who the author was, he was a Yorkist partisan, in his own words 'a servant of the king's, that presently saw in effect a great part of his exploits, and the residue knew by true relation of them that were present at every time.' Where the *Mémoire* is the sparest of narratives, *The Arrival* is a much fuller and more elaborate account, which often tells both sides of the story, recounting events happening simultaneously in different places, and explaining them at length.

The story commences with Edward's invasion across the North Sea from Zeeland. Adverse weather held up Edward's initial departure for nine days and his first landing at Cromer was abortive. Sailing northwards to Ravenspur, there 'fell great storms, winds, and tempests upon the sea' and he was 'in great torment,' observes our author – obviously no mariner – as his ships were scattered along the Holderness coast. Coming ashore, he found the country altogether hostile. How the king's small force was allowed to pass between much larger local levies, to enter York and proceed southwards is elaborately explained in terms of Edward's audacity, his deceit – his claim being only for his duchy of York, not the crown – and the role of the Earl of Northumberland in restraining his retainers. *The Arrival* faithfully reports Edward's dealings with the improbably (but correctly) named Michael of the Sea, the recorder, and other emissaries of York, and the disappointing numbers who joined him at this stage. Only once across the Trent did Edward secure numbers enough to confront Warwick who, however, declined to fight. *The Arrival* records both Edward's attempts to shame Warwick into battle by parading his army in formation and by occupying his home town of Warwick, and his negotiations, at Clarence's instance though probably insincere, 'to avoid the effusion of Christian blood,' which put Warwick further in the wrong. When these tactics failed, Edward marched to London – *The Arrival* reports a miracle of St Anne at Daventry, 'a good prognostication of good adventure that should befall the king' – and captured the City, the Tower, King Henry VI and Archbishop Neville. When Warwick rushed southwards, hoping to pin Edward against the walls and to surprise him at Easter, the king confronted him near Barnet. Our informant surely shared the noisy night in a hollow, overshot by Warwick's artillery, and actually saw the king beating down those in front of him, then those on either hand, 'so that nothing might stand in the sight of him and the well-assured fellowship that attended truly upon him.' Assuredly he saw little else: his account faithfully records confusion in the fog as the two armies were misaligned and the Lancastrians mistakenly fought one another.

Following thanksgivings at St Paul's, where the bodies of Warwick and his brother were displayed, *The Arrival* records the western campaign against Queen Margaret, when the king marched to Bath, but Margaret retreated into Bristol. Thereafter he records some cunning manoeuvring, as each army sought to outfox the other, which culminated in their race for the Severn crossing into Wales at Tewkesbury. The Lancastrians marched through dust in the vale, whilst the Yorkists took the easier Roman road across the Cotswolds. The Lancastrians marched 30 miles on a very hot day and their sufferings were acute: 'his people might not find, in all the way, horse-meat nor man's meat nor so much as drink for their horses, save in one little brook, wherein was full little relief [because] it was so muddied with the carriages that had passed through it.' Though the Lancastrians won the race, they were obliged to stand and fight. Again *The Arrival*, best informed on the king's movements, is confused, unable to explain precisely how Somerset in the Lancastrian van managed to attack their flank, but clear enough about its disastrous consequences. Harpsfield was with the king as he progressed to Worcester and to Coventry, and *The Arrival* is full of news of further northern disturbances, their dissolution, and the toing and froing of messages between the king and his northern and London agents.

The Arrival recounts here, from outside, the Bastard of Fauconberg's uprising. It is likely that the author accompanied the king on suppression duty on 26 May, for he was explicitly not with Richard, Duke of Gloucester, at Sandwich that day.

Probably a southerner, the author of *The Arrival* is as unfamiliar with Yorkshire as the Cotswolds. His account lacks the insight into terrain and tactics, the technical jargon of a military commander or a professional soldier, and the interest in individuals, their feats of arms, coats of arms and casualties appropriate to a herald. Vivid though *The Arrival* is, historians have found it hard to convert this narrative into concrete accounts either of the two battlefields or the course of the two battles. It is the version of a layman, a combatant in an inferior role, who tells us nothing about his own exploits, yet witnessed those of the king at first hand and knew little of what else happened on the battlefield; perhaps the king did not either. Our author was evidently on the central staff, au fait with calculations, comings, goings and negotiations alike, being particularly well informed on the political dimensions, on strategy and on morale. If he was indeed Harpsfield, his authorial achievement did him little good for, having slain one of his own colleagues in 1471, he pleaded benefit of clergy to save his life, suffered brief imprisonment and disgrace, and in mid-1474 had to seek employment abroad. But he was forgiven, returning as chancellor of the exchequer, and lived out his last years until about 1489 in secure employment and relative prosperity surrounded by a growing family. Harpsfield's legacy is the most complete and vivid account of any of the Wars of the Roses.

16TH AND 17TH CENTURIES

It seems to me that such fine deeds ought not to be forgotten, so that those who follow the profession of arms may learn to imitate them and avoid the cruelties and base acts which many of them perpetrate because they do not know or do not wish to know how to curb their hatred.

(François de La Noue)

TWO SOLDIER-WRITERS AND A HUGUENOT CAPTAIN

French Religious Wars

Robert J. Knecht

BLAISE DE MONLUC

Blaise de Monluc was born in 1501 in Gascony, a province reputed to be fertile only in soldiers. His earliest experience of war was gained in the Italian Wars, a series of conflicts involving the Italian city-states and other nations from 1494–1559. In 1525 he was taken prisoner at Pavia, but soon released as he was not worth a ransom. Two years later he shared Marshal Lautrec's defeat at Naples and was seriously wounded. In 1534 he served in one of Francis I's provincial legions and in the 1540s fought in Piedmont. Under King Henry II, he attached himself to the rising star of François, duc de Guise, and in 1554 defended Siena, which had rebelled against its Florentine overlord. On returning to France, he was appointed colonel-general of the infantry and knighted. After the peace of Cateau-Cambrésis, however, he fell upon hard times. He thought of joining the Huguenots in south-west France, but decided that his interests would be better served by supporting the Catholic cause. As the king's lieutenant-general in Guyenne, he kept the peace for five years at the cost of much cruelty. Two executioners accompanied him everywhere, administering summary justice at his bidding. Monluc boasted that his passage through Guyenne could be easily plotted on a map thanks to the bodies which he left hanging from trees lining the roads. When a rebel leader at Saint-Mézard begged Monluc to spare his life, he seized the poor man by the throat, screaming: 'How dare you ask for mercy when you have disobeyed your king?' Throwing him down onto a stone cross, he had him instantly beheaded. The sword blow was so violent that part of the cross was broken off. At Fumel, in 1562, Monluc ordered 30 or 40 Huguenots to be hanged or broken on the wheel without trial. At Gironde, he ordered 80 prisoners of war to be hanged from pillars in the market hall. In September 1562 he was responsible for a massacre at Terraube, when a deep well was filled to the top with bodies.

Cruelty was essential to the effective conduct of war, according to Monluc. His nights, on his own admission, were never peaceful: he was always fighting enemies in his sleep. Doctors blamed his imagination, but perhaps this was a sign of a guilty conscience. Disfigured at the age of 70 by a shot from an arquebus, Monluc had to wear a mask for the rest of his days. On being relieved of his governorship, he turned to writing his memoirs between 1570 and 1576, calling them *Commentaires* in imitation of Julius Caesar. The French Wars of Religion produced many military autobiographies. If their aristocratic authors felt uneasy about taking up the pen in place of the sword, they could take comfort from the example of Caesar, who had combined a brilliant military career with authorship. 'The greatest captain that ever lived,' wrote Monluc, 'was Caesar, and he has shown me the way, having himself written his own commentaries, and being careful to record by night the actions he had performed by day.' Monluc wrote long after the events he described and his memory sometimes let him down. Writing, however, enabled him to relive his wartime experiences and also to impart lessons to his fellow captains. He warned them against the perils of gambling, drink, avarice – 'and there is a fourth,' he wrote – 'it is the love of women. If you cannot avoid it, at least approach it soberly. Do not lose your head or commit yourself. That is the exact opposite of a stout heart. When Mars is campaigning, put aside love; you will have time enough for it later.'

Monluc thought artillery was more frightening than effective and shared Machiavelli's distrust of foreign mercenaries. Historical truth, he believed, could be found not in abstract speculation but in the smell of gunpowder and blood. Even so, like the proverbial Gascon, he was inclined to exaggerate and boast. The doctrinal issues dividing Catholics from Protestants did not interest him. The only religious test he understood was whether his faith was that of the king. Viewing religion and politics as indivisible, Monluc refused to allow freedom of conscience precedence over obedience to the monarch. Monluc died, a lonely and embittered old man, in 1577.

FRANÇOIS DE LA NOUE

François de La Noue was born in 1531. Though trained as a soldier, he was also well-read in the classical historians, Scriptures, Church Fathers and contemporary authors. Although he became a Protestant in about 1559, he remained on good terms with the duc de Guise and was chosen to accompany Mary Stuart to Scotland in 1560. In the first religious war, he fought at Dreux under Condé. In the second, he lost an arm, which was replaced by an iron one – hence his nickname 'bras de fer.' In spite of his chosen career, La Noue hated war. He also deplored the divisions among his countrymen. In 1572 he fought in the Low Countries. Later, he was given the impossible task of persuading his co-religionists to surrender La Rochelle to the king, and instead took over command of the town's defences. After that he commanded the Huguenots in western France. In 1578 he followed the duc d'Alençon to the Low Countries, and in 1580 was taken prisoner by the Spaniards. It was during his captivity, which lasted five years, that he wrote his *Discours politiques et militaires*. This, unlike Monluc's *Commentaires*, is not an autobiography. La Noue's personal recollections form only the 26th part of his book, the rest being concerned with ethical, religious, political, economic and military matters. The *Discours* is a kind of encyclopaedia, intended to warn La Noue's fellow nobles and soldiers of the perils facing France and to point to the remedies available to them. La Noue believed that the army, like much else in France, had degenerated since his youth, its discipline especially having crumbled away. Two monsters, he claimed, were devouring France: *la picorée* (pillage) and massacre. He advocated a revival of the feudal levy and the creation of a standing army of 2,500 infantry. He was critical of the traditional way of disposing cavalry, favouring compact blocks instead. Regarding fortification, he thought earthworks were cheaper and more effective than the elaborate structures favoured by Italian military engineers. By saving money on one fortress, he wrote, ten more could be built. But La Noue's memoirs range beyond military matters. They are remarkable especially for their tolerance and humanity. Thus he praises the duc de Guise for his courteous treatment of the prince de Condé after the battle of Dreux. As there were few beds left after the destruction of the prince's baggage, the victorious duke invited his defeated prisoner to share his own. 'It seems to me,' writes La Noue, 'that such fine deeds ought not to be forgotten so that those who follow the profession of arms may learn to imitate them and avoid the cruelties and base acts which many of them perpetrate because they do not know or do not wish to know how to curb their hatred.' It has been said that he did not know how to hate. He never forgot that Jesus died for all Christians, not just a few, and that all Frenchmen were brothers. The contrast between him and Monluc could not be greater.

FRANÇOIS DE BEAUMONT, BARON DES ADRETS

François de Beaumont, Baron des Adrets (1513–87) was a lesser nobleman from Dauphiné whose military career began in the Italian Wars. Having been captured by the Spaniards at Montcalvo, he was set free after paying a ransom that left him destitute. Like other veterans of the Italian Wars, he viewed the peace of Cateau-Cambrésis as a betrayal. He challenged the governor of Montcalvo to a duel, but it was banned by the Guises who controlled the government of Francis II. This may have turned des Adrets into a Protestant. In the first religious war he fought under Condé, capturing Valence in April 1562 and some smaller towns. He committed atrocities allegedly in reprisal for Catholic excesses. In May the baron set up a veritable dictatorship in Lyon. He seized Grenoble in June after sacking the abbey of Saint Antoine, then captured Romans and Saint-Marcellin. At Montbrison, he allegedly ordered 300 or 400 prisoners of war to be thrown off a tower into a burning brazier. Des Adrets was criticised for spreading his activities too widely instead of attending to the defence of Lyon. In July 1562 Condé appointed the seigneur de Soubise in his place. Early in 1563 des Adrets was arrested and taken to Nîmes for trial, only to be set free by the Peace of Amboise. Angered by Condé's snub, des Adrets decided to switch sides. In the second religious war, he besieged Mâcon (1567) and La Côte-Saint-André (1568) for the king. His admission to the order of St Michael suggests that he had reverted to Catholicism. In 1569 he led 17 enseignes of Dauphiné to the duc d'Aumale in

Trajan's Column in Rome illustrates campaigns of the early 2nd century AD, but many of the features shown, especially engineering skills and camp building, were just as important in the conquest of Gaul. In the top scroll, soldiers build a camp from turves to ensure the army is not attacked at night. (Ancient Art and Architecture)

This modern statue of the Spartan king, Leonidas, stands in the centre of the town of Sparta. Inscribed below is a famous two-word reply he is said to have given when the Spartans were invited by Xerxes at the battle of Thermopylae to surrender by laying down their arms. Leonidas answered him in Greek, 'Molon labe,' meaning, 'Come and take them.' (Ancient Art and Architecture)

Byzantine mosaic in St. Apollinare Nuovo, Ravenna, depicting the palace of Theoderic, the Goths' great war leader and last monarch to rule a unified Italy until the nineteenth century. This mosaic dates from around the 6th century AD, originating in Italy. (Ancient Art and Architecture)

The battle of Varna 1444. These victorious Ottomans look down on the body of the Polish King, Wladislaw III. In 1444 the Ottoman sultan had signed a ten-year truce with Hungary, however only months later the Hungarians organised a new Crusader army to fight against the Ottomans. The battle shown here was the last battle in the Crusade for Varna. On the left of the picture the treaty that the Christians broke is flown from a spear. (Stephen Turnbull)

The death of Mongol General Sartaq at the battle of Cho'in in 1232 marked the end of the second Mongol invasion of Korea. (Stephen Turnbull)

This image shows tactical single combat with sword and spear during the decisive battle of Sekigahara, 1600. The origins of this battle can be found in the split of the Japanese *daimyō* into two armed groups in the 1590s. (Stephen Turnbull)

This statue of Kato Kiyomasa that can be found outside Kumamoto Castle. In this depiction of him he is shown wearing his famous tall helmet. (Stephen Turnbull)

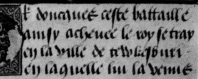

Top left: Hereward and his men attack the Normans. In later times perceived as an English hero, he was seen as a rebel and a bandit by the Norman regime and ended his days as an outlaw in the forest. (Ann Ronan Picture Library)

Top right: Bertrand du Guesclin, a French hero, royal chamberlain and Count of Longueville, fought in many campaigns and proved that you did not have to come from a wealthy background to rise up the ranks, but instead is an example of meritocracy. His tomb, depicted here, was placed close to that of Charles V in the royal necropolis of Saint-Denis. The effigy may give some idea of the constable's appearance. (Roger-Violett)

Left: The execution of Lancastrians after the battle of Tewkesbury, 4 May, 1471. King Edward IV (left) looks on. The battle is recorded in *The Arrival of Edward IV*, potentially written by Nicholas Harpsfield. (Geoffrey Wheeler Collection)

Effigy of Othon de Grandson. Othon was one of those who survived the fall of the Crusader city of Acre to the Mamluks in 1291. He then continued his very successful career in the service of the English crown. Military equipment, though old-fashioned, is shown in very interesting detail. Even the bulge caused by the knight's ears beneath the mail of his coif, and almost certainly a partially padded coif beneath, has been accurately shown. (In situ Cathedral Lausanne, Switzerland. David Nicolle photograph)

This Osprey artwork by Gerry Embleton shows a Teutonic knight c.1230-83 (left), a Hochmeister, Teutonic Order c.1219 (middle) and a Schwerbrüder c.1270 (right). (Gerry Embleton, Osprey)

A group of mounted warriors practise the tactic of the close-order charge with lances couched. Holding the weapon tightly under the arm united man and horse into a single projectile. This enabled the rider to unhorse an opponent in the cavalry skirmishes that made up much of the warfare of northern France. These warriors were called chevaliers, but in England became known as knights. From left to right are two figures wearing mail armour, then scale and lamellar, both constructed from small metal plates sewn onto a leather backing. (Christa Hook, Osprey)

'Cromwell after the battle of Marston Moor,' by Ernest Crofts. Crofts was one of several Victorian artists who specialised in civil war scenes, a very popular genre during the 19th century, though the images often owe more to a romantic and dramatic licence than to strict historical accuracy. (Bridgeman Art Library)

The equipment of a mounted arquebusier during the Civil War, including a leather buff coat, armour protecting the chest and the bridle arm, an open-fronted helmet and, carried at his side and attached to belts across both shoulders, a broadsword and a carbine. (Royal Armouries)

The Château of Estillac-en-Agenais (Lot-et-Garonne). This was the home of Blaise de Monluc, who acquired a reputation for savagery during the French religious wars. Triangular in plan, it has two bastions at the eastern and southern angles, based on designs by Italian military engineers. (David Nicolle)

The battle of Lexington, 19 April, 1775, was one of the first engagements of the War of American Independence. Thirteen united 'states' sought independence from Great Britain. The war ended in 1782 with the signing of the Treaty of Paris. (National Army Museum)

Sir William Henry Dillon (1780–1857) aged 72, one year before he reached the rank of Vice-Admiral of the Red. He spent six decades on active service in the Royal Navy, during which he produced the letters which became the basis for his memoirs. (Lithograph by Bauginet, National Maritime Museum, Greenwich, London)

Rogers' Rangers, as described by Thomas Brown, was an independent company of rangers that fought for Great Britain in the French-Indian War. They were formed in the winter of 1755 under the command of Major Robert Rogers. This artwork shows an elite rangers officer. (Gerry Embleton, Osprey)

This painting of the French-Indian War shows Braddock's Column under attack. The image is viewed from the positions of the French and allied Indians firing into the British positions. Braddock has come under fire for his lack of knowledge of warfare in North America, however, he was only partly to blame for the British defeat. (State Historical Society of Wisconsin)

On 8 May 1846, the first major battle between the Mexican and American armies was fought on the coastal plain of Palo Alto. On the first day of battle American artillery beat off Mexican assaults. The following day, American infantrymen cracked the Mexican lines and sent them into retreat. President Polk told Congress: 'American blood has been shed on American soil' and the war was on. (Painting by Carl Nebel, Archives Division, Texas State Library)

Lorraine, but on being suspected of corresponding secretly with the young Protestant princes of Condé and Navarre, he was arrested and imprisoned in Lyon. He was set free following the Peace of Saint-Germain and Charles IX assured him that he had never doubted of his loyalty. Henry III, however, was less forthcoming when the baron called on him at Lyon in 1574. Des Adrets retired to the château of Romanesche, but in 1585, at the start of the eighth religious war, he returned to Lyon to give advice to the sieur de la Valette, who commanded the king's army. Des Adrets died in 1587. He is mainly remembered for his cruelty, although he claimed that he never broke the laws of war. Some of his misdeeds have not been proven, but he was certainly an unpleasant man who reacted violently to any offence, alleged or real. Religion seems not to have mattered greatly to him.

COLONEL ROBERT MONRO, SCOTS MERCENARY

Thirty Years' War

Richard Bonney

Colonel Robert Monro (*c.*1590–1680) commanded a Scots mercenary regiment called Mackay's Regiment, and later Monro's during the Thirty Years' War. Mercenaries were a typical feature of the war, and we know more about Monro than others because he left his memoirs, which are in essence a regimental and social history. He considered that an army career offered the possibility of achieving one's potential through hard work, diligence and ability. It was far better to 'live honourably abroad, and with credit, then to encroach (as many do) on their friends at home.' For Monro, the profession of arms was 'a calling,' and his service in the German conflict was in part for his 'better instruction,' and in part a matter of principle, supporting as he did the Bohemian and Protestant cause. He was wounded three times, at Oldenburg in 1627, at the siege of Stralsund in 1628 and at Nuremberg in 1632.

Monro was a Presbyterian whose military service in the Thirty Years' War was given to successive Lutheran monarchs, first Christian IV of Denmark, then Gustavus Adolphus of Sweden, fighting against the Roman Catholic emperor. Proud of both his nationality and religion, he attributed victory over the Catholic imperial forces at Breitenfeld largely to 'the invincible Scots, whose prayers to God were more effectual through Christ, then theirs through the intercession of Saints.' Unlike many mercenaries, Monro based his choice of side firmly on religious principle and opposition to 'Catholique Potentates' who would overthrow 'our estates at home' and 'make shipwracke of our consciences' by 'leading us unto Idolatry.' Gustavus Adolphus' example of 'Piety and religious exercise' was particularly commended by Monro: 'as His Majesty was religious himselfe, so he maintained good lawes and good discipline, grounded on religion and holiness of life.' The king sought to employ both Lutherans and Calvinists, and thus to heal the rift within the evangelical cause. Monro was much impressed by Gustavus' speech to his troops, in which the Swedish king:

> was perswaded, that though God should call him out of the world, yet the Lord would not abandon his owne Cause ... he had no other intention in prosecuting these warres, but onely to pull downe the tyranny of the house of Austria; and to obtain a solid and settled peace unto all men, that were interessed in he quarrell.

For Monro, it was Gustavus '... and none other under God, who helped them [the Germans] to their liberties, He it was and none other releeved Israell.'

That, at least, was Monro's understanding of the politics of the war, but it was a particular understanding, and it was not necessarily shared even by recruits from the British Isles. Another mercenary, Sydnam Poyntz, changed both sides and religion but did not specifically match the two, enlisting with Protestant Saxony soon after his own conversion to Catholicism. Poyntz rose to the rank of captain in the Saxon Army, but when taken prisoner by the Imperialists he 'lost againe all that I had.' Making the best of his circumstances, he changed sides, and finding favour with his capturer, Colonel Butler – the principal murderer of Albrecht von Waldstein, a leading figure on the Catholic side – he was able to rebuild his career and finances and 'send home often tymes Mony to my Wife, who its seemes spent at home what I got abroad.' Similarly, the very different Monro was as keen to have the potentially Catholic Irish join his forces as the English and Scots.

In Poyntz's case, career and profit came before conviction, but with Monro, the career of arms was also the progress of the soldier of Jesus Christ. It was the duty of the Christian soldier to 'walke in his wayes without wearying' and to bear his own cross and suffer misery in patience. His duty was to prepare for death 'by unfained repentance, thinking more often of death than of long life, call[ing] to minde Gods judgements, and the pains of Hell' so that his conscience was clear and he had no reason to fear death. Monro was aware, however, that mercenaries did not necessarily display the same degree of 'vertue' that he advocated. He criticised the 'crueltie and inhumanitie' of General Tilly's Catholic League army and condemned the immoderate conduct of Field Marshal Pappenheim's forces after the failure at Maastricht. Looting was permissible to the Swedish Army in occupied Bavaria, but burnings were unauthorized acts of revenge by soldiers. Hostages were taken, but as a guarantee of payment of contributions. The difference between success and failure on the battlefield was critical in securing contributions: 'the Townes of Germanie are best friends ever to the masters of the field, in flattering the victorious, and in persecuting of the loser.' Good commanders were those who gave their troops 'some liberty of booty: to the end that they might prove the more resolute another time, for Souldiers will not refuse to undergoe any hazard, when they see their Officers willing to reward them with honour and profit.' Sometimes, as at Breitenfeld, supposed friends, the Saxons, were as acquisitive as foes: 'they made booty of our wagons and goods, too good a recompence for Cullions that had left their Duke, betrayed their country and the good cause.'

Gustavus Adolphus was specially praised for ensuring that his armies did not 'oppresse the poore, which made them cry for a blessing to his Majesty and his Army' and his willingness to expand the size of his forces by recruiting prisoners, as after Breitenfeld. The encouragement of desertion in the opposing army was a deliberate tactic. The securing of food supplies was critical to Gustavus, 'knowing well how hungry men could be contented with little, in time of need.' For Monro, hunger was the great enemy, 'for oftimes an Army is lost sooner by hunger than by fighting… For to hunger, and to fight valiantly, doth not agree with nature… Armes doe resist Armes, but to resist hunger, no Fort, no Strength, no Moate or Fossie is able to do it.' Service under Christian IV was made more palatable by good quarters and good wine and beer, while the march from Würzburg to Frankfurt in 1631 'being profitable as it was pleasant to the eye, we see that Souldiers have not always so hard a life, as the common opinion is.' Yet soldiers also needed their pay: on another occasion, Monro records that '… we were all of us discontented; being too much toyled with marching, working and watching, without any pay or gaines for honest men.' Graf von Mansfeld, leading the army, was a notoriously bad paymaster: Poyntz recalls that he and his comrades had 'nothing from our Generall but what we got by pillage which as the Proverb is lightly come as lightly goes.' Mutiny was inevitable, as was the case with Swedish troops at Donauwörth for three months in the spring of 1633, when the army commanders rewarded themselves but did not pay the troops their year's back pay. Some mutinies, such as those of the Dutch ('not the best Souldiers in extremitie of danger') were a cover to avoid danger, however, and no more than 'a Cloake of discontentment.'

NEHEMIAH WHARTON, PARLIAMENTARIAN AND RICHARD ATKYNS, ROYALIST

English Civil Wars

Peter Gaunt

NEHEMIAH WHARTON

Nehemiah Wharton, a London apprentice, marched off with the parliamentary army in summer 1642. He wrote a series of letters about the English Civil War that throw light upon the opening weeks of the conflict, covering the period from mid-August onwards. Sergeant Wharton's letters are dominated by an ostensibly mundane round of marching, scavaging and minor skirmishing as he and his fellow soldiers marched from London to Worcester via Coventry and Northampton. He was not present at the battle of Powick Bridge – though he was anxious to discover accurate details of the engagement – and the series of letters closes on 7 October, well before the battle of Edgehill. However, they are full of the fascinating minutiae of the opening phase of the war, as troops got used to the hardship of military life, of foraging for food and drink – Wharton acquired a taste for poached venison as well as strong beer, including a barrel of 'ould Hum' – and of 'long and tedious' marches and the strain of sentry duty. His letters are littered with references to 'foule weather,' noting on one occasion that 'before I marched one mile I was wet to the skin,' on another that he was 'up to the ancles in thick clay.' Marching to Hereford in early October, he and his men were assailed by 'rain and snow, and extremity of cold,' which killed one of them. On several occasions he failed to get a billet at the end of the day and spent the night with his men in the open air, picking and eating any available fruit, huddled around fires made from hedges and uprooted fences and gates, singing psalms through the night. Wharton was 'exceeding sick' on one occasion, but soon recovered. He saw the dead and the dying en route, a royalist drummer with his arm shot off and another dead drummer by 'our knapsack boyes rifled to the shirt, which was very louzy,' and he helped bury 28 corpses found when they entered Worcester. He reported several fatal accidents, fellow soldiers or civilian bystanders killed when muskets went off accidentally, as well as the rough treatment of a prostitute who had followed the troops to Coventry – she was paraded, pilloried, caged and ducked in the river. On a happier note, in Coventry Wharton had a winter suit made up, trimmed with gold and silver lace.

Two broader traits emerge from Wharton's letters. Firstly, he and many of his colleagues were motivated by a strong godly or puritan zeal. Uplifted by several 'famous,' 'worthy' or 'heavenly' sermons preached to the troops, they seized the opportunity to attack their religious opponents. Joint pressure secured the removal of their lieutenant-colonel, who was felt to be ungodly. 'Papist' gentlemen were routinely threatened and plundered en route, relieved of food, drink and game, though senior officers tried to curb this activity. Particularly in the opening fortnight of the march, a string of parish churches were visited and 'purified' by removing Arminian elements. Prayer books and surplices were destroyed, painted windows smashed, altar rails ripped out and burnt. Wharton reported how a group of soldiers used plundered surplices, hoods and caps to dress up as the Archbishop of Canterbury. He was shocked to see shops open and people at work in Worcester on a Sunday and berated the ignorant townsmen. Secondly, Wharton was in wonder at the various sites he visited and was anxious to record what he saw – 'the passages of my pilgrimage' as he put it. Thus Buckinghamshire was 'the sweetest country that ever I saw.' Although he did not have time to visit Warwick itself, he saw and noted its hilltop castle as he marched by and did explore the surrounding countryside, seeing chapels, springs and gardens. He was very impressed with the streets, houses, churches and walls of Coventry, which he felt compared favourably with London, though he found Northampton in many ways more impressive still. Worcestershire clearly delighted Wharton, who became quite lyrical about the 'pleasaunt, fruitfull, and rich countrey, aboundinge in corne, woods, pastures, hills and valleys, every hedge and heigh way beset with fruits,' especially pears 'whereof they make that pleasant drinke called perry,' which was better than anything he had tasted in London. Although he thought the townspeople godless and popish, he liked Worcester itself, describing its walls, gates and bridge and its 'very stately cathederal' – the tombs of King John and Prince Arthur had particularly caught his eye – and was anxious to view and sketch the earthwork defences being thrown up around the town. Twice he rode to Malvern and, 'after much toyle,' climbed the hills above the town to take in the view, which on a clear day Wharton reckoned extended 'neare thirty miles round.'

RICHARD ATKYNS

Richard Atkyns was a country gentleman from Gloucestershire, in his late 20s at the time of the civil war. Early in 1643 he accepted an invitation to be a captain in a cavalry regiment being raised for the king and for around six months, between March and September 1643, he campaigned in southern England under Prince Maurice. He left a brief account of his fairly short military career within his much longer *Vindication*, written and published in the late 1660s. As a retrospective account, written a quarter of a century later, it lacks some of the breathless immediacy of Wharton's letters and also contains a few factual errors, though Atkyns' memory was generally good and his account often colourful and vivid. His first action was a scrappy fight with Sir William Waller's parliamentarians at Little Dean in Gloucestershire on 11 April. His horse gave way, perhaps reduced by the sight and sounds of battle to hopeless 'trembling and quaking,' but on a borrowed mount Atkyns was one of a dozen or so junior officers who charged a body of parliamentary musketeers; they turned and fled without firing a shot. However, in over-exuberant pursuit, Atkyns and his colleagues fell into a parliamentary ambush and he was lucky to escape – his buff coat was slashed by enemy swords and a musket ball fired by one of his colleagues took off a bar of his helmet and 'went through my hair' but 'did me no hurt.' Later in April, he was present at the unsuccessful royalist attempt to relieve besieged Reading. He was horrified at the sight of crack royalist troops, ordered to attack a strongly defended parliamentary position, dropping 'like ripe fruit in a strong wind' in the face of withering musket fire. On the evening of 10 June, in the course of a skirmish around Chewton Mendip in Somerset, Atkyns played a prominent role in a counter-attack which rescued Prince Maurice, who had been wounded and briefly captured by Waller's men. In the evening gloom and mist, Atkyns' groom lent Maurice his horse to make good his escape and was richly rewarded by the prince. Atkyns next encountered this fellow 15 years later, 'begging in the streets of London, with a muffler before his face, and spoke inwardly, as if he had been eaten up with the foul disease,' a fate which probably befell many damaged and unemployed veterans.

The high points of Atkyns' account are probably his descriptions of the battles of Lansdown and Roundway Down in July. Atkyns provides vivid descriptions not only of the bitter, dour struggle at Lansdown, 'the air so darkened by the smoke of the powder that … there was no light seen, but what the fire of the volleys of shot gave,' but also of the catastrophic explosion of an ammunition cart after the battle, caused by parliamentary prisoners careless with a match given them to light their tobacco. Atkyns, who was near the cart at the time, apparently escaped unscathed, though he noted the deafening noise, the darkening of the air and the 'lamentable screeches' of the survivors, many of them 'miserably burnt.' Falling back to Oxford after the battle, Atkyns was so tired that he fell asleep leaning on a post while his horse was reshod, fell off his horse repeatedly thereafter and, reeling as if drunk, eventually reached the house of a relative and slept for 14 hours. In his description of Roundway Down, he gives a superb account of the difficulty of harming a cuirassier, for no matter how he slashed at Sir Arthur Heselrige with his sword or discharged pistols at point blank range against his helmet, Heselrige's armour was impregnable. Eventually surrounded by other royalists and with his horse repeatedly stabbed and giving way beneath him, Heselrige agreed to surrender, but at that point he was rescued by parliamentary colleagues and Atkyns was forced away. The sudden departure of his groom, a 'rogue,' taking with him Atkyns' spare clothes and other belongings, left him for a time without a change of clothes, and he was forced to go around in dirty and blood-stained clothes so that 'I became so lousy in three or four days, that I could not tell what to do with myself.' When he eventually procured a change of clothes, the old ones were so rotten through blood and sweat that they fell off him in tatters. Thereafter Atkyns' account trails off. He was present at the capture of Bristol in late July, but gives a rather brief and colourless description and, soon after, apparently thinking that the king's cause was safe and overall royalist victory assured, he left the army, never to return.

MARIE MAGDELAINE MOURON, DESERTER

The French Wars

John A. Lynn

An extraordinary document from 1696 records the interrogation of a deserter imprisoned in the fortress of St Omer. The officer in charge of hearing the case of this unfortunate individual was in a quandary and requested guidance from Paris.

What so perplexed the officer was the nature of the deserter in question, because at a time when the army put only men in uniform, his prisoner had been revealed to be a woman.

Born Marie Magdelaine Mouron, she had grown up on the French coast near Boulogne. Her father first worked as a butcher and later bore arms, but not in a king's regiment. Rather, he served as a kind of armed guard and private soldier for the financiers who enforced and collected the salt tax, an important revenue for the Sun King. After Marie's mother died, her father remarried, but apparently the new wife turned out to be the wicked stepmother of legend. Not only was Marie's home life unhappy, but she had little hope for the future. A poor girl in her circumstances had few options; some menial employment – perhaps even prostitution – was all that awaited her. But Marie was a girl with a taste for adventure, and she decided that she could only break free of her destiny by assuming a man's identity.

There is no way of knowing for sure, but Marie may very well have heard the stories of women who had disguised their identities to serve as soldiers. Highly embellished tales of warrior women circulated in print: for example, the story of Geneviève Prémoy, who was supposed to have taken the name of Chevalier Balthazar and performed so well under fire that the king himself allowed her to maintain her rank even after her true sex became known. Beyond this, there was the fictionalized account of Christine de Meyrac, published as the *Héroïne mousquetaire*.

Probably sometime in 1690 – the record is not clear – Marie left home, slipped away to a nearby town, bought used men's clothing, discreetly changed into them, cropped her hair, and answered the recruiter's call. Her high voice and lack of facial hair could be explained as typical of an adolescent lad; perhaps 'he' was a bit underage and physically immature, but the expanding army needed troops, and so few questions would have been asked. Adopting the name 'Picard,' Marie signed on in a company commanded by Captain Destone of the Royal Walloon Regiment.

Marie soldiered as 'Picard' for a year and a half, ending up in the garrison at Sisteron, a fortress guarding the Durance River in Provence. There, as her interrogation reveals, she quarrelled with another soldier and had to leave the army. The details are unclear, but she may have become unacceptable to the men of her unit, perhaps showing cowardice or perhaps being recognized as a woman. Even common soldiers at this time could approach an officer and ask that one of their fellows be banished from the regiment.

Be that as it may, from Sisteron she drifted to Avignon, where she once again enrolled, now as a dragoon in the Morsan Regiment. This time she took the name 'St Michel.' The fact that she was accepted as a dragoon suggests that Marie was a big girl, since dragoons put a premium on physical size. Her regiment saw service in Spain as part of the duc de Noaille's small army in Catalonia.

From late May through mid-June 1693, the Morsan dragoons took part in the successful siege of the Catalonian port town of Rosas and its supporting fort of La Trinité. Marie's regiment anchored the extreme right flank of the French Army. We have no account of Marie's actions during the siege, but she certainly took part in the foraging and skirmishing required of dragoons. While Noaille's campaign went well in Catalonia, the pressures against Louis' armies in Italy increased, and he was forced to dispatch five battalions to Marshal Catinat in Italy. This weakened Noaille's army to the point that it had to revert to the defensive, so after securing Rosas, he withdrew his army across the French border into Roussillon. The Morsan dragoons quartered in Collioure; there 'St Michel' became embroiled with another dragoon named St Jean, and the dispute led to a duel. In the fight, she received a sword cut so deep that she was unable to stop the flow of blood and had to seek medical attention, thus revealing her sex to the regimental surgeon.

As luck would have it, this was the day when Marshal Noailles was to review the regiment. Marie, once more openly a woman, pleaded with the marshal, telling him of her adventures, and he took pity on her, giving her to the care of the wife of an artillery officer. Noailles also arranged that upon her recovery Marie would go to be schooled, or 'instructed,' in Perpignan. However, Marie did not fit in. By now she was as much a dragoon as a young woman, and mistreatment at the hand of the headmistress drove Marie to rebel. In one final dispute, Marie heaved a plate of salad at the headmistress' head and ran away. She now undertook an epic journey on foot. By modern roads, the distance from Perpignan to St Omer is about 680 miles, but Marie's travels along country paths must have been much longer. The first stage of her trek took her only as far as Montpellier, where she became so desperately ill that she had to remain in a hospital for several months, during which time she was bled 13 or 14 times by her account. Eventually she reached St Omer, but the record is mute on how long it took her and on how she supported herself along the road. It is clear, however, that at least two and a half years passed between the time of her duel and her return to the ranks in 1696.

The final drama came when she once again enlisted, now as 'La Garenne,' in the company of Desbrière of the du Biez infantry regiment in March 1696. She appears to have taken a recruitment bounty at this time, the usual reward for enlisting. She was obviously taken with the military life, but the clock was running out for her. By now Marie had spent at least five years in the army and on the road, and sun and toil had undoubtedly weathered her face. It must have been increasingly hard for her to convince others that she was a beardless adolescent lad. Her fellows in the Desbrière Company began to remark publicly that 'La Garenne' must really be a woman.

'La Garenne' began to pass 'his' off-duty hours with two other soldiers from the company, Langenois and Languedoc, who planned to desert. Marie testified later that she tried to dissuade them but failed. Her knowledge of their intentions, she said, convinced her to flee lest she be punished because of her close association with them. She slipped away from the regiment by herself on 1 May. Hiding her coat and stockings, which would give her away as a soldier, she walked the 12 miles to Aire and tried to enlist in the Sanzé Regiment. The lieutenant-colonel of the regiment, La Bussière, into whose company Marie tried to enroll, challenged her, doubting that she was a man. At this point Marie broke down and admitted that she was a woman, but it did not stop there. La Bussière recognized the vest she wore as uniform issue in the du Biez Regiment, and she further admitted that she was a deserter. La Bussière arrested her.

What were her sins? The most obvious charge could have been sexual misconduct; prostitutes, when apprehended, received harsh treatment. However, there was no evidence that Marie was guilty of liaisons with men, or women for that matter. When a woman jailer inspected Marie to ensure that she was a woman, she also probably confirmed Marie's virginity, for the court accepted her statement on oath that she had never had sexual relations with any man. With her propriety established, the simple fact that she was a woman in the ranks would have led only to her dismissal.

Her captain, Desbrière, maintained charges against her less because he had lost a soldier than because he had been robbed of an investment. Marie had certainly received a recruitment bounty, and Desbrière stated that she received pay for March and April – money gone to no purpose now. In addition, he would make a loss on any uniform items or equipment she took with her, since it was the captain's responsibility to replace these in the case of desertion. Making it all worse, in trying to enroll in another regiment, she would have accepted another bounty. Thus she was a *rôleur*, someone who went, or 'rolled,' from one regiment to another to pocket several bounties.

The penalty inflicted on male deserters was draconian – branding the cheek, cutting the nose and ears, and condemnation to service on the king's galleys for life. It was recognized from the start that this was not on the cards for Marie, and that she would face only incarceration. While her fate is uncertain, an undecipherable scrawl in the margins of her file seems to direct that she be committed to prison for a long term.

Beyond its novelty, this story provides a good deal of information on life in the ranks. Marie's life demonstrates that a woman could stand up to the toils and duties of military life in the 17th century. More profoundly, it speaks of the proximity but privacy of military life. Men lived in close confines; when quartered they regularly slept two to a bed, but they did not disrobe. Marie's interrogation reported that 'although she has almost always slept with some comrade,' she 'always did it so well that she had never been recognized for what she was.'

Obviously Marie did not disrobe or bathe with her fellows, and this fact was not regarded as so unusual as to draw notice. Urination clearly posed certain issues. One reason why it seems necessary that she had heard of other women soldiers before becoming one herself is that she must have figured out how to urinate standing up. We know from other accounts that this could be done by using a bored-out animal horn or a metal tube; some device must have been part of her kit from the first day. The fact that she was recognized as a deserter because of her clothing tells us that uniforms in the French Army had become common by the 1690s. Her disputes, one ending in a duel, imply a sense of honour among the rank and file that mimicked that among officers. But perhaps the most important fact that we learn from Marie's career under arms is the mobility enjoyed by the troops. At a time when a peasant might never travel more than a few miles from his place of birth, Marie marched from the English Channel to the Mediterranean, from Provence to Catalonia. Today, the military is associated with patriotic sentiment; however, Marie lived in a time when parochialism, not nationalism, was the rule. The fact that hundreds of thousands of individuals left their homes and visited the length and breadth of France helped to create a sense of the land and people of France. The much-expanded armies of the 17th century not only defended the state but helped to create a sense of nationhood.

18TH CENTURY

By the time our regiment began to embark, the shot flew both thick and hot, and every boat made to the first ship they could reach, the boat that I was in got on board one of the bomb ketches, who the minute we came along side of her, discharged a 13 inch mortar, the shell of which I saw fall in the middle of a troop of French horse. By this time the action became general among the troops we had on shore and a dreadful scene it was!

(A soldier of the British 68th Foot Regiment)

A SOLDIER OF THE BRITISH 68TH FOOT REGIMENT

Seven Years' War

Daniel Marston

This unnamed soldier wrote a journal that describes the British attacks on the coast of France in 1758, which attempted to draw off French forces from the western European theatre of operations of the Seven Years' War. The soldier describes the events of that summer, giving excellent insight into camp life, rations in the fleet and lack of training. He also highlights the difficulty of combined operations, when troops are caught without artillery support. Sadly, the author never mentioned his own name in the journal or its date of publication, so we can determine very little about the person who wrote this account.

The soldier was born in Oxford in 1743. In April 1758 he enlisted at the age of 15 into the 68th Regiment of Foot. He may have made a mistake about the regimental number, since although the 68th did serve in the coastal operations of 1758, it was not involved in the first embarkation of which he was part, but only the second and third operations. He describes how in May he set out with other recruits to travel to the Isle of Wight from Dover, seeking to attract other recruits on the way.

The soldier describes his arrival on the Isle of Wight, and mentions, interestingly for the era, that the regiments were placed in tented towns and not quartered with the population. A very detailed account is given of how the camps were set up, including the following relevant items: all of the men were given equipment to set up their tents, and were to gather straw for their own beds; six men were assigned to each tent, and two blankets were given to each man; the usual arrangement for sleeping was head to foot, so that three faced one way and three the other and the accepted rule was that the oldest soldier slept farthest away from the entrance, and the youngest slept next to it, which obviously meant being trodden upon.

When the soldier first arrived, he was examined by a doctor. The men then paraded in front of the officers, who allocated them to regiments by drawing numbers from a hat. He was drawn for the second battalion, the 68th Foot, and provided with a red coat, laced hat, cap, gun, sword, etc. The next day he was taken out to learn how to walk (the art of learning manoeuvres), and then to learn how to use a musket. All this happened in one day, and he had been in camp for only 11 days when orders arrived to embark. If this few days' instruction was the norm for learning very complicated manoeuvres, it is not surprising that newly arrived recruits were considered to be deficient in training.

The soldier's journal next gives a very detailed list of provisions on board ship. On Mondays, six men were given 4 pounds of bread, half a pound of cheese, and three-quarters of a pound of butter. On Tuesday they received 4 pounds of beef, 4lbs of flour, and 1 pound of fruit plus bread. On Wednesday the men were given the same menu as Monday. On Thursday the men were given 2 pounds of pork instead of beef. The Saturday menu was the same as Tuesday, and the Sunday menu was the same as Thursday. The men appear to have been better fed than is commonly believed today.

The fleet numbered 24 ships of the line and the army strength was numbered at 13,000 men. The fleet arrived on 5 June opposite Cancalle Bay near St Malo and the troops were landed the following day. The soldier wrote that he was 'given provisions for three days.' He also describes how 'for six hours the ships kept ferrying men ashore.' He comments that there were only about 100 French in the area, and describes how in the town of Cancalle, 'all the people fled so the sailors and soldiers plundered and some were caught and one was hung.' Most of the army then marched off toward St Malo, but his regiment, along with one other, remained at Cancalle. The troops advancing on St Malo destroyed shipping in the area.

The soldier mentions that 'from 3am to late in the evening the two regiments in Cancalle were busy building defensive works.' The troops sent to St Malo were re-embarked as news arrived of a larger French force, and the soldier states that his regiment re-embarked also from Cancalle. The fleet headed toward Cherbourg, 'weather intervened however and the ships sailed back to Portsmouth.'

The soldier briefly mentions the second embarkation, which arrived off Cherbourg on 6 August. A force was sent ashore and fought an engagement on 7 August, repelling the French and allowing the rest of the force to land the next day. The town of Cherbourg surrendered and the port installations were destroyed. The troops were then re-embarked.

On 3 September the fleet arrived at St Lunaire Bay, near St Malo. The force was again unable to mount a proper siege of St Malo, and the soldier spends most of his time describing the coming disaster. He explains how, as the British formed a camp after an engagement with the French, they captured French deserters. The deserters warned that a large French force was soon to arrive. He passed this information along to his officers, but they did not express much concern. On 11 September orders were given to embark the troops, but boarding proceeded in a casual fashion. He describes what followed:

The French army appeared, and in the short time they began to cannonade us, which we could not return, having no artillery on shore, but the shipping did for us all that was possible to be done; by the time our regiment began to embark, the shot flew both thick and hot, and every boat made to the first ship they could reach, the boat that I was in got on board one of the bomb ketches, who the minute we came along side of her, discharged a 13 inch mortar, the shell of which I saw fall in the middle of a troop of French horse. By this time the action became general among the troops we had on shore and a dreadful scene it was! To see so many brave fellows lose their lives, and we not able to give them any manner of assistance, at last the few who remained were obliged to throw down their weapons and surrender.

The 68th Foot returned to England, and the soldier's regiment spent the winter at Rochester. In April 1759 the regiment served garrison duty on the island of Jersey, then it was shipped to Guadeloupe to fulfil the same role in the spring of 1760. There it remained for more than three years, returning to England on 23 August 1763. The soldier was discharged on 28 September of the same year, at the age of just 20.

BENJAMIN GOULD, MASSACHUSETTS PROFESSIONAL

The American Revolution

Daniel Marston

Benjamin Gould's story originates from a manuscript written in his own hand at the end of the war. It provides an interesting account of an American soldier of the period who served during the siege of Boston, as well as in operations in New York City and near Saratoga. Gould begins his story with his enlistment in Captain John Beecher's company, which was part of Colonel Moses Little's regiment, a Continental infantry regiment. Gould's regiment was part of the army that occupied Boston following the British withdrawal on 17 March 1776. Gould claims that he joined the army as a sergeant. If this is true, then he must have had previous military experience as a private soldier, although he does not provide any background information.

Gould's regiment was ordered to New York City as the threat to that area increased. He describes how his regiment arrived in the New York area just as battle began on Long Island: 'in the morning we heard a heavy cannonading ... it was the enemy, taking Long Island and New York and our army retreating from it.' Following the defeat on Long Island, his regiment was ordered to proceed to Fort Washington, on Manhattan Island. His regiment was ordered to make carriages and to supply the fort with additional material in preparation for a possible siege. The regiment arrived as the artillery began preparations for the British arrival.

Gould comments that supplies ran low during the regiment's tenure at Fort Washington. He reports when Royal Navy ships appeared off the west side of the fort on the Hudson River, and records that a detachment of British troops was reported to be only 3 miles from the fort. He states that '[we] could not spare a man to draw provisions and [were] obliged to live upon potatoes and cloves for several days.' Instead of attacking right away, however, the main British force headed north to White Plains in an attempt to catch the Main Continental Army. It is at this point that the manuscript becomes somewhat confusing. Up to now, Gould described his regiment as if it were an infantry unit. The manuscript, however, raises the possibility that Gould had been transferred to an artillery unit. He describes orders 'to make the best grape [shot] I could.' His regiment was ordered to proceed to White Plains to support the Main Army. His subsequent description of the battle of White Plains supports the theory that he fought with an artillery unit, especially as he describes how 'when our army retreated I struck the left tent and took the last cannon from our lines.'

This description ends the narrative of the 1776 campaign. Gould mentions the ongoing problem of keeping the numbers of men in the Continental service constant for a long period of time. At the end of 1776, his own Continental service comes to an end, and he is offered service with the Massachusetts Militia, with the proviso that he could 'leave at any time for service with the Continentals if he wished.' He notes, 'taken from the Continental Service and placed in the militia in the summer of 1777.' His new militia unit was sent to fight against the British advance down Lake Champlain and along the Hudson River, but he does not make it clear in which of the several Massachusetts militia regiments involved in this campaign he served.

Gould's unit most likely arrived during the month of September when American units were operating behind Burgoyne's line of advance to disrupt his supply networks. His unit was given four days' supplies and ordered to operate on Lake George. American forces had seized Fort George on 18 September, and from there they had pushed north to Fort Ticonderoga. Gould's unit operated in the area around Lake George 'for 17 days.' His narrative is unclear, but it appears that his unit marched south towards Bemis Heights, since he next describes a major action on the 7th (presumably of October, when an engagement took place at that location). Although he was with a unit of Massachusetts militia, they are not specifically mentioned in accounts of the battle. Massachusetts Continental regiments and various New England militia units were present, however, and his unit may have been attached to one of these groups for the battle.

Gould describes how on 'the seventh [October] at about one o'clock we were laid by the cannon of the enemy who were marching to attack us.' He appears to be describing the last British attack against Bemis Heights on 7 October. He goes on to record that:

we returned to our places and was immediately ordered to march … it was but a few minutes before the enemy fired upon us … a second shot our men seemed terrified at this but soon received and stood their ground nobley [sic] … the enemy made no refrain but retreated precipitately.

He also describes coming across an abandoned British camp and his actions: 'I took nothing out of it but a bottle of beer which was very exceptible [sic] as we were very dry.'

Gould's unit was given its discharge on 1 November 1777, but he stayed in the area to settle accounts. He next refers to 1780, when he notes receiving command of a militia company. This implies that he received a commission, either after the battle of Bemis Heights or when he was called up for the militia in 1780. Gould and his company were ordered to West Point; where they arrived on 20 June 1780. He spent the remainder of his service on garrison duty at West Point. Gould was discharged at the end of the conflict.

THOMAS BROWN, ROGERS' RANGER

The French-Indian War

Daniel Marston

The Roger's Ranger Corps that developed in New England and Nova Scotia was considered to be an elite force. The rangers drew most of their men from the frontier regions, selecting those considered capable of enduring the hardships of fighting in the forest. They were considerably feared by their French and Indian enemies. One ranger's journal provides us with detail of their actions during the French-Indian war.

Thomas Brown was born in Charlestown, Massachusetts in 1740. He decided to go to war fairly early in the conflict; while serving as an apprentice, at the age of 16 he enlisted in 'Major Rogers' Corps of Rangers,' joining Captain Speakman's Company in May 1756. The way the text is written implies that this was a newly raised unit. Brown describes how he and others marched to Albany, New York, where they arrived on 1 August, and then moved on to Fort Edward.

Brown's narrative relates how, upon arrival at Fort Edward, he and other Rangers were sent out on 'Scouts,' which today would be defined as patrols. He mentions that, during one of these Scouts, he managed to kill an Indian. He does not, however, provide any information about the amount or type of training that he received, and the text implies that the Rangers learned their trade of scouting and ambushing on the job.

Brown's Scouts expeditions took place during the late summer, autumn and early winter months of 1756 and 1757, during the same period that French and Indian raiding parties were operating in the area. Both sides were seeking intelligence on the preparations of the forces operating around forts William Henry and Carillon (Ticonderoga), as well as carrying out raiding parties on convoys travelling to the forts.

Although Thomas Brown does not provide details concerning his training, he describes in great detail a long-distance 'scout' to ambush French and Indian supply columns operating in the Fort Carillon and Crown Point region. This Scout, which left Fort William Henry on 18 January 1757, is very likely the battle of the Snowshoes. According to Brown, the Scout consisted of 60 Rangers, including Major Robert Rogers, the Corps commander. All of these Rangers, according to Brown, were volunteers. In other words, unlike other operations, the men on this Scout chose to go rather than being ordered to do so.

Brown relates how the Rangers arrived on the road leading from Fort Carillon to Crown Point. As they came in sight of Lake Champlain, Major Rogers spotted some 50 sleighs on the lake's frozen surface. He ordered the Rangers to lay in ambush and, when the French sleighs were 'near enough ... to pursue them.' He describes his proximity to Major Rogers as the Rangers ambushed the party, as well as the Rangers' capture of seven Frenchmen in the raid. (He also notes that many men from the sleighs managed to escape, either to Crown Point or Fort Carillon, alerting the French and Indians based at both forts to the presence of Rogers and his Scout.)

The Rangers interrogated the prisoners and learned that there were 500 French Regulars based at Fort Carillon. Major Rogers decided that the Scout should return to Fort William Henry and that, due to the amount of snow on the ground, they would return the same way they had come, outfitted with snowshoes. The French and Indians in the area, alerted to the Rangers' presence, set out to destroy Rogers and his men.

Within a few hours of the march, the Scout was spotted and attacked. Brown describes how:

> We march'd in an Indian-File and kept the Prisoners in the Rear, lest we should be attack'd: We proceeded in this Order about a Mile and a half, and as we were ascending a Hill, and the Centre of our Men were at the Top, the French, to the number of 400, besides 30 or 40 Indians, fir'd on us before we discovered them.

Major Rogers ordered his Rangers to advance, sending them into withering fire. Brown describes what happened to him and some of the other men, highlighting the brutal reality of eighteenth-century forest warfare. He states that:

I receiv'd a Wound from the Enemy ... thro' the Body, upon which I retir'd into the Rear, to the Prisoner I had taken on the Lake, knock'd him on the Head and killed him, lest he should Escape and give Information to the Enemy.

Brown was almost killed by two Indians as he withdrew to the rear of the column. However, he was able to form himself, with other Rangers, into a small box of men. The fighting in the area was intense, as Brown describes:

[I] got to the Centre of our Men, and fix'd myself behind a large Pine, where I loaded and fir'd every Opportunity; after I had discharged 6 or 7 Times, there came a Ball and cut off my Gun just at the Lock. About half an Hour after, I receiv'd a Shot in my Knee; I crawled again into the Rear, and as I was turning about receiv'd a Shot in my Shoulder.

Brown speculates that the fighting lasted for five and half hours, and notes that, while they were surrounded, the Rangers were not overwhelmed during the daylight hours. Brown contends that the Rangers inflicted more than 60 casualties on the French and Indian troops, and describes what happened as night drew in:

The Engagement held, as near as I could guess, 5 and half Hours... By the Time it grew dark and the Firing Ceased on both Sides, and as we were so few the Major [Rogers] took the Advantage of the Night and escaped with all the well Men, without informing the wounded of his Design, lest they should inform the Enemy and they should pursue him before he had got out of their Reach.

Brown was able to make it to Captain Speakman; they and another badly wounded Ranger, named Baker, were able to make a small fire. They could not hear or see any other Rangers in the vicinity; at one moment, Captain Speakman called out to Major Rogers but received no answer. The wounded men were unable to travel, and hope of escape began to dwindle as they heard the enemy approaching. The men decided to surrender to the French, at which point Brown appears to have slipped away from the other two men at the fire. Brown's account of what occurred next says:

I crawl'd so far from the Fire that I could not be seen, though I could see what was acted at the Fire; the Indian came to Capt. Spikeman [Speakman], who was not able to resist, and stripp'd and scalp'd him alive; Baker, who was lying by the Captain, pull'd out his Knife to stab himself, which the Indian prevented and carried him away.

Speakman, who was still alive after this attack, pleaded with Brown to kill him. Brown refused, and moved off in order to avoid a similar fate. (Speakman was later beheaded by the Indians.) Since Brown had no shoes, and the snow was quite deep, he found progress difficult. He attempted to move around various French sentry positions, and at one point came close to being seen by a French soldier. Brown survived the night in an agony of discomfort, without adequate clothing or shoes. Around 11am the next morning, he was spotted by a small group of Indians. They rushed him and he thought it would be best to be killed outright instead of being scalped alive. He describes how:

> I threw off my Blanket, and Fear and Dread quickened my Pace for a while; but, by Reason of the Loss of so much Blood from my Wounds, I soon fail'd. When they were within a few Rods of me they cock'd their Guns, and told me to stop; but I refus'd, hoping they would fire and Kill me on the spot; which I chose, rather then the dreadful Death Capt. Spikeman [sic] died of. They soon came up with me, took me by the Neck and Kiss'd me... They took some dry Leaves and put them into my Wounds, and then turn'd about and ordered me to follow them.

Thomas Brown served out the remainder of the war as a captive, both of French military officers and various Indians. He travelled as far as the Mississippi River, to the west, and the Montreal region, to the north. He was returned to the British forces on 25 November 1759, after more than two years of captivity, and returned to Charlestown at the beginning of January 1760.

MIDSHIPMAN WILLIAM HENRY DILLON, RN

French Revolutionary Wars

Gregory Fremont-Barnes

William Henry Dillon was born in August 1780, the illegitimate son of a middle-class family of Irish descent. His mother died in his infancy and his father, not wishing William to join a profession, sent him into the navy in 1790 at the age of 10. When Britain entered the French Revolutionary Wars in 1793 he already had three years' experience at sea, having served aboard HMS *Saturn*, a 74-gun ship of the line. He was still only 13, but a midshipman nonetheless, now aboard the frigate *Thetis*.

Dillon's wartime experiences were exceptionally wide. He served on convoy and blockade duty, he was involved in the search of neutral vessels for war contraband, and he visited practically every West Indian island under British, and many others under enemy, control. He witnessed mutinous behavior, punishments aboard ship, and men growing sick from tropical disease. He fought in two major and many minor naval engagements, was wounded in battle, was injured several times in the ordinary course of duty, and fell ill from fatigue and disease. He had experience of capturing enemy ships and, like all his contemporaries, eagerly sought the prize-money that these represented.

Dillon's memories of his campaigns may have gained a little lustre with the benefit of hindsight, but in general they provide a fascinating insight into life at sea during the French Revolutionary Wars. Among the countless anecdotes that fill his memoirs, Dillon vividly recalls the rite of passage through which all seamen crossing the 'Equinoctial line,' or Equator, underwent. There was the obligatory appearance of Neptune and his 'myrmidons,' who put the uninitiated through a series of unpleasant dunkings, the whole episode enlivened with music and drink. The account Dillon gives of a seaman's life aboard ship is of a hard, often monotonous existence and, apart from the strenuous task of working the rigging and navigation, men passed countless hours with nothing to see on the horizon and the prospect of weeks at sea with only such entertainment as they could devise for themselves: cards, singing, dancing, carving, drinking.

The rigours of long years at sea often took their toll on a man's health. In the first year of the war Dillon lived for several months on salt meat without so much as a piece of fruit. 'I was obliged to be very careful in my diet, as symptoms of the scurvy had begun to show itself in my legs,' he recalled many years later. Living conditions on board were at best basic and sometimes barely tolerable. For some months black ants infested his ship, attacking anything edible, before they finally sprouted wings and disappeared without a trace. The cockroaches, lice, rats and other vermin remained on board.

Some months later Dillon was transferred to the *Defence*, a 74-gun ship of the line, under Captain Gambier, who received Dillon well and promised him that 'if you attend to your duty, you will find a friend in me.' Patronage was all-important in the navy, and throughout his career Dillon always kept this in mind. In September 1793, the *Defence* joined the Channel Fleet under Lord Howe, the navy's most distinguished admiral, who had made his reputation in the War of American Independence. Discipline, hard work, attention to duty, and a strict code of morality were the order of the day aboard the *Defence*, whose seamen privately referred to their captain as 'Preaching Jemmy.' Dillon recalled how Gambier evinced a determination to enforce his religious principles on board the ship under his command.

> He had prayers in his cabin twice a day, morning and evening. I was obliged to attend every morning… As I had no Bible, he obliged me to provide myself with one, and

he did not fail to examine as well my book of prayers, at the same time asking many questions upon religious subjects.

Of the 25 ships of the line in Howe's fleet in the spring of 1794, the *Defence* was the first vessel involved in the first major naval engagement of the wars known as the battle of the Glorious First of June. Dillon, still only 14 at the time, commanded three of the lower-deck guns. Initial contact with the French was made on 29 May and on receiving the signal to chase, the crew grew eager for the opportunity to come to grips with the enemy: 'No one thought of anything else than to exert himself to his utmost ability in overcoming the enemy,' Dillon recalled. 'Death or Victory was evidently the prevailing feeling.' Shots soon came flying over the quarterdeck, killing one man and wounding nine. The captain was nearly hit, but after recovering his composure after a shot whistled past him he calmly removed a piece of biscuit from his pocket and began to eat it. 'He had evidently been shook by the wind of the shot. He had on a cocked hat, and kept walking the deck, cheering up the seamen with the greatest coolness.' But as casualties mounted, so too did damage to the ship, and just as the wounded were being taken below and the first fatalities thrown overboard, 'a volley of shot assailed the Poop, cut away the main brace, and made sad havoc there.'

Dillon witnessed with shock the death of a seaman in action. 'It was a most trying scene. A splinter struck him in the crown of the head, and when he fell the blood and brains came out, flowing over the deck.' But this was just the beginning; two days later the main action took place. At dawn the rival fleets were shrouded in heavy mist, but as the sun gradually broke through, visibility was restored and the great, floating engines of war, their canvas sails billowing in the wind, offered an impressive spectacle to the opposing crews. 'The weather became fine, and we enjoyed one of the most splendid sights ever witnessed – the two Fleets close to each other in line of battle, only waiting for the signal to commence the work of destruction…'

Howe's ships slowly closed on the French, and when the enemy was 10 miles off to leeward Dillon was roused from a brief slumber and summoned to his station on the lower deck. Up went the colours and the gun ports; his crews rammed home powder and shot, ran out the guns and impatiently awaited the signal to issue the first broadside.

We retained our fire till in the act of passing under the Frenchman's stern, then, throwing all our topsails aback, luffed up [put the bow to windward] and poured in a most destructive broadside. We heard most distinctly our shot striking the hull of the enemy. The carved work over his stern was shattered to pieces.

As the battle raged with increasing ferocity, the death toll began to mount. Dillon witnessed one of the crew killed by a shot that cut his head in two. At 10.30am the mizzenmast came down and the *Defence* began to drift to leeward. An hour later the mainmast collapsed across the starboard side of the poop deck with a tremendous crash, and all the while, on the lower deck, where Dillon continued to shout commands above the din of roaring cannon, smoke billowed everywhere from the fire of the guns, making it almost impossible to see. The crews kept up the pace of fire so rapidly that the guns began to overheat and on recoiling they nearly struck the upper deck beams. The risk of the guns bursting became so great that Dillon ordered the crews to use less powder and lengthen the intervals between discharges.

After over an hour and a half of furious activity, the men were growing weary. Often stripped to the waist, wide-eyed with excitement or terror, barefoot and covered in black powder, blood, and sweat, the gun crews must have looked dreadful. Keeping these poor wretches at the guns and working them to maximum efficiency was the responsibility of the officers, one of whom, on sensing signs of fatigue, drew his sword and, brandishing it in the air, threatened to 'cut the first man down that did not do his duty.' On being satisfied with their replies, he returned his weapon to its scabbard and the men resumed their fire.

Immediately afterward Dillon and two other men were blown down from the wind of a shot. 'I thought myself killed, as I became senseless, being jammed between these men.' Dillon was lucky to survive, but the others were dead; no sooner was he back on his feet with the help of his men than there came a call to repel boarders. However, in the end the enemy vessel passed the *Defence*, the immediate threat subsided, and the order was cancelled. The French, at last, had been beaten and were making off. At a cost of 1,100 men Howe had captured six enemy vessels and inflicted 3,500 casualties.

When the fighting had ended, Dillon must have been a pitiful sight. His clothes were soaked through from water that had burst through a port during the action, his shoes were covered in blood, and his face and hands smeared with burnt powder. Fourteen of the men under his command had been either killed or wounded and one gun had been disabled. After shaking hands with the men to congratulate them on their survival, he went to the quarterdeck, which he found covered in musket shot from enemy marksmen. Below deck, the surgeon reported the ship's losses: 91 killed and wounded, a heavy toll. Dillon concluded, mournfully: 'The number of men thrown overboard that were killed, without ceremony, and the sad wrecks around us taught those who, like myself, had not before witnessed similar scenes that War was the greatest scourge of mankind.'

Later in the year, aboard the *Prince George*, Dillon went to the West Indies. This was not a popular destination. The other midshipmen 'were talking of nothing else but the yellow fever. Indeed, death stared them in the face.' But Dillon stayed on, anxious to 'see the world,' gain experience, and, above all, to achieve promotion through active service. He sensibly prepared his will, well aware that the West Indian climate and insect-borne diseases accounted for thousands of lives every year.

Dillon went on to take part in numerous landing operations, as well as in the siege and capture of St Lucia in 1796, after which he was promoted to acting lieutenant. At Antigua he watched as sickness spread among the ships' crews. 'Violent vomiting attacked our seamen, the witnessing of which was truly distressing, as they brought up large worms.' He himself fell ill, probably with sunstroke, which left him 'in a state of stupefaction' for four days. He was fortunate to recover, for various diseases, especially yellow fever, ravaged British ships in climates too harsh for the delicate dispositions of Europeans. There were compensations, however, and in the course of his years in the West Indies Dillon assisted in the capture of numerous prizes – mostly merchantmen and privateers – which over the years earned for him a respectable share of prize-money. On one occasion he won about £20, while on another – with the capture of a valuable merchant vessel – he earned several hundred pounds. Considering his pay was only about £2 a month, this was equal to many years' ordinary income, and some fortunate men – particularly the captain and other officers, who received a disproportionately high share – could retire on such proceeds.

In 1798, while stationed in Irish waters aboard an armed cutter, he was able to take a small part against the rebellion there, storming a rebel fort with cutlass in hand and later apprehending one of the principal rebel leaders. He returned to the Jamaica station in April 1799 and served again throughout the West Indies for the remainder of the war, taking more prizes, including a 12-gun brig whose French crew had mutinied and taken their captain prisoner. When the captain attempted to blow up the ship by taking a candle to the magazine, Dillon claims to have seized him and saved the ship – and himself.

Shortly after the end of the war he went to London to see his father, who had scarcely seen his son in 12 years. Now 22, deeply tanned, and wearing plain clothes, Dillon was at first unrecognizable. His homecoming was a joyous one. 'The war was over,' he wrote in his memoirs. 'I had had twelve years of toil and anxiety.' But he could not know that the peace was to be very brief and the country would soon need him back at sea. He spent the remainder of his career on active service, including several years as a prisoner of the French and, after the Napoleonic Wars, commanding ships in several South American navies. He was knighted and retired a vice-admiral. While Dillon's experiences cannot be said to typify those of an ordinary sailor aboard ship – as such men were almost always illiterate and first-hand accounts are rare – Dillon's junior rank nevertheless placed him in close contact with ordinary ratings and his memoirs certainly give us a fascinating insight into what life must have been like.

WAR
IN THE
AMERICAS

You felt like you were somebody when you were on a good horse... You were a part of a proud outfit that had a fighting reputation, and you were ready for a fight or a frolic.

(Sergeant Charles Windolph)

JUAN ALMONTE, SOLDIER AND DIPLOMAT

The Texas War of Independence 1835–1836

Alan C. Huffines

Juan Almonte was born the bastard son of Mexican federalist revolutionary Father José María Morelos y Pavón, and an Indian, Brigida Almonte, on 15 May 1803. From this ignominious birth he became involved in the final Mexican revolution and allied himself with the forces for independence from Spain, and finally with the nationalist–centralist faction of Mexican politics. Mexican folklore records that Fr Morelos y Pavón was marching with his soldiers past a village when an Indian woman appeared and held up a baby boy, declaring that the priest was the father of the child. Allegedly Morelos y Pavón, embarrassed, dismissed her by waving her off with the word 'Almonte' – 'to the mountains' – and that is the legend of his name. Whether the story is true or not will never be known, but at some point the rebel priest assumed responsibility for the boy and sent him to be educated in America amongst expatriate Mexican republicans. His father's execution in December 1815 ended Almonte's education and he then became a clerk in New Orleans.

When Mexico achieved independence, Almonte returned to his native country from Nacogdoches, Texas where he had been working, and was appointed to the staff of Don José Felix Trespalacios, headquartered in Texas. In 1824 he was assigned to Great Britain as a member of the Mexican Legation and was largely responsible for Mexico's first commercial agreement with a foreign nation.

In 1830, while working as a newspaper editor, he criticized President Anastasio Bustamente for allowing foreign intrigue into the new republic and was forced into hiding. This brought him into contact with Antonio López de Santa Anna Perez de Lebron.

Santa Anna sent him to inspect Texas in 1834 (the only official Mexican report from this period) to determine its potential as an agricultural and industrial holding and, possibly, for colonial insurrection. His instructions were in two parts, one public and the other secret.

The second and secret portion contained 12 articles that required Almonte to assess everything from the mood of the colonies, the size of their militia and numbers of armaments, to who were the men of influence. He was to return to Mexico City and deliver his report in person.

Aside from the skullduggery, Almonte's inventory of ports, populations, rivers, towns and soil types is superbly succinct and at the same time, informative. Interspersed with the valuable details of the flora and country's potential, he wrote a warning to his superiors in Mexico District Federal (DF):

the climate in Texas is perfectly adaptable for the people of [northern] Europe, and the immigration is so considerable that in less than ten years the [American] population has multiplied five times. Finally, Texas is the most valuable possession that the [Mexican] Republic has, and God grant that our neglect does not cause us to lose so precious a part of our territory.

Almonte remained meticulous, thorough and brief. He served as Santa Anna's chief of staff during the Texas War of Independence, and kept a daily journal beginning in February 1836 and ending a few days before the Mexican's defeat at San Jacinto. In the entire journal he made no ideological commentary; and he neglected to record the inter-staff quibbling and backstabbing so common among his peers in that army, which is rare in an officer, especially one so loyal to Santa Anna. Throughout the war, he recorded the weather (it never rained during the Alamo siege) and various troop and supply issues consistent with a chief of staff's duties. His last journal sentence on 6 March was 'I was robbed by our soldiers.' A traditional robbery is unthinkable, and it is more likely he felt he had been disappointed by their conduct in some respect, possibly in the summary execution of Texan prisoners. His journal is possibly the single most important historical record of the war.

While pursuing the retreating Texan Army, Santa Anna sent Almonte to New Washington to capture the rebel government. Almonte and 50 dragoons arrived as the rowing boat carried interim President David G. Burnet and his wife from the Morgan Plantation warehouse to the Texas schooner *Flash*, anchored about quarter of a mile from the shore in Galveston Bay. Burnet had desired that the flatboat hauling cargo out to the schooner be used to transport his entire party, horses included. But a Texan came riding into town warning that the Mexicans were just behind him. Burnet had no time to load the flatboat, so a small rowing boat was commandeered. One of the *soldados* managed to touch Burnet with his lance, but the boat was too far from shore, and Burnet was uninjured. The dragoons raised their weapons to fire at the fleeing politician, but Almonte halted their fire and admonished his *soldados* never to fire on women. Burnet had been within easy musket range and would no doubt have been killed or wounded, but with Almonte, humanity overrode expediency. Burnet and his escort arrived safely at Anahuac and went on to Galveston Island. It is impossible to determine how the Texas War of Independence would have turned out had Almonte captured the Texan president rather than the Texans capturing his.

He commanded the Mexican right at San Jacinto, comprised of three cazadore companies, and after they broke he was seen swimming Peggy Lake with one hand, the other holding his sword out of the water. During the slaughter Almonte gathered several officers around himself and said: 'Gentlemen, you see that our men will not fight, they are panic stricken; let us get them together and surrender them.'

His timely leadership and cool head no doubt kept these *soldados* from the butcher's bill that day. At dusk he surrendered himself and 250 *soldados* on the southwest side of the battlefield, near the Old Washington Road. General Thomas Jefferson Rusk, Texas secretary of war, took charge of the prisoners and recorded this meeting with Almonte:

> It was probably Almonte whom I saw before me. I therefore observed to him [in Spanish] 'You must be Colonel Almonte.' He replied in English, 'You speak [Spanish] well.' I then rode up to him and gave him my hand, saying to him, 'It affords me great pleasure to see you, Colonel.' With great presence of mind and his customary politeness he responded, 'The pleasure is reciprocated.'

One of his guards, a Tejano, who was not so hospitable as Rusk, said to the prisoners in their native tongue:

> Now you shall see, contemptible and faithless assassins, if you do not pay with your vile blood for your murders at the Alamo and La Bahia. The time has come when the just cause that we defended triumphs over you; you shall pay with you heads for the arson, robberies, and depredations that you have committed in our country.

Almonte remained with Santa Anna during his captivity and served as his translator during the negotiations. He was friendly and courteous to his captors, which must have had some impact on the resolution of his president's fate.

He became minister of war in 1840 in the cabinet of President Anastacio Bustamente. In July General Urrea and several *soldados* met Almonte on the street, demanded his sword, and announced that President Bustamente was to be placed under arrest. Almonte drew his blade and fought through the *soldados*. Once safe, he quickly organized forces to suppress the revolution, although another revolution that autumn eventually overthrew the Bustamente government. Almonte became destitute and earned his income by science lecturing.

When Santa Anna returned to power in 184, Almonte was named minister to the United States and once again he became involved in the affairs of Texas. In November of 1843, he wrote the US Secretary of State and declared Mexico's intent for war if the United States annexed Texas. In his letter, he reminded the secretary that the revolution had been caused, at least in part, by US intervention. He made a further argument that when the US had recognized Mexican independence from Spain, that recognition extended to Mexican rule over the Texan province. He reminded the government that, regardless of US goals in the region, Mexicans would not be deterred from what was rightfully theirs. If the US Congress voted for annexation, he would immediately return to Mexico, sever diplomatic ties, and help prepare Mexico for a war against the United States. Unwilling to become embroiled in another war, America decided against annexing the Republic of Texas at that time.

Almonte continued to work as a diplomat and in subsequent years was twice minister to Great Britain, and minister to the United States again in 1853. While he was in Europe, he gained sympathy for the Mexican monarchists and supported foreign intervention in Mexico to restore the throne. He returned home in 1862 with French soldiers. He was named 'El Jefe Supremo,' and President of the French Executive Council by the French government. He was exiled after the failure of French intervention and died in Paris on 21 March 1869, aged 65.

ULYSSES S. GRANT, SOLDIER AND US PRESIDENT

The Mexican War

Douglas V. Meed

General William Tecumseh Sherman said it best: 'Grant's whole character was a mystery even to himself; a combination of strength and weakness not paralleled by any whom I have read in ancient or modern history.'

Ulysses Simpson Grant was born on an Ohio farm in 1822 and spent his early years helping his father bring in crops. As a youth he showed no interest in the military, but when his father secured for him an appointment to West Point Military Academy, he grudgingly agreed to enter the school. He disliked the academy, with its spit and polish and difficult curriculum. He did, however, shine in mathematics, but was a diffident scholar in other studies. On horseback he became transfigured: a shy, smallish man on the ground, he was a commanding equestrian in the saddle. The man who would later command all the armies of the United States did not like the army. After graduating in the middle of his class in 1843, Grant informed his classmates that he planed to resign his commission at an early date and find a job as a mathematics teacher. The delicate, fair-skinned, 5ft 8in. tall lieutenant, who was once described as looking 'like a doll,' was not rated highly enough to be assigned to the coveted engineers or field artillery branches. He was instead assigned to the 4th Infantry to quartermaster and commissary duties.

When war broke out between the United States and Mexico, Grant determined to do his duty in spite of his opposition to the conflict. He later wrote: 'I regard the war as one of the most unjust ever waged by a stronger against a weaker nation.' Grant considered the war 'a conspiracy to acquire territory out of which slave states might be formed for the American Union.'

In September 1845, the 4th Infantry joined Zachary Taylor's army near Corpus Christi, Texas. Camping there to pass the time before marching to the Rio Grande, the officers formed a theatrical troupe. In a production of *Othello*, Grant played the gentle lady Desdemona. Pictured in well-known photos taken during the Civil War, it is difficult to imagine the rumpled, bearded, grim-faced general who, one observer remarked, 'looked like he was about to ram his head through a brick wall,' playing the part of the delicate wife of a Moorish general. When the fighting started, Grant wrote that he was determined to do his duty as a soldier to bring victory to his country. Before Fort Texas on the Rio Grande on 2 May 1846, he first heard the sound of hostile cannon, and later recalled: 'I felt sorry that I had enlisted.'

His baptism of fire came on 8 May during the battle of Palo Alto, when a cannon ball decapitated a soldier standing near him. The following day, Grant was given command of his company as they marched to the relief of Fort Texas.

During the ensuing battle of Resaca de la Palma, he led his company in a successful charge, backed up by the flying artillery. In August, when Taylor began his march to Monterey, Grant, much to his disgust, was placed in charge of the regimental mule train. Frustrated, Grant wrote that he had never used a profane expletive in his life, but 'I would have the charity to excuse those who may have done so, if they were in charge of a train of Mexican pack mules.'

After his regimental adjutant was killed during a charge before Monterey, Grant took over those duties and by 23 September, his opinion of combat had undergone a metamorphosis and he was to battle his way into the city alongside his regiment.

During house-to-house fighting, the 4th ran low on ammunition and Grant volunteered to ride through gunfire to bring up additional supplies. Through shot and shell, hooking a foot over his saddle with one arm around his horse's neck, he clung to the side of his mount Comanche-style and galloped back to the supply waggons. He soon returned to the fight with a waggon-load of ammunition.

In March 1847, Grant, who had been transferred to Scott's army, splashed ashore with the first troops to land on the beach south of Vera Cruz. To his dismay, his efficiency as a mule-train driver resulted in his being made permanent quartermaster for his regiment. During the battles of Cerro Gordo, Contreras and Churubusco, Grant was relegated to guarding the mules and the supply waggons.

When the American Army advanced toward Mexico City, he volunteered to help reconnoitre the city's defences. In his memoirs written some 40 years later, Grant praised the reconnaissance reports of his future nemesis, Robert E. Lee as 'perfect.' Lee, in his report, noticed the work of 'Lieutenant Grant ... who was usefully employed.' Ironically, when the Civil War erupted 15 years later, Lee refused the command of the Union armies that Grant would lead to victory against him after four years of bitter fighting.

In the attack on Molino del Rey, Grant left his mules and joined in the assault. By nightfall, the battle had been won, but at a terrible cost in casualties. For his gallantry during the attack, Grant was brevetted a first lieutenant.

He missed the fighting during the assault on Chapultepec, but when that position was taken, he was one of the first to arrive before the gate of the San Cosme causeway, which led to the centre of Mexico City. The San Cosme was the same elevated road that Cortez had used during his retreat from the Aztec capital 300 years previously. The defenders had placed guns and infantry to sweep the approaches along the road. Grant realized that the enemy position had to be destroyed if the American attack was to succeed.

He later wrote: 'I found a church … that looked to me as if the belfry would command the ground back of … San Cosme.' The young lieutenant commandeered a mountain howitzer and a number of men from the Voltiguers Regiment. He ordered the gun disassembled and parcelled out the components to his men. To dodge the road, which was swept by enemy fire, Grant and his men slipped to the south and carried the howitzer parts through several ditches, wading through waist-deep water. Coming up behind the church, Grant politely knocked on the door. When a priest opened the door and peeked out at the muddy, sweat-soaked lieutenant, he at first refused admittance.

In his memoirs, Grant was perhaps too polite to write about his persuasive measures, merely stating that the priest 'began to see his duty in the same light that I did and opened the door.'

The Americans manhandled the howitzer parts up the winding, narrow stairway to the belfry and reassembled the gun. Grant later wrote: 'We were not more than two or three hundred yards from San Cosme.' Opening fire, the Americans dropped shell after shell on to the heads of the San Cosme defenders. In the meantime, the American troops who had been tunnelling through adobe houses on the north side of the causeway reached the San Cosme gate. After Grant's bombardment had silenced the Mexican guns and raked and spread panic among the infantry defenders, the Americans were able to carry the position by assault. At the same time, other troops captured the Belen Gate and by the evening of 13 September, Scott's army had advanced to the heart of Mexico City. The following day, the capital capitulated as the remaining Mexican troops retreated from the city. As a result of his action, Grant was brevetted captain. For all practical purposes, the fighting was over.

When the war ended Grant returned home and, on 22 August 1848, he married his long-time sweetheart, Julia Dent. A few years later, while stationed in California and separated from his wife, out of loneliness and boredom, he took to the bottle. In 1854, under a cloud caused by his excessive drinking, he resigned his commission.

Grant rejoined Julia and with his family settled in St Louis, Missouri, for the next six years. During that time, he failed miserably both as a businessman and as a farmer. In 1860, he and his family moved to Galena, Illinois, where he worked as a clerk in his father's small leather store. In 1860, Grant was a broken, middle-aged man, cursed with failure and disappointment. Behind his back, neighbours referred to him not as Ulysses, but rather as 'Useless Grant.'

When the Civil War broke out in 1861 and the Union was desperate for experienced officers, Grant was commissioned a colonel of Illinois volunteers and was quickly raised to brigadier-general. He had early successes, particularly in forcing the surrender of Fort Donelson, an important Confederate fort on the Cumberland River in Tennessee. He was promoted to major-general, but in April 1862, his fortunes plummeted and he was nearly shelved when he barely escaped defeat during the bloody battle at Shiloh, Tennessee.

President Lincoln, suffering from incompetent and reluctant generals, supported Grant. When told of Grant's drinking, Lincoln asked for the name of his brand of whisky so he could send a keg to all of his generals. 'That man fights,' said Lincoln.

In July 1863, Grant captured the fortress of Vicksburg, the key to control of the Mississippi River. Shortly afterwards, he was given command of all the more than one million Union troops. Attacking Robert E. Lee in Virginia, Grant suffered appalling casualties: more than 6,000 Union soldiers fell in less than one hour at Cold Harbor. Grant weathered the cries of 'Butcher' and gradually wore down the thinning Confederate forces. Hailed as the hero who won the war, Grant was elected President in 1868 and was re-elected in 1872. After retirement, he made bad investments and became bankrupt and deeply in debt. Although suffering horribly from throat cancer, he wrote his memoirs to pay his debts. Four days after he finished them, he died, in July 1885.

BLACK HAWK, SAUK WAR CHIEF

The War of 1812

Carl Benn

In 1833, the Sauk war chief, Black Hawk, looked back over his life and dictated his memoirs, which were translated into English for publication, a fascinating first-hand account of one warrior's life around the time of the War of 1812.

Black Hawk was born in 1767 at Saukenuk, the principal tribal town, on the east bank of the Mississippi River. At the age of 15, he took up the ways of the warrior and wounded his first enemy. Shortly afterwards, he joined his father in a campaign against the Osages, a tribe that lived to the south-west of his own people, and was

WAR IN THE AMERICAS

'proud to have an opportunity to prove to him that I was not an unworthy son, and that I had courage and bravery.' Excited with 'valour and ambition,' Black Hawk 'rushed furiously upon another, smote him to the earth' with his tomahawk, ran his lance through his body, and took his scalp, while his father watched, said nothing, but 'looked pleased.' Upon returning home, he joined the other warriors in his first triumphal scalp dance, then continued fighting to protect his tribe's access to hunting lands from other aboriginal challengers and to avenge the killing or capture of members of his nation.

A new period of challenge began in 1804, when American officials assumed control of the fur trade community of St Louis following the 1803 Louisiana Purchase in which the United States acquired sovereignty over the vast territories on the west side of the Mississippi River from France. Although Sauk territory had fallen within the boundaries of the United States previous to that time, American influence had been minimal. However, in 1804, the newcomers invited four Sauk leaders to St Louis, where they used alcohol to befuddle them into signing a fraudulent treaty, alienating an enormous amount of Sauk (and Fox) land as a condition for restoring peace with the settler population following an outbreak of low-level hostility between natives and the newcomers. The Sauks were allowed to remain in the ceded territory until the US sold it to settlers. This treaty, combined with tensions arising from increasing settlement, led Black Hawk and many in his nation to maintain friendly relations with the British in Canada in the hope that the British might help the Sauks overturn the treaty and secure the independence of their homeland. However, another Sauk group, the peace band, chose the path of neutrality and accommodation, partly because the growing American presence was changing their trade and other relationships, and partly because its members did not believe they could oppose the United States successfully.

Black Hawk then learned about the efforts by Tecumseh and Tenskwatawa to form their pan-tribal confederacy, remembering ruefully how

> … runners came to our village from the Shawnee Prophet … with invitations for us to meet him on the Wabash. Accordingly a party went from each village. All of our party returned, among whom came a Prophet, who explained to us the bad treatment the different nations of Indians had received from the Americans by giving them a few presents and taking their land from them. I remember well his saying, 'If you do not join your friends on the Wabash, the Americans will take this very village from you!' I little thought then that his words would come true! Supposing that he used these arguments merely to encourage us to join him, we agreed that we would not.

Despite his coolness to the Shawnee brothers, Black Hawk remained hostile to the Americans and rejected the legitimacy of the 1804 treaty. Naturally, he participated in the slowly escalating opposition to the United States, which exploded into war in 1811 at Tippecanoe. Once the Anglo-American war had broken out in 1812, Black Hawk led a war party in an attempt to take Fort Madison near his village, but it failed. In early 1813, he responded to a call by British officials to lead 200 men away from his homeland to the Detroit frontier, where he saw action at Frenchtown and at forts Meigs and Stephenson. When he returned to the Mississippi early in 1814, he learned how the conflict had transpired there during his absence. In many ways, this was a classic frontier struggle with both the natives and settlers organizing small-scale raids against each other and attacking non-combatants. Perhaps the best news from Black Hawk's perspective was the burning and evacuation of Fort Madison by its American garrison in September 1813 following a summer of aboriginal harassment. This 'pleased' him because 'the white people had retired from our country.'

As the 1814 campaigning season opened in the spring, the locus of American strength in the west was St Louis. To the north, the British occupied the fur-trade village of Prairie du Chien and used it to encourage and supply native allies along the Mississippi who continued to oppose the Americans (unlike many of the tribesmen of Tecumseh's alliance, who had been knocked out of the war after the battle of Moraviantown). The fighting that ensued repeated the patterns of raids and harassment set earlier, and also saw a more energetic American response to try and subdue the tribes and evict the British. The Americans sent troops up the Mississippi in fortified gunboats to intimidate the tribes, and, in June, they entered Prairie du Chien without resistance because the small garrison had abandoned the village in the face of their advance. They then built Fort Shelby but surrendered it after a short British siege in July. (The victors renamed the post Fort McKay.)

Black Hawk fought in the 1814 Mississippi campaign, including an engagement at Campbell's Island in July and the battle of the Rock Island Rapids in September. At the latter, he defeated Major Zachary Taylor, the future president, who retreated downriver after the fighting. At the former, high winds drove one of the American vessels aground. Black Hawk declared: 'This boat the Great Spirit gave us!' and led an assault against it. He remembered: 'We approached it cautiously and fired upon the men' who had come ashore from the stricken vessel. Faced with the attack, the Americans 'hurried aboard, but they were unable to push off, being fast aground.' Black Hawk continued:

> We advanced to the river's bank, under cover and commenced firing at the boat. Our balls passed through the plank and did execution, as I could hear them screaming in the boat! I encouraged my braves to continue firing. Several guns were fired from the boat, without effect.

Then he prepared a bow and arrows 'to throw fire to the sail, which was lying on the boat; and after two or three attempts succeeded in setting the sail on fire. The boat was soon in flames!' Then one of the other vessels in the flotilla attempted to rescue the stranded soldiers. Black Hawk recalled that it 'swung in close to the boat on fire, and took off all the people except those killed and badly wounded. We could distinctly see them passing from one boat to the other, and fired on them with good aim. We wounded the war chief in this way!'

At this point, another American vessel came by and dropped anchor to assist the beleaguered boat, but the anchor did not take hold and the gunboat drifted ashore while the first rescue boat abandoned the fight. With another vulnerable target, Black Hawk's band 'commenced an attack' and 'fired several rounds' but the crew did not shoot back. Thinking his enemy was afraid or had only a few men on board, he ordered his men to rush the stricken craft. 'When we got near, they fired, and killed two of our people, being all that we lost in the engagement.' Then: 'Some of their men jumped out and pushed off the boat, and thus got away without losing a man!' This show of bravado impressed Black Hawk, who declared: 'I had a good opinion' of the boat commander because he 'managed so much better than the other,' and in fact Black Hawk noted that it 'would give me pleasure to shake him by the hand.'

Word of the war's end reached the upper Mississippi in May 1815, when an American vessel from St Louis carried the news up to Prairie du Chien. The British invited their aboriginal allies to a council and told them that they had to end their hostilities. An angry and defiant Black Hawk held up a black wampum belt that had been given to him early in the conflict and declared: 'I have fought the Big Knives, and will continue to fight them till they are off our lands. Till then my father, your Red Children can not be happy.' He then led his followers against the Americans, with the most notable action of 1815 being a skirmish known as the 'battle' of the Sink Hole. Other Sauks, however, signed a treaty with the United States in 1815. A year later, Black Hawk acknowledged the wider peace and he too agreed to stop fighting.

After the war, whites pressured the Sauks to move to the west side of the Mississippi. Black Hawk told the story of one friend that symbolized the tensions of the era, recalling how, on an island in the Rock River, he 'planted his corn; it came up well – but the white man saw it! – he wanted the island, and took his team over, ploughed up the corn, and replanted it for himself. The old man shed tears; not for himself, but the distress his family would be in if they raised no corn.' In 1831, with Black Hawk's band continuing to oppose removal, troops surrounded Saukenuk, opened fire with artillery and then moved in. The village, however, was empty; its people had fled across the Mississippi during the previous night. The Americans torched their homes and desecrated their graves, perhaps knowing how important sites associated with the spiritual world were to the Sauks.

A cowed Black Hawk agreed to live in the west, but when the Americans failed to live up to promises to provide food in compensation for the loss of crops at Saukenuk, he and other leaders brought 1,000 or more Sauks, Foxes and other native men, women and children home again in April 1832. The so-called 'Black Hawk War' ensued, but it amounted to little more than a brutal series of tragedies for a short time and culminated in the butchering of the majority of Black Hawk's followers when they tried to swim back across the Mississippi River under fire. Black Hawk gave himself up to the Americans, who toured him through the eastern United States to demonstrate their power and thereby prevent further troubles. It was upon his return to the Mississippi that he dictated his memoirs.

Black Hawk lived out his remaining days quietly in the shadow of the sadness of all that his people had lost, passing away in 1838. Shortly afterwards, a white man broke into his grave and stole his remains. They were put on display in a museum, and then were lost in a fire.

JOHN BEATTY, UNION SOLDIER

American Civil War: the War in the West

Stephen D. Engle

In many ways, John Beatty was typical of the common soldier of the Union army, and his journal details army life in the Western theatre throughout the early years of the war. Beatty was born on 16 December 1828 near Sandusky in the western region of Ohio, a region known for its strong anti-slavery sentiments. At the outbreak of war, he raised a company of local volunteers, which joined the 3rd Ohio Volunteer Infantry Regiment. When the unit was mustered into service, Beatty, recently promoted to lieutenant-colonel, became the regiment's commander. In November 1861, however, his regiment was transferred to General Don Carlos Buell's Army of the Ohio in Kentucky. Throughout 1862 and 1863 he campaigned across the Bluegrass state, Tennessee, northern Mississippi and northern Alabama, participating in many of the battles. At 33 years of age, Beatty was older than the typical soldier who mustered into the army in 1861, and at 5ft 11in., he was taller than most mid-19th-century Americans. He was thin, possessed dark hair and wore a moustache, characteristic of Civil War soldiers.

Like most soldiers, Beatty typically began his journal entries with comments about the climate. 'The weather has been delightful, warm as spring time. The nights are beautiful' is representative of the remarks he frequently made. The landscape was also a source of interest. 'This is peculiar country,' he remarked while in Louisville, 'there are innumerable caverns, and every few rods places are found where the crust of the earth appears to have broken and sunk down hundreds of feet.'

Beatty was also struck by the obvious and routine role that slavery played in the lives of the Southern people. Upon arriving in Louisville, Beatty came across a sign that read 'Negroes Bought and Sold,' and this struck a cord with the Ohioan. 'We have known to be sure, that negroes were bought and sold, like cattle and tobacco, but it nevertheless, awakened new, and not by any means agreeable, sensations to see the humiliating fact announced on the broad side of a commercial house.' To this he added, 'These signs must come down.'

Beatty found camp life both rewarding and a nuisance. It was rewarding to enjoy the weather of the South and to hear the pleasantries of music under moonlit nights. 'The boys are in a happier mood, and a round, full voice comes to us from the tents with the words of an old Scotch song.' Still, it was difficult to keep the men out of trouble. 'The boys, out of pure devilment, set fire to the leaves, and to-night the forest was illuminated.' In August 1862, he wrote: 'I am weak, discouraged, and worn out with idleness.' Excessive drinking often brought retribution and insubordination from the soldiers. When Beatty arrested a half-drunk soldier and strapped him to a tree for being insolent, the soldiers reacted scornfully. 'It was a high-handed outrage upon the person of a volunteer soldier,' Beatty observed, and the common soldiers never let their commanders forget they were volunteers.

There were also casualties beyond the battlefield for the soldiers of Beatty's regiment. When a soldier got a letter from home that his girlfriend had married someone else, Beatty remarked that the news made this soldier 'crazy as a loon.' The poor soul 'imagined that he was in hell, thought Dr Seyes the devil, and so violent did he become that they had to bind him.' Worse yet was the disease of the soldiers, particularly during the winter months. 'There is a great deal of sickness among the troops; many cases of colds, rheumatism, and fever, resulting from exposure,' Beatty observed. 'Passing through the company quarters of our regiment at midnight, I was alarmed by the constant and heavy coughing of the men. I fear the winter will send many more to the grave than the bullets of the enemy, for a year to come.' It surely did.

Beatty also noted that the Union army had become a haven for runaway slaves. 'We have much trouble with the escaped negroes … the colored folks get into our regimental lines, and in some mysterious way are so disposed of that their masters never hear of them again.' Near Murfreesboro, Tennessee, he remarked: 'We have in our camp a superabundance of negroes.'

During spells of boredom, Beatty usually turned his thoughts

to the cottage home, to wife and children, to a time still further away when we had no children, when we were making the preliminary arrangements for starting the world together, when her cheeks were ruddier than now, when wealth and fame and happiness seemed lying just before me, ready to be gathered in, and farther away still, to a gentle, blue-eyed mother – now long gone – teaching her child to lisp his first prayer.

Religion often found expression in music and was a way for the men to escape the boredom of camp life. 'Surely nothing has the power to make us forget earth and its round of troubles as these sweet old church songs, familiar from earliest childhood,' commented Beatty.

Beatty read the newspapers and was particularly interested in the politics of the war. In July 1862, the Ohioan commented on the Confiscation Act passed by the Congress. 'I trust the new policy indicated by the confiscation act, just passed by Congress, will have a good effect… It will, at least, enable us to weaken the enemy,' he argued, 'and strengthen ourselves, as we have hitherto not been able to do.' 'Slavery is the enemy's weak point, the key to his position. If we can tear down this institution, the rebels will lose all interest in the Confederacy, and be too glad to escape with their lives…'

He clearly viewed the institution of slavery as the cause of the war and the root of the evils of Southern society. By the end of 1862, the Emancipation Proclamation had clearly changed the war. In February 1863, Beatty remarked that the 'army is turning its attention to politics somewhat,' particularly when it came to Lincoln's Proclamation. 'Generals and colonels are ventilating their opinions through the press. I think their letters may have a good effect upon the people at home, and prevent them from discouraging the army and crippling the Administration.'

Beatty also wrote about commanders. For the most part he liked his division commander, General Ormsby Mitchel. Mitchel was a professional and proper gentleman who 'never drinks and never swears,' and in Beatty's estimation was 'indefatigable.' But Beatty came to detest Don Carlos Buell for his slowness in campaigning and for his apparent sympathy with the Southern people during the summer of 1862. Buell 'is inaugurating the dancing-master policy,' was Beatty's sarcastic expression for Buell's lethargy, which he declared was the policy of an 'idiot.'

Campaigning gave Beatty plenty of things to react to, not the least of which was the unexpected cheering of citizens for the Union soldiers. 'We passed many fine houses, and extensive, well improved farms,' he penned in 1862, 'but few white people were seen. The negroes appeared to have entire possession.' The sight of a pretty woman warmed his heart. While marching in Tennessee, Beatty came upon a scene where 'a young and very pretty girl stood in the doorway of a handsome farm-house and waved the Union flag. Cheer after cheer arose along the line;

officers saluted, soldiers waved their hats, and the bands played "Yankee Doodle" and "Dixie."' 'That loyal girl,' he wrote, 'captured a thousand hearts.'

Murfreesboro, Tennessee, was quite a place for Beatty. He remarked:

> Murfreesboro is an aristocratic town, many of the citizens have as fine carriages as are to be seen in Cincinnati or Washington. On pleasant week-day evenings they sometimes come out to witness the parades. The ladies, so far as I can judge by a glimpse through a carriage window, are richly and elegantly dressed. The poor whites are as poor as rot, and the rich are very rich. There is no substantial well-to-do middle class. The slaves are, in fact, the middle class here.

By April 1863, however, Murfreesboro had undergone a transformation. The fine houses and trees of the city had been 'cut or trampled down and destroyed.' 'Many frame houses, and very good ones, too,' he remarked, 'have been torn down, and the lumber and timber used in the construction of hospitals.' Even the air had changed: 'There is a fearful stench in many places near here, arising from decaying horses and mules.'

Perhaps nothing caught Beatty's attention more than the ordeal of the battle. In February 1862, he wrote that although it was bitterly cold, 'the conviction that a battle was imminent kept the men steady and prevented straggling.' The evening before the battle of Stone's River (Murfreesboro) in December 1862, Beatty wrote: 'To-morrow, doubtless, the grand battle will be fought, when I trust the good Lord will grant us a glorious victory, and one that will make glad hearts of all loyal people on New-Year's Day.' At one point during the battle, he glanced up to see a soldier who was heading to the back of the line struck in the back between the shoulders, killing him instantly.

After the battle he walked the battlefield and found the dead and wounded scattered for miles. As he walked across the terrain, he commented: 'we find men with their legs shot off; one with his brains scooped out with a cannon ball; another with half a face gone; another with entrails protruding … another boy lies with his hands clasped above his head, indicating that his last words were a prayer.' 'How many poor men moaned through the cold nights in the thick woods, where the first day's battle occurred,' he penned, 'calling in vain to man for help, and finally making their last solemn petition to God!'

The fact that Beatty survived the Civil War was a testament to his fitness as an officer and to a significant degree the result of simple luck. When he resigned his commission in January 1864 and returned to Sandusky, the Civil War had become central to his life. An everyday banker from Ohio who had witnessed the drama of the Civil War, Beatty was no longer an ordinary citizen.

McHENRY HOWARD, CONFEDERATE SOLDIER

The American Civil War: the War in the East

Robert K. Krick

McHenry Howard did not hesitate about going to war against the Star-Spangled Banner when Northern troops invaded his home town of Baltimore in 1861. Federal authorities simply threw into jail those of Maryland's elected legislators who would not do as they were told. Howard and thousands of other young men from the state hurried southward, eager to fight for restoration of self-government. Their purpose, Howard wrote, was 'not merely to aid the cause of the Confederacy as it was constituted, but believing that they were serving their own State – in subjection – in the only way that was left to them.'

When war interrupted Howard's civilian pursuits, he had been studying law after graduating from Princeton University. The 22-year-old lawyer in training belonged to a volunteer organization, the 'Maryland Guard,' that served both military and social purposes. The guardsmen affected gorgeous uniforms of the 'Zouave' variety, modelled after the outfits of French colonial troops who had caught the popular fancy in North America. Howard later described his garb with amusement provided by hindsight:

> The full dress was a dark blue jacket, short and close fitting and much embroidered with yellow; a blue flannel shirt with a close row of small round gilt buttons (for ornament merely), down the front, between yellow trimming; blue pantaloons, very baggy and gathered below the knee and falling over the tops of long drab gaiters; a small blue cap, of the kepi kind, also trimmed with yellow; and, finally, a wide red sash ... kept wide by hooks and eyes on the ends.

Private Howard would soon discover, in the world of a real soldier in the field, that 'this gaudy dress, which made a very brilliant effect on street parade ... was totally unsuitable for any active service.'

For nearly a year Howard served (more suitably attired, of course) in the ranks as an enlisted man with the 1st Maryland Infantry, Confederate States Army, made up of 1,000 young men who had escaped across the Potomac River to join the Southern cause. In the spring of 1862 he won a commission as lieutenant and aide-de-camp to fellow Marylander General Charles S. Winder. Lieutenant Howard remained at that lowest of the commissioned ranks for the final three years of the war. In his staff role, he had an opportunity to observe much of the conflict's most dramatic events, and many of its most significant leaders. After a Federal shell killed General Winder at Cedar Mountain in August 1862, Howard did staff duty with generals Isaac R. Trimble, George H. Steuart, and George Washington Custis Lee, son of commander General Robert E. Lee.

When Lee's Army of Northern Virginia headed north after the battle of Chancellorsville, Lieutenant Howard followed as a supernumerary. His chief, General Trimble, had not reported back to the army after convalescing from a bad wound. That left Howard without a role, but he could not ignore his comrades' aggressive move northward and headed across country toward the Potomac to catch up with the army. When he splashed up the left bank of the river, the exiled Marylander noted sadly that it was the first time he had been on the soil of his native state in more than two years.

In Greencastle, Pennsylvania, Howard and half a dozen other stray Confederates wound up in a hot street fight against mounted Yankees. Pistol bullets shattered windowpanes on all sides, dust obscured galloping horses and the little band of rebels had to flee. Later Howard and his mates chased a lone horseman for miles, only to discover that he was a Confederate major and an old friend.

During the army's subsequent retreat back toward Virginia, Howard rode through a Maryland town and thought wistfully, 'Oh, that it was Baltimore!' On 14 July, as the Army of Northern Virginia abandoned Maryland, Howard wrote in his diary: 'Feel very much depressed at the gloomy prospect for our State. I look around me constantly to see as much of it as I can before leaving it.' As the army crossed the Potomac into Virginia, bandsmen gladly struck up 'Sweet Home,' but that seemed 'a mockery' to the Marylanders. Howard 'could not refrain from some bitter tears as I … looked back to our beloved State.'

For ten months after Gettysburg, the exiled lieutenant performed staff duty under General George H. Steuart, a West Point graduate with 'Old Army' ideas about organization and discipline. The summer after Gettysburg passed without a major engagement. During the lull, Howard and his mates fought against the elements and against logistical defects – just as has every army in every era. In September 1863, he wrote disgustedly in his diary: 'Raining like pitchforks – very disagreeable… Regular equinoctial storm – have had nothing to eat for almost twenty-four hours.' Violent downpours had drowned every fire for miles. Through one uncomfortable day, Lieutenant Howard, General Steuart, and three others huddled unhappily in a storm-shaken tent all day long, hungry and miserable.

Howard missed the campaigning around Bristoe Station in October 1863 because he had gone to the Confederate capital for religious reasons – to be confirmed in the Episcopal faith in Richmond's elegant St Paul's Church. He had returned to duty by the time of the battle of Mine Run, where his staff chores brought him under heavy fire: 'the bullets coming through the switchy woods sounded somewhat like the hissing of a hail or sleet storm.' He also noticed in that engagement one of the benchmarks of the war's evolution. Confederate soldiers had reached the conclusion that substantial protective fortifications made really good sense in the face of rifled musketry. They used 'their bayonets, tin cups, and their hands, to loosen and scoop up the dirt, which was thrown on and around the trunks of old field pine trees' that they cut down and stretched lengthwise.

During the winter of 1863–64, genuine hardship became a constant companion of Southern soldiers. Lieutenant Howard described his diet, at a point in the food chain well above the privates and corporals, as consisting mostly of 'corn dodgers' – corn meal cooked with water – for both breakfast and dinner. In good times, dinner also included 'a soup made of water thickened with corn meal and mashed potatoes and cooked with a small piece of meat, which … was taken out when the soup was done and kept to be cooked over again.'

Events in the spring campaign in 1864 threw McHenry Howard into the cauldron of combat, then yanked him out of action as a prisoner of war. At the battle of the Wilderness, the night of 5 May echoed mordantly with the 'moans and cries' of wounded men from both armies who lay between the lines and beyond succur. 'In the still night air every groan could be heard,' Howard wrote, 'and the calls for water and entreaties to brothers and comrades by name to come and help them.' The next morning, fires started in the underbrush by muzzle flashes spread through the Wilderness and burned to death some of the helpless wounded.

Spotsylvania followed Wilderness immediately. On 10 May 1864, a brutal crossfire caught and pinned down Howard and his friends. They had no option but to hug the ground and wait for darkness. 'A more disagreeable half hour,' he wrote in retrospect, 'with a bullet striking a man lying on the ground every now and then, could not well have been spent.' Two days later a Federal assault swept over the nose of the Confederate works near the point soon to be christened 'the Bloody Angle.' Yankee bayonets surrounded Howard and he went into a captivity that would last for six months. Howard's concise sketch map of the Angle at Spotsylvania remains an important artifact for studying the battle.

As his captors herded Lieutenant Howard to the rear at Spotsylvania, he began a prison experience shared by hundreds of thousands of Civil War soldiers. Howard wound up at Fort Delaware, in the middle of the Delaware River downstream from Philadelphia. There he enjoyed reasonably civilized treatment, by the uncivilized standards of the day. The fort's commander liked Howard and others of the Confederates, but some of his subordinates took the opportunity to abuse their power. In November 1864, Howard went back south under a programme for the exchange of prisoners. Once released in Georgia, he used a flask of brandy to bribe his way into a good railroad car on a Confederate train and by the end of 1864 had reached Richmond again.

Through the war's waning weeks, young Howard assisted General G. W. C. Lee in the effort to turn an accumulation of home front troops, raw levies and naval ratings into a hotchpotch brigade for emergency use. The emergency arose on 2 April 1865. The lieutenant was sitting in a pew at St Paul's, where he had been confirmed a few months earlier, for the 11am Sunday service, when a courier informed Jefferson Davis that the army's lines had been broken. Richmond must be abandoned. For four days the ersatz brigade under G. W. C. Lee took part in the retreat west and south from Richmond. In a mix-up that especially depressed and horrified Howard, the green troops loosed a volley against friends that killed several men, victims of mistaken friendly fire just a few hours before the army surrendered.

Howard fell into enemy hands again on 6 April at Sayler's Creek. This time his prison camp was Johnson's Island in Lake Erie. There he took the oath of allegiance to the United States on 29 May and made his long way home. Awaiting him in Baltimore was a demand, dated September 1862, that he report to Yankee conscript officers to be drafted into Federal service. Men had come to his mother's house and asked the names and occupations of all the family's males. McHenry's mother responded that her husband and eldest son were being held unconstitutionally as political prisoners in northern Bastilles. Four sons were serving in the Confederate army. 'McHenry,' she told her interrogators, was 'with Stonewall Jackson and I expect he will be here soon.' The officials wrote out the conscription demand and left. McHenry kept the souvenir the rest of his life.

Lieutenant Howard enjoyed a long and fruitful career after the war. He completed his legal training and practised law in Baltimore for decades, finding time also to write extensively about his Confederate experiences. McHenry's lively, urbane recollections appeared in periodicals in both the North and South. He eventually turned his story into a charming and important – and sizable, at 423 pages – book that is a classic piece of Confederate literature: *Recollections of a Maryland Confederate Soldier and Staff Officer under Johnston, Jackson and Lee* (Baltimore: Williams & Wilkins Company, 1914). Howard died in his native Maryland on 11 September 1923, two months before his 85th birthday.

SURVIVORS OF THE BATTLE OF LITTLE BIGHORN

The Plains Wars – The Battle of Little Bighorn 1876

Charles M. Robinson III

The battle of Little Bighorn was a pivotal event. For the Indians, it was perhaps their greatest single victory, one in which they completely annihilated five companies of a modern army. Yet it was a hollow victory because it outraged the nation and assured the ultimate destruction of the Indian way of life. As such, Little Bighorn left an indelible imprint on those who fought there. Well into the 20th century, both Indian and white survivors had vivid recollections of that day. Among them were the

Cheyenne warrior Wooden Leg (1858–1940), and Sergeant Charles Windolph (1851–1950), Company H, Seventh Cavalry, who is believed to have been the last white survivor.

WOODEN LEG

Wooden Leg began relating his story to Dr Thomas Marquis, former physician to the Northern Cheyenne Agency in Montana, in the 1920s. Although Marquis did not speak Cheyenne, he was reasonably fluent in Plains sign. This was the primary means of communication, although Wooden Leg would sometimes emphasize a point with words from his limited English vocabulary, and augment his gestures with pencil sketches. Other Cheyennes who were either present at the fight, or among the bands hostile to the government in 1876, often participated in the discussions, corroborated Wooden Leg's experiences and offered their own views on the subject

Wooden Leg was born on the Cheyenne River in the Black Hills of South Dakota in 1858. His name referred to physical stamina – the ability to walk long distances without tiring as though his legs were made of wood. He earned it when he and some companions lost their mounts to Crow horse thieves. On foot, they overtook two of the Crows, rushed and killed them, and recovered their horses.

Growing up, Wooden Leg was typical of a Cheyenne boy training to be a warrior and provider. He learned to ride and hunt and, through painful experience of snow blindness and frostbite, how to handle himself outdoors. The only hostile encounter with whites came when he was about seven or eight years old, when members of his band fought soldiers – probably Colonel Connor's – on Lodgepole Creek near its confluence with the North Platte River. His own first combat experiences were against Crows and Shoshones, the traditional enemies of the Cheyennes. When Wooden Leg was about eight, his older brother, Strong Wind Blowing, and another Cheyenne were killed in the Fetterman massacre of 1866, in which 80 white men under the foolhardy Captain William Fetterman were killed by 2000 Indians.

'There was rejoicing in our camp on account of the victory,' he said, 'but our family and all relatives of the two dead Cheyennes were in mourning. We wept and prayed for the spirits of our lost ones.'

Wooden Leg was in Two Moon's camp when Colonel Joseph Reynolds attacked it on 17 March 1876. He had no ammunition for his old muzzle-loading rifle, and he had loaned his revolver to his cousin, who had gone out with the scouts the night before. He had a borrowed bow and arrows, and grabbed the first pony he saw to go out and fight. It soon became obvious that the camp was lost, so he returned to his lodge to gather his valuables. As he rode out he picked up two children, carried them to safety, and then went back into the fray. When he and three companions killed and stripped a soldier, he came away with the man's blue coat. From a distance, they watched as the soldiers burned their village. Later, they recovered what they could from the wreckage, and that night Wooden Leg was among the group that stampeded the horses.

The Cheyennes joined Crazy Horse's Oglalas, and together the two groups travelled up and joined the giant camp of the Hunkpapas under Sitting Bull. Wooden Leg participated in the battle of the Rosebud, after which the camp moved toward Little Bighorn. The Cheyenne camp circle was at the north end, downriver from Major Marcus Reno's attack, and so these warriors were primarily concerned with Lieutenant-Colonel George Custer. Describing the fight, Wooden Leg recalled:

> Most of the Indians were working around the ridge … occupied by the soldiers. We were lying down in gullies and behind sagebrush hillocks. The shooting at first was at a distance, but we kept creeping in closer around the ridge. Bows and arrows were in use much more than guns. From the hiding-places of the Indians, the arrows could be shot in a high and long curve, to fall upon the soldiers or their horses. An Indian using a gun had to jump up and expose himself long enough to shoot…
>
> I saw one Sioux walking slowly toward the gulch, going away from where were the soldiers. He wabbled [sic] dizzily as he moved along. He fell down, got up, fell down again, got up again. As he passed near to where I was I saw that his whole lower jaw was shot away. The sight of him made me sick. I had to vomit.

After the battle, the tribes split up. In November, while the main Cheyenne band camped on the Red Fork of the Powder River, Wooden Leg and nine other warriors went out searching for Crow Indians. They passed through Little Bighorn, and collected unfired cartridges and souvenirs scattered about the battlefield. As they headed back toward their camp, they encountered their people who, during their absence, had been attacked by General Ranald Mackenzie.

'They had but little food,' Wooden Leg said. 'Many of them had no blankets nor robes. They had no lodges. Only here and there was there one wearing moccasins. The others had their feet wrapped in loose pieces of skin or of cloth. Women, children and old people were straggling along over the snow-covered trail down the valley.'

Following the surrender, Wooden Leg was among the group exiled to the Indian Territory. He did not, however, join Dull Knife or Little Wolf in the outbreak, but waited until he and other Northern Cheyennes were allowed to repatriate. He later became a baptized Christian and a judge of the Indian Court.

SERGEANT CHARLES WINDOLPH

Wooden Leg's army counterpart, Sergeant Charles Windolph, was with Captain Frederick Benteen's battalion at Little Bighorn. He was in his 80s and living in Lead, South Dakota, when historian Frazier Hunt first contacted him in the mid-1930s. Over the next ten years, until 1946, he related his story to Hunt and his son, Robert. The following year it was published 'with explanatory material and contemporary sidelights on the Custer Fight,' as *I Fought With Custer*. Although Windolph commented that the 70 years since the fight had given him plenty of time to remember the details and fix them in his mind, he acknowledged his account might not match those of other survivors. 'Even the men who were with Benteen and Reno and lived to tell the tale, didn't come anywhere near telling the same stories about what they did, and what they saw,' he explained, adding, 'I had only one pair of eyes, so, of course, all I can tell is what I saw myself.'

Windolph was born in Bergen, Prussia, on 9 December, 1851. He reached military age as Prussia was preparing to go to war with France, and to avoid conscription he escaped first to Sweden and later to the United States. Like many other young German draft dodgers, he found it difficult to earn a living in the United States and so ended up with the only job available – enlistment in the US Army.

Company H, 7th Cavalry, was posted to Nashville, Tennessee, when Windolph joined in 1870. Three years later, his battalion was sent to Dakota Territory (North Dakota), where he took part in the Yellowstone Expedition to explore a route for the railway into Montana. He was not present in the expedition's only Indian fight on 4 August because Company H had been left behind to guard the supply depot on the lower Yellowstone. In 1874, he participated in Custer's Black Hills Expedition. After a brief stint in New Orleans during the winter of 1875–76, his company was sent to Fort Abraham Lincoln. On 17 May, the 7th rode out of Fort Abraham Lincoln as part of General Terry's Dakota Column. Windolph remembered the day:

> You felt like you were somebody when you were on a good horse, with a carbine dangling from its small leather ring socket on your McClelland [sic] saddle, and a Colt army revolver strapped on your hip; and a hundred rounds of ammunition in your web belt and in your saddle pockets. You were a cavalryman of the Seventh Regiment. You were a part of a proud outfit that had a fighting reputation, and you were ready for a fight or a frolic.

The Dakota Column linked up with Colonel John Gibbon's Montana Column, and on 22 June, the 7th separated and started on its scouting expedition. Windolph recalled that although the men expected a hard fight, they were not particularly worried. Each man believed that if anyone died, it would be someone else, not himself. On 25 June, after a hard three days, the 7th located the Indian village and prepared to attack.

About noon, Benteen took his battalion, including Company H, up the valley and scouted the hills, while Custer and Reno moved down the valley toward the village. After about two hours, Benteen ordered the battalion to turn about and rejoin the others. As they drew closer, they heard gunfire. Benteen ordered his men to draw pistols, and they charged up the bluffs at a gallop to find Reno and his men fleeing up the hill.

'I'll never forget that first glimpse I had of the hilltop,' Windolph said. 'Here were a little group of men in blue, forming a skirmish line, while their beaten comrades, disorganized and terror stricken, were making their way on foot and on horseback up the narrow coulee that led from the river, 150 feet below.'

For the next few hours until sundown, the two battalions held off the Indians, all the while wondering why Custer didn't come to support them. It never occurred to them that Custer and the remaining five companies of the 7th were already dead. After a cold, rainy night the shooting began again. By now the wounded were crying for water, and Benteen called for volunteers to make the near-suicidal rush to the river. Windolph was one of 17 who came forward, and Benteen detailed him and three other good marksmen to draw fire and keep the Indians distracted while the others went for water. Several of the water party were wounded, but Windolph and his three German countrymen emerged unscathed. All four received the Medal of Honor. After the Indians withdrew, and General Alfred Terry and Gibbon arrived, the men learned of Custer's fate. Windolph was a member of the detail that buried Custer and his brother, Tom. After the Great Sioux War, Windolph participated in the Nez Percé campaign of 1877. He left the army in 1883, and worked for Homestake Mining Company in Lead, for 49 years. He died on 11 March 1950 at the age of 98.

WARS OF EMPIRE

Soldiers! The eyes of your country are upon you.
Be steady, be cool, be firm in the assault. The town
must be yours this night.

('Black Bob' Craufurd, Light Division)

I shall never forget the scream the poor lad gave when
struck. It was one of the last they fired, and shattered his
left arm to pieces as he stood between the waggons.
That scream went to my very soul, for I accused
myself of having caused his misfortune.

(Cavalié Mercer, Royal Horse Artillery)

PRIVATE EDWARD COSTELLO, 95TH RIFLES

The Peninsular War 1807–1814

Gregory Fremont-Barnes

Edward 'Ned' Costello was born in Ireland in 1788 and joined the 95th Rifles in 1808, while a shoemaker. In May 1809 his battalion embarked for the peninsula, where his experiences over the next five years were a series of hardships, adventures, narrow escapes, wounds and desperate combats. Throughout his many years' of unbroken campaigning he remained a private, and his experiences, recorded for publication in 1841, provide a valuable insight into the lives of ordinary British soldiers in Wellington's army.

The 95th was a recently raised regiment, armed with the Baker rifle rather than the Brown Bess musket, and sporting distinctive dark green uniforms trimmed with black leather. 'I was highly delighted with the smart appearance of the men, and with their green uniform,' Costello wrote. The 95th (nicknamed the 'Sweeps' because of their dark appearance) not only wore different uniforms from the line regiments, but their weapons provided unrivalled accuracy and their loose open-order tactics, known as skirmishing, quickly brought the 95th into prominence as an elite unit within that already distinguished element of the army, the Light Brigade, later renamed the Light Division.

Costello had hardly arrived when the Light Brigade began one of history's greatest forced marches when it left to join Wellington's main body at Talavera, 70 miles south-west of Madrid, where a battle was shortly expected. 'Our men suffered dreadfully on the route, chiefly from excessive fatigue and the heat of the weather. The brain fever soon commenced, making fearful ravages in our ranks, and many dropped by the roadside and died.' Despite being light troops, the 95th still carried 70–80lb of equipment, provisions, ammunition and a rifle, and the blistering July heat took a terrible toll. In 26 hours the Light Brigade had marched 62 miles, only to arrive at Talavera after the battle was over. Nevertheless it had been an epic achievement.

> As we advanced … the heights of Talavera burst upon our sight. With three loud huzzas, we hailed the news… The scene, however, was appalling… The field of action … was strewn with the wreck of recent battle. The dead and dying, thousands of them, conquerors and conquered, lay in little heaps, interspersed with dismounted guns, and shattered ammunition waggons. Broken horse trappings, blood-stained shakos [infantry helmets], and other torn paraphernalia of military pomp and distinction, completed the battle scene.

After suffering a severe fever for six weeks Costello rejoined his regiment at Barba del Puerco in March 1810. There, on the windy night of the 19th, while defending the bridge over the River Águeda over a deep chasm studded with jagged rocks, the French attacked, taking the sentries prisoner and surprising Costello and 43 other riflemen, who were on picket duty. The men sought cover in the rocky and broken ground and kept up a regular fire at those attempting to take the heights from below. Costello's company kept 600 French infantry at bay for half an hour until the colonel of the regiment brought three more companies to assist.

In July 1810, following the French capture of Ciudad Rodrigo, the French attacked the Light Division with overwhelming numbers, in the course of which Costello and a small group of riflemen became surrounded by cavalry:

> While hotly engaged with the French infantry in our front, one or two troops of their hussars … whipped on our left flank… A cry of 'The French cavalry are upon us' came too late, and they charged in amongst us. Taken unprepared, we could offer little or no resistance, and our men were trampled down and sabered on every side.

A French dragoon grabbed hold of Costello's collar and aimed his sabre at his chest, only to be killed by a volley fired by soldiers of the 52nd Foot:

> This tumbled the horse of my captor and he fell heavily, dragging me down with him. The animal was on the dragoon's leg. Determined to have one brief struggle for liberty, I freed myself from his grasp, dealt him a severe blow on the head with the butt of my rifle, and rushed up to our 52nd.

Costello, however, was shot in the right knee and while being evacuated on the back of a comrade, that man was shot, whereupon Costello dragged himself over the bridge spanning the Coa River. He was lucky to have escaped with his life, and this was only one of a number of similar occasions.

The retreat was typically awful, and Costello eventually reached the hospital at Belem, near Lisbon. The experiences of the sick there and at Figueira, en route, were quite horrendous:

> The heat of the weather was intense and affected our wounds dreadfully. Doctors were scarce … maggots were engendered in the sores, and the bandages, when withdrawn, brought away lumps of putrid flesh and maggots. Many men died on board, and others were reduced to the necessity of amputation, but by care, and syringing sweet oil into my wounds, I managed to get rid of the maggots.

With a better standard of care in Belem, he soon recovered and remained to convalesce until October, when he left to rejoin his unit at the Lines of Torres Vedras.

Costello fought in numerous skirmishes and minor actions during the course of the year, pursuing the French, seeing the desolation and suffering left in their retreat, and the dreadful vengeance of the guerrillas as bodies of their victims were discovered and smoking villages marked the progress of the army. Costello fought at Fuentes de Oñoro in May 1811 and continued the advance through Spain. Like many of his comrades, he amused himself between marches and combat with wrestling and boxing matches with the peasantry, while the officers went hunting and dancing with village girls, who exchanged lessons in Spanish dance for those of England and Ireland.

At the beginning of 1812 the army laid siege to the border fortress of Ciudad Rodrigo, and when two breaches had been made in the walls Costello volunteered for the 'forlorn hope,' which was to be the small party leading in the main assault against the Lesser Breach. A second attacking party would attempt the Greater Breach. He noted that 'many of our men came forward with alacrity for this deadly service. With three officers from my company I had, as I then considered, the good fortune to be chosen. This was a momentous occasion in the life of a soldier, and so we considered it.' Shot and shell roared overheard and each man considered his chances of survival. They shook hands with each other; Costello went so far as to give his father's address to a comrade in the event he did not survive the experience. 'As darkness descended over the city,' Costello relates, 'our imaginations became awake to the horrors of the coming scene.'

'Black Bob' Craufurd, that grim but highly respected commander of the Light Division, came forward to lead the stormers in person. With a clear and distinct voice he addressed the troops:

> Soldiers! The eyes of your country are upon you. Be steady, be cool, be firm in the assault. The town must be yours this night. Once masters of the wall, let your first duty be to clear the ramparts, and in doing this keep together.

Costello records that his heart beat powerfully as he and his comrades anxiously watched for the signal, while further to the rear thousands of troops of his division stood in readiness to follow up the storming party. 'We were on the brink of being dashed into eternity,' he recalled, 'and among the men there was a solemnity and silence deeper than I ever witnessed.'

On the appearance of the signal rocket Craufurd cried 'Now lads, for the breach!' and the men raced to the objective. 'As we neared the breach, the shot of the enemy swept our men away fast. Canister, grape, round-shot, and shell, with fireballs to show our ground, and a regular hailstorm of bullets, came pouring in and around us.' Craufurd fell mortally wounded, but the attack never faltered. The men scrambled up ladders placed in the ditch and ascended against a storm of fire. The attackers pushed on undaunted, though when the French sprung a mine many were killed and others scorched by the explosion. Costello himself was nearly killed by a French artillery gunner with whom he grappled until support arrived, but the whole scene was one of bitter hand-to-hand combat. In only half an hour the fight was over. The fortress was in British hands and Costello had again escaped with his life, though there were other 'scrapes' to come.

Costello would go on to participate in the even greater assault on the fortress of Badajoz in April. He again volunteered for the forlorn hope detachment, and said of the two commanders: 'There was never a pair of uglier men, but a brace of better soldiers never stood before the muzzle of a Frenchman's gun.' Costello was wounded in the breach and 'for the first time for many years, I uttered something like a prayer.' He eventually heard the sound of firing diminish, and above the cries of the wounded he detected cheering from the town. The place had fallen, though Costello was himself wounded in the right leg, while two musket shots had perforated his helmet. Badajoz was not to be his final action, however. He would continue his march with the Light Division and go on to serve at Salamanca, the retreat from Burgos, and at Vittoria, where he took away more than £400 worth of booty from the abandoned waggons. 'All who had the opportunity were employed in reaping some personal advantage from our victory,' he wrote, 'so I determined not to be backward.' There followed the various struggles for the Pyrenees, the action at Tarbes and finally the battle of Toulouse.

Costello also served in the Waterloo campaign, losing his finger to a musket ball at Quatre Bras, and for several years in the occupation of France. He spent many years again fighting in Spain during the Carlist War as part of the British Legion before becoming a yeoman warder at the Tower of London in 1838. He died in 1869, with two of the musket balls from which he was wounded still inside him. One, which had buried itself in his leg at the Coa in 1810, was, by his request, removed after his death. In addition to his printed recollections, 'Ned' Costello can truly be said to have carried the Peninsular War with him well into the Victorian era.

BARCLAY DE TOLLY, RUSSIAN COMMANDER, AND JACOB WALTER, NAPOLEONIC SOLDIER

Napoleonic Wars

Todd Fisher

BARCLAY DE TOLLY, RUSSIAN COMMANDER

Michael Andreas Barclay de Tolly was born on 24 December 1761 in Polish Lithuania. He was descended from a minor Scottish nobleman who had gone to the Baltic to seek his fortune. The Barclays had prospered in the Germanic Lutheran provinces and Michael's father had served in the Russian Army prior to receiving his patent of nobility from the tsar.

Michael grew up in St Petersburg where he was raised by his aunt. This was a common occurrence among the German Protestants and gave the young man the exposure to upper society unavailable in the Baltic provinces. His foster-father was also in the military and enrolled the young Barclay in a cavalry regiment at the age of six. He would spend the rest of his life within the military.

Barclay's schooling was basic, but he was a voracious reader and pursued studies beyond the normal requirements. Among his acquired talents was a fluency in Russian and French, to accompany his native German. He also devoured anything that would expand his military knowledge. During his youth he developed a quiet, taciturn personality quite in keeping with his German upbringing. His contemporaries described him as meticulous, brave, honest, modest, bright and somewhat humourless.

Barclay joined the Jaegers in 1787 and his unit joined the army of Prince Potemkin (of Potemkin Village fame). Here the captain caught the attention of his superiors and became an aide to one of the wing commanders, Prince Anhalt-Bernburg. During the victorious siege of Ochakov against the Turks, Barclay participated in the desperate sortie in which most of his fellow officers were casualties.

Barclay continued to serve with distinction until 1789, when he was transferred to the Finnish front.

He was married to his cousin the next year before a posting as major and battalion commander of the St Petersburg Grenadier Regiment sent him to Poland. The war lasted until 1793 and flared up again the following year when the Poles under Thaddeus Kosciuszko, who had fought for the Americans in the War of Independence, revolted. Distinguishing himself at the battles of Vilna and Grodno, he continued the campaign under General Suvorov when the Warsaw suburb of Praga was stormed. This brutal event ended the rebellion and led to the final destruction of what remained of Poland. Barclay was promoted to lieutenant-colonel for his conduct and to full colonel in 1796. He remained in Russia commanding the 3rd Jaegers, missing Suvorov's campaigns in Italy and Switzerland but performing with such efficiency that he was promoted to major-general in March 1799.

When war against Napoleon came in 1805, Barclay was posted under Count von Bennigsen. Fortunately Bennigsen's army avoided the debacle of Austerlitz, though its arrival there may have swung the balance. There was to be no promotion for battlefield heroics, but neither was there any blame.

The war came to life again for the Russians in 1806 as they moved to support their Prussian allies. Unfortunately, they were unable to arrive before Napoleon crushed the Prussians at Jena-Auerstädt and the pursuit that followed. The leading Russians took up their positions around Warsaw and awaited the French and their supporting armies. Napoleon moved upon them quickly, and after forcing a river crossing, fought the twin battles of Pultusk and Golymin. It was at the battle of Pultusk that Barclay, by now a lieutenant-general, received his baptism of fire as a commanding general. Leading one of the advance guards, his men faced the brunt of the redoubtable Marshal Lannes' attack. A desperate fight in the woods swung back and forth. Lannes, realizing the French were facing the main Russian Army and not a rearguard, broke off the attack. Barclay won praise for his calm, skilful performance.

The three advance guards were consolidated under the command of Prince Bagration. Barclay led the most active troops of this command. He continued the campaign and covered himself with glory in several rearguard actions. At Eylau on 7 February 1807, his men defended the village against determined assaults by the French. It was only an attack of the Old Guard that finally expelled Barclay's men. Once more he mounted a counter-attack. Barclay, leading cavalry, was hit in the arm by canister and narrowly avoided being crushed by the stampede of horses before one of his men scooped him up.

After being rushed to a hospital in Königsberg, Barclay's arm was saved. However, this wound would never fully heal, and Barclay never again had the full use of the arm. It was serious enough that he would not be fit for action again until after Friedland and the Russian surrender at Tilsit. During his convalescence Barclay became friends with the tsar. Visiting his wounded general in the hospital, Alexander was struck by Barclay's modest and honest character – a welcome contrast to the vain, preening degenerates who so often surrounded the young tsar.

Following the Peace of Tilsit, Napoleon suggested an attack on Sweden to his new Russian allies. This served French needs in two ways: first it would close one of Britain's most lucrative ports left in Europe, and secondly it would draw Russia away from central European affairs. An attack on this traditional enemy was very appealing to Tsar Alexander. The campaign got under way, with Barclay commanding a column in the main army. After initial successes, the tide turned against the Russians as all of Finland rose up in a guerrilla war. Barclay showed initiative to the point where he disobeyed a direct command in order to save a contingent that was about to be crushed. Demands were made in the army hierarchy to have him court martialled, but defenders arose to support Barclay. In the end the tsar sided with Barclay and he was promoted to governor of Finland.

The second phase of the war called for a crossing of the frozen Gulf of Bothnia. This scheme seemed insane since it demanded crossing the frozen waters – a march of 24 miles, a brief rest on a snowy islet, then another 36 miles over the ice. Throughout they would be subjected to the near-arctic winter with no possible protection. Despite these tremendous obstacles, Barclay led his men safely to the Swedish side of the gulf and captured the fortified city of Umea. This legendary effort was temporarily lost in the news that a *coup d'etat* had overthrown the King of Sweden and peace had been declared.

Barclay remained as governor of Finland until the end of 1809. His careful and efficient performance earned him Alexander's praise and promotion to minister of war on 20 January 1810. He immediately set about reforming the field regulations. This massive effort was compiled and distributed in what became known as the *Yellow Book* because of the colour of its cover. This was the first change to be made to the regulations since the days of Peter the Great in the early 1700s.

He next lobbied to establish a series of defensive fortifications along the frontier. While he started the programme, little was completed prior to the 1812 campaign. It was his belief that the Russians should be passive in the campaign and grudgingly fall back upon their lines of communication until they could effectively counter-attack. This policy set him at odds with Bagration, who felt that any abandonment of Russian soil was a sin.

When the war began, he was directly under the command of the capricious tsar and dutifully fell back on the camp of Drissa. It was only after the tsar's departure that he was able to formulate his own plan. He fell back toward Smolensk and prepared to take the initiative. Bagration joined him with his army and graciously placed himself under Barclay's command.

It was only now that Barclay seemed to lose his nerve. He vacillated between attack and a further retreat. He sent confusing orders and had his troops marching in circles. When Napoleon made a move on Smolensk, he regained focus and orders became firm and clear. Following the battle, Barclay decided on a further retreat, and the generals around him became enraged.

He had been under suspicion for being a 'foreigner' and his behaviour brought this criticism to a new height. Tsar Alexander felt a change was required and placed Mikhail Kutusov in overall command. Barclay took this demotion with equanimity and performed heroically at the following battle of Borodino. At that battle, Bagration was mortally wounded. With his great rival gone, Barclay continued to act as the 1st Army commander. A fortnight after the fall of Moscow, the two armies were consolidated. Soon thereafter Barclay left the army and Kutusov for reasons of health, but in reality, with the joining of the two armies, his role was at an end.

He took no further part in the 1812 campaign, but was placed in charge of the Russian 3rd Army in February 1813. He manoeuvred skilfully and once more earned the confidence of the tsar. Following the twin defeats of Lützen and Bautzen, Barclay was made commander-in-chief of all Russian armies. He remained in the field at the tsar's side throughout 1813 and entered France for the campaign of 1814. He was promoted to field marshal for his service.

In 1815, Barclay organized the army for a second invasion of France following Napoleon's return. Though he saw no fighting, he was made a prince of Russia. He continued his role as commander-in-chief for the next three years, when ill health caused him to ask for a leave of absence. The tsar, wishing to reward this most loyal servant, granted him a two-year leave and 100,000 rubles for expenses. Barclay was not to enjoy this rest, however, for on his way to a spa in Bohemia he stopped at one of his homes near Riga for a rest. He died that night, 25 May 1818, apparently of a heart attack.

In the end it was his organizational skills, more than his bravery, which had proved most valuable to Russia. By preserving the army, he set the stage for Napoleon to make the fatal error of advancing too far and remaining too long in Russia. His steadying influence may have made the crucial difference in Russia's struggle.

JACOB WALTER, NAPOLEONIC SOLDIER

Jacob Walter, from Württemberg (now in south-west Germany) was drafted into the army in the autumn of 1806. He was inducted into the 4th (or Franquemont) Infantry Regiment and sent to guard Napoleon's line of supply as the campaign moved into old Poland. During 1809 he fought the rebels in the Vorarlberg who were attacking Napoleon's rear. During the campaign of 1812 his regiment was part of Ney's Corps. Apart from fighting at the battle of Smolensk, he participated in no major action. He followed the army during the retreat and was mustered out of the regiment for reasons of poor health upon returning home in 1813. There was nothing remarkable about him and he contributed little to the war effort, but he was an honest chronicler of his experiences and he recorded the attitudes common among the German soldiers of his day.

Walter had been brought up a Catholic, the brother of a priest. This had allowed him the opportunity to learn to read and write. It is interesting that Walter sowed his wild oats in 1806, 'an element of my youth,' but became religious during the retreat from Moscow.

In 1807, Walter was guarding a rear area when a spy was brought in. The evidence seemed clear enough, so the man was whipped 150 times prior to being shot. There seemed to be no purpose for the flogging other than the amusement of the soldiers and officers, but Walter found nothing odd in this. Following this incident, he was sent out to requisition food from the local villages. Not having a map, he sought a local guide. Naturally, he picked on the most downtrodden section of society, the Jews, to find his man. The man tried to hide but was found and dragged down two flights of stairs. His misery was of great amusement. Walter's attitude was typical of the time, and he never noted any disapproval among his comrades.

The process of finding food often differed little from outright theft. The peasants in their huts made of straw could not defend themselves against pillaging troops. On one occasion, Walter shot a pet dog for his own amusement and then was surprised that the locals were uncooperative.

Walter had contempt for other beliefs, including Prussian Lutheranism. He observed that these people were superstitious, while exhibiting his own superstitions on repeated occasions. The ideas of the Enlightenment had not penetrated far beyond the upper and educated classes.

Walter's fondest recollections were of his family. The highlight of a campaign was when his regiment was stationed in the same place as his brother's.

In 1809 Walter's battalion was sent to put down the rebellion in the Vorarlberg, which had risen in sympathy with the Tyrol. He saw action in the fighting around Bregenz on 29 May, where he gained experience as a skirmisher. Taking a position on the staircase of a building, he shot off most of his ammunition before making a mad dash to the rear. In the subsequent fighting in the town, he shot a man at point blank range. At no other time does he mention that he actually hit an opponent. At Bregenz, where his men made a hurried withdrawal, Walter makes it quite clear that he considered his running ability his key asset. Complaints about the local breads and grain, which differed from those at home, were typical among soldiers at the time and Walter makes repeated comments throughout his memoirs.

In 1812 his regiment marched to the Russian border. Throughout the march, he was unaware of the ultimate destination. This was the only time he remembered seeing the high command. The crown prince ordered his Württembergers to go through manoeuvres when it was a holiday. This was pointed out by one of the lesser-ranking Württemberg generals and the prince threatened to arrest him. It seems that the prince was annoyed that he had his command placed under Ney, and was taking out his displeasure on his men.

Walter remembered the march into Russia for its heat, choking dust and long downpours. He soon began a campaign-long effort to find food. Often the only food available had to be purchased from the despised Jews. The irony that his salvation lay in their willingness to sell to him was lost on him.

At Smolensk, Jacob Walter fought in the only major battle of his military career. Along with his blue-coated comrades, he assaulted the bridgeheads in an effort to cut off the city's defenders. Breaking into the city, he saw the devastation of the fires caused by the battle. His impression was one of total chaos. Finally he rested near a hospital station, to be treated to the sight of piles of amputated limbs. Walter did march past the carnage of the battle of Borodino, but made little comment about it. By the time he reached Moscow, his company was down to 25 men, from a starting strength of about 175.

During the retreat, Walter became the servant or batman of a major. This he hoped would provide him with a better chance of survival, but it soon was clear that the major depended more on Walter than vice versa. Hunger was a daily concern and the resulting weakness led to disease and death all along the march. Lice covered every part of his body and the cold wore him down. If he had not stolen a horse, he thought he would have perished; instead someone else did. Indeed, Walter claimed that no one survived without a horse. This was an exaggeration, but clearly it was important, since the soldiers kept stealing each others' horses.

Near Borisov he was reunited with a fellow Württemberger, cold and wet from fording a river, who shared his loaf of bread with Walter. For this Walter pledged a lifetime's devotion. They finished their meal and mounted their horses to continue the journey, but the generous friend was dead by morning. The horror of the Beresina crossing is told, with dazed men sitting down in the snow, never to rise. It was here that Walter saw Napoleon. He comments on the unmoved expression on the emperor's face, though it is hard to believe that he got close enough to get a good look. It is more likely that he projected his own disillusionment.

Near Vilna, he was with a small group of men when the Cossacks came upon them. At first he tried to flee, but he was stabbed at and knocked off his horse. He lay in the snow and did not move while his compatriots were massacred. Finally the Cossacks rode off and Walter stole away to rejoin the army.

At the Niemen River he met up with some Westphalian soldiers. Offered hospitality by some local peasants, the men were plied with alcohol and soon set upon and murdered. Walter escaped only by sensing a trap at the last moment.

On Christmas Eve, he finally reached a place where he could bathe and get a change of clothes. The filth and lice were caked on like 'fir-bark.' Soon he had his first square meal in months and headed back home with a supply and hospital train. On reaching Württemberg he was mustered out of the army for reasons of ill health. He returned home and made a full recovery within a couple of weeks.

CAPTAIN CAVALIÉ MERCER, ROYAL HORSE ARTILLERY

Waterloo: the fall of the French Empire

Gregory Fremont-Barnes

Cavalié Mercer was born in 1783, the second son of General Mercer of the Royal Engineers, who had served in the War of American Independence on the staff of General Henry Clinton, and afterwards spent the next two decades as commanding engineer in the west of England. The younger Mercer attended the Military Academy at Woolwich, was commissioned into the Royal Artillery as a second lieutenant at the age of 16, and was posted to Ireland during the rebellion of 1798. He became a captain in December 1806 and in the following year was dispatched to South America with the expeditionary force under General Whitelocke (1757–1833), which suffered ignominious defeat. To his great personal regret Mercer did not see service in the

Peninsular War, but was sent abroad during the Waterloo campaign while still a captain, in which capacity he commanded G Troop, Royal Horse Artillery.

Mercer, who related his experiences in his *Journal of the Waterloo Campaign*, was a candid, colourful and accurate observer of the events around him. Unlike many diarists both before and since, Mercer fully acknowledged the fact that most soldiers have a limited view of the battlefield and seldom know anything of events occurring even a few hundred yards away:

> Depend on it, he who pretends to give a general account of a great battle from his own observation deceives you – believe him not. He can see no farther (that is, if he be personally engaged in it) than the length of his nose; and how is he to tell what is passing two or three miles off, with hills and trees and buildings intervening, and all enveloped in smoke?

On the morning of the battle of Waterloo (18 June 1815) Mercer's troop was camped in an orchard, where his men busied themselves filling their canteens with rum, preparing oatmeal, cooking soup and digging up potatoes. When firing began he noticed that the bivouacs on the hillside suddenly became deserted, and as the firing grew louder he ordered the troop to be readied for manoeuvre. The kettles of soup were overturned and the troop was ready to move, but Mercer was entirely without orders. 'It appeared to me we had been forgotten. All except only ourselves, were evidently engaged; and labouring under this delusion, I thought we had better get into the affair at once.'

Reaching the battlefield, Mercer surveyed attractive open country, covered in fields of corn and dotted with thickets and woods. It was a relatively quiet position, left of the heavily fortified farm of Hougoumont. But as the battle intensified he watched as French cavalry and artillery became more active and round-shot began to fall on his position. He briefly exchanged fire with a French battery, in the course of which one of his gunners was struck by a cannon shot:

> I shall never forget the scream the poor lad gave when struck. It was one of the last they fired, and shattered his left arm to pieces as he stood between the waggons. That scream went to my very soul, for I accused myself of having caused his misfortune. I was, however, obliged to conceal my emotion from the men, who had turned to look at him; so, bidding them 'stand to their front,' I continued my walk up and down, whilst Hitchins [the troop surgeon] ran to his assistance.

Round-shot continued to plough into the soft mud around him, one striking a horse from the gun team, depriving it of the whole of its face below the eyes. Yet the beast remained alive and standing, leaving Mercer to order the farrier to end his misery, which he performed with a thrust through the heart with his sabre. Shortly thereafter a senior officer, his face blackened from smoke, his sleeve torn open from French fire, galloped up, calling out, 'Left limber up, and as fast as you can.' In moments Mercer's troop was trundling toward the main ridge between Hougoumont and the Charleroi ridge, where the French were massing a large body of heavy cavalry in preparation for a charge.

Wellington's orders, the officer informed Mercer in clear terms, were explicit: if the cavalry were certain to reach the guns, Mercer and his men were to fire for as long as possible before retiring into the safety of the adjacent squares of infantry. As Mercer's troop ascended the reverse slope of the main Anglo-allied position, the full spectacle and sound of battle burst upon him:

> We breathed a new atmosphere … the air was suffocatingly hot, resembling that issuing from an oven. We were enveloped in thick smoke, and, malgré the incessant roar of cannon and musketry, could distinctly hear around us a mysterious humming noise, like that which one hears of a summer's evening proceeding from myriads of black beetles; cannon-shot, too, ploughed the ground in all directions, and so thick was the hail of balls and bullets that it seemed dangerous to extend the arm lest it should be torn off.
>
> Hitchins, unaccustomed to such a cacophony, watched and listened with utter astonishment, twisting and turning in his saddle, declaring, 'My God, Mercer, what is that? What is all this noise? How curious! – how very curious!'

When a cannon shot came hissing past, Mercer ordered him to withdraw, for the troop would need its surgeon intact.

Still, the troop reached the summit without loss, and the guns were unlimbered between two squares of Brunswick infantry to await the expected onslaught. No sooner had the first of Mercer's guns been manoeuvred into position in the interval between the squares than he perceived through the smoke the leading squadron of the advancing column coming on at a brisk trot. He immediately issued the order 'case shot!' and the guns unlimbered and were ready for action in moments. 'The very first round,' Mercer observed, '… brought down several men and horses. They continued, however, to advance.'

Meanwhile the Brunswickers had begun to issue musket fire, but as the square appeared unsteady he knew that he must remain with the guns and repulse the attackers or watch the infantry dissolve in panic. In this he knew that he must disobey Wellington's explicit order, and face the consequences later, '… a resolve that was strengthened by the effect of the remaining guns as they rapidly succeeded in coming to action, making terrible slaughter, and in an instant covering the ground with men and horses.'

The horsemen nevertheless persevered, and though their progress was slowed to a walk they carried on, leading Mercer to the unpleasant conclusion that they would ride over him, though 'the carnage was frightful.'

In a hurried effort to retreat, the cavalry jostled and pushed through the debris, becoming:

> … a complete mob, into which we kept a steady fire of case-shot from our six pieces. The effect is hardly conceivable, and to paint this scene of slaughter and confusion impossible. Every discharge was followed by the fall of numbers, whilst the survivors struggled with each other, and I actually saw them using the pommels of their swords to fight their way out of the mêlée. Some, rendered desperate at finding themselves thus pent up at the muzzles of our guns, as it were, and others carried away by their horses, maddened with wounds, dashed through our intervals – few thinking of using their swords, but pushing furiously onward, intent only on saving themselves. At last the rear of the column, wheeling about, opened a passage, and the whole swept away at a much more rapid pace than they had advanced… We then ceased firing; but as they were still not far off, for we saw the tops of their caps, having reloaded, we stood ready to receive them should they renew the attack.

One of the first men of Mercer's troop to fall was a gunner named Butterworth, responsible for sponging one of the guns. Having just finished ramming down a shot, he was in the process of stepping back away from the mouth of the cannon when his foot became stuck in the mud, thus pulling him forward just as the gun was fired.

> As a man naturally does when falling, he threw out both his arms before him, and they were blown off at the elbows. He raised himself a little on his two stumps, and looked up most piteously in my face. To assist him was impossible – the safety of all, everything, depended upon not slackening our fire, and I was obliged to turn from him.

Eventually Butterworth brought himself to the rear, but was discovered dead by the roadside the following day, having bled to death on the way to Waterloo while in search of medical attention.

Meanwhile, the French launched a second determined charge:

> None of your furious galloping charges was this, but a deliberate advance, at a deliberate pace, as of men resolved to carry their point. They moved in profound silence, and the only sound that could be heard from them amidst the incessant roar of battle was the low thunder-like reverberation of the ground beneath the

simultaneous tread of so many horses. On our part was equal determination. Every man stood steadily at his post, the guns ready, loaded with a round-shot first and a case over it; the tubes were in the vents; the port-fires glared and sputtered behind the wheels; and my word alone was wanting to hurl destruction on that goodly show of gallant men and noble horses...

I ... allowed them to advance unmolested until the head of the column might have been about fifty or sixty yards from us, and then gave the word, 'Fire!' The effect was terrible. Nearly the whole leading rank fell at once; and the round-shot, penetrating the column, carried confusion throughout its extent. The ground, already encumbered with victims of the first struggle, became now almost impassable. Still, however, these devoted warriors struggled on, intent only on reaching us. The thing was impossible...

The discharge of every gun was followed by a fall of men and horses like that of grass before the mower's scythe ... until gradually they disappeared over the brow of the hill. We ceased firing, glad to take breath.

Mercer, on seeing yet a third attack on its way, cried: 'There they are again!' But it was a pathetic, or perhaps more appropriately, tragic display:

This time, it was child's play. They could not even approach us in any decent order, and we fired most deliberately; it was folly having attempted the thing. I was sitting on my horse near the right of my battery as they turned and began to retire once more. Intoxicated with success, I was singing out, 'Beautiful! – Beautiful!'

G Troop suffered 18 casualties at Waterloo, three of whom were killed in the battle, two others missing and presumed killed and the rest wounded, among them gunner Philip Hunt, whose left arm was shattered by a round-shot. Mercer's troop lost 69 horses, nearly three times as many as any other troop, and had expended an extraordinary amount of ammunition – about 700 rounds.

After the Napoleonic Wars Mercer was placed on half-pay until 1824, when he briefly served in Canada as a brevet major. In 1837, having attained the rank of lieutenant-colonel, he was again ordered to Canada, where he commanded the artillery in Nova Scotia during the border dispute that nearly led to war between the United States and Britain. He became a colonel in 1846 and major-general in 1854. Afterwards he was commander of the Dover garrison and retired from active service, though continued as colonel-commandant of the 9th Brigade of Royal Artillery. He spent the remainder of his life at his cottage outside Exeter and died in 1868 at the age of 85, immensely proud of having been present at the century's most decisive battle.

CAPTAIN LEWIS EDWARD NOLAN, CAVALRY OFFICER

The Crimean War

John Sweetman

'Attack, sir! Attack what? What guns, sir?' Flinging his arm towards the end of the valley, Captain Nolan replied: 'There is your enemy! There are your guns!' According to Lord Lucan, commanding the Cavalry Division, these comprised the final, fateful words between the two men, which sent the Light Brigade to destruction. But by the time that he recalled them, Lucan had been accused by Lord Raglan of losing the brigade, and having been killed at its outset, Nolan could no longer defend himself.

A slim, dark-haired figure with a trim moustache, Lewis (or Louis) Edward Nolan was an unusual junior officer. He spoke five European languages and several Indian dialects. An outstanding horseman, he had served in a foreign army and published two books about the cavalry, acting as model for their illustrations. He had also designed a cavalry saddle to the satisfaction of the duke of Cambridge. Born in 1818 in Canada, the second son of an infantry captain, John Babington Nolan, his grandfather, Babington Nolan, had been a light cavalryman. Lewis therefore had a strong military background.

After returning from Canada and living for a short while in Scotland, the family moved to Milan, then part of the Austrian Empire, where now on half-pay Lewis' father became British vice-consul. At the age of 14, as a cadet Lewis joined the 10th Imperial and Royal Hussars, a Hungarian unit in the Austrian Army, where he was known as Ludwig. Tutored by a renowned riding instructor, Colonel Haas, at the Engineer School near Vienna, he went on to serve with his regiment in the Hungarian and Polish provinces, earning official praise for his expert swordsmanship and riding ability. While in England during 1838, he took part in Queen Victoria's coronation celebrations, and the following year he returned to his family in Scotland, ostensibly on sick leave. Nolan never went back to Austrian service.

On 15 March 1839 he purchased a commission in the 15th Light Dragoons of the British Army and sailed with that regiment to India. His stay there was short. In March 1840, he obtained two years' sick leave, though there is no evidence of illness. Back in England, in June 1841 he purchased advancement to lieutenant and in March 1842 was posted to the cavalry depot at Maidstone for a riding master's course.

There he impressed Sergeant R. Henderson, an instructor, with his 'thoroughly amiable temper, kindness of disposition and really fascinating manner,' besides a transparent devotion to soldiering. Nolan returned to India in May 1843 and the following year became riding master of the 15th Light Dragoons. His 'active and zealous' work brought commendation from an inspecting general. Socially, he was being noted as an accomplished competitor at military race meetings and a conscientious attender at levees, balls and reviews. Appointment as aide-de-camp (ADC) to the commander-in-chief in Madras was followed by that of extra ADC to the governor.

At 31 Nolan had clearly made a name for himself, but he had so far seen no action and would not do so until the Crimea. In March 1850, two months after his father's death, he purchased a captaincy and in January 1851 again secured two years' nominal sick leave. He stayed in for Britain a few months before travelling on the continent of Europe to observe cavalry manoeuvres in Russia, Sweden and Prussia. Command of the 15th Light Dragoons' depot troop at Maidstone and of the regiment's detachment at the funeral of the Duke of Wellington followed in 1852. Whilst at Maidstone for the second time, he published his two books: *The Training of Cavalry Remount Horses, A New System* (1852) and *Cavalry: Its History and Tactics* (1853). The *Illustrated London News* proclaimed the latter 'a capital book, written with full knowledge of the subject, both practical and theoretical,' and the American Major-General G. B. McClellan praised Nolan's analysis, based on an exhaustive study of military history.

Raglan's ADC and great-nephew, Somerset Calthorpe, considered Nolan 'an officer who, most justly, is very highly thought of by the authorities.' Such was his reputation that he was sent in advance of the expeditionary force's arrival in Turkey to buy horses for the cavalry in that country and Syria. He was appointed ADC to Brigadier-General Richard Airey, commanding the first brigade of the Light Division, and went with Airey when he moved to Raglan's headquarters as quartermaster-general.

The day after the allied armies commenced their advance southwards from the landing beaches in the Crimea, 'the brave and daring Captain Nolan' came under fire during the skirmish on the Bulganek River, reputedly remarking that 'The Russians are damn'd bad shots.' 'The impetuous Nolan,' according to one contemporary, carried messages and orders back and forth during the battle of the Alma on 20 September. Afterwards, to *The Times'* correspondent W. H. Russell, Nolan angrily denounced Lucan for not sending cavalry after the fleeing Russians.

He accompanied the allied force as it marched round Sevastopol to besiege the naval port from the southern upland. There Nolan continued to decry unimaginative use of the cavalry arm, especially the light cavalry. He considered its traditional role of foraging, pursuing beaten enemy troops after a battle and carrying out reconnaissance forays far too restricting. Years later, Sergeant Henderson recalled:

> I remember, strange as it may appear, that in putting a case hypothetically of cavalry
> charging in a plain, Captain [then Lieutenant] Nolan drew with a piece of chalk on

the wall of the Quartermaster's store in Maidstone barracks a rough sketch which as nearly as possible represented the relative positions of the Russian artillery and the British light cavalry at the battle of Balaclava; the only thing he was not quite right in was the result. He assumed in such a case the certain capture of the guns.

Nolan believed that, after the first discharge, the slowness of artillerymen rearming muzzle-loading cannon would allow charging cavalrymen to overrun a battery. Not aware of this, but irritated by Nolan's criticisms in the field, Lord George Paget, Cardigan's second-in-command, observed disparagingly: 'He writes books and was a great man in his own estimation and had already been talking very loud against the cavalry.'

Throughout the morning of 25 October 1854, Nolan sat above the Plain of Balaclava and saw the inaction of the Light Brigade on the flank of the heavies, when they swept the Russian squadrons back over the Woronzov (Causeway) Heights. His volatile nature and anger at Lucan's perceived incompetence was a dangerous combination, as he plunged down the slope with the decisive Fourth Order. Before he rode off with the message, 'to prevent the enemy taking away the guns,' Nolan received 'careful instructions' from Raglan and his immediate superior, Airey. It is inconceivable that either of them briefed him that the brigade was to advance up the valley to attack the Russian guns at its far end. Situated between his two brigades, themselves divided by the Woronzov Heights, Lucan could see neither the redoubts nor the guns at the head of the valley... hence the reputed sharp scene between him and Nolan.

Having delivered the order, Nolan joined the 17th Lancers and rode with them behind Lord Cardigan, the brigade commander. Before the advance had gone far, he galloped beyond Cardigan, shouting and waving his sword as he looked back towards the brigade. Almost at once he was killed by a shell burst, and his intentions will never be known. It has always been assumed that he suddenly realised Cardigan was moving towards the wrong guns. But, according to Henderson, Nolan thought that light cavalry charging guns at speed could succeed in carrying them. This leaves the intriguing possibility that, when he died, Nolan was not trying to redirect the Light Brigade, but attempting to get Cardigan, inexperienced in warfare and following the text-book procedure of gradually building up speed, to go faster.

Like the precise content of the exchanges between him and Lucan, the truth can never now be known. Initially, Lucan blamed Nolan for the ensuing debacle. He may have been right, after all. Perhaps justifiably, therefore, a memorial in Holy Trinity church, Maidstone, records that Nolan 'fell at the head of the light cavalry brigade in the charge at Balaklava [sic].'

CAPTAIN LÉONCE PATRY, 6TH INFANTRY REGIMENT OF THE LINE

The Franco-Prussian War

Stephen Badsey

Marie Gabriel Léonce Patry, born in Paris of Norman origins and 29 when the war began, was the son of a schoolmaster who had obtained a free place for him at the officer training academy at Saint-Cyr on hardship grounds. Promoted to lieutenant in 1867, he served in the 1st Battalion of the 6th Infantry Regiment of the Line. In July 1870 he was at the regimental depot at Charleville, while the regiment was garrisoned some distance away at Mézières. Disregarding orders to report to Saint-Cyr as an instructor, Patry was determined to fight, and managed to be put in charge of 300 reservists assembling at Mézières to rejoin the regiment, which had already departed by train for Lorraine. Throughout the war, he kept a notebook that became the basis of his later memoirs.

On 29 July Patry and his men disembarked at the railhead at Thionville, north of Metz, but were unable to find their regiment. Joining other troops marching eastwards, they reached the regiment the next day, forming part of IV Corps. Patry actually crossed over the frontier into the Palatinate, near Ittersdorf west of Saarlouis, on 2 August, before taking part in the retreat to Metz with his regiment, reaching the eastern outskirts of the city on 13 August. Typical of French mobilization problems was that on this date his regiment numbered 1,807 compared to its notional full strength of more than 2,400 men. Patry's account is a litany of complaints, poor staffwork, poor food and marching weather that was either hot and dusty, or too wet. He is particularly critical of the captain commanding his company, whom he depicts as a coward and a fool.

Patry was under fire for the first time on 14 August at the battle of Borny. His regiment was hardly involved in the battle of Mars-la-Tour, of which he recorded only his own confused impressions. 'I heard the episode narrated in five or six different ways,' he wrote of one general's death in action. 'I became certain that most of the great feats so preciously reported by history were nearly always invented.' Two days later at the battle of Gravelotte-St Privat, Patry's regiment was heavily engaged just south of St Privat itself. Patry describes the strain of being under fire in his third battle in five days. 'Was it bad morale?' he wonders. 'When we were lying in the furrow, inactive and impotent under that hellish fire which tried us without our being able to return blow for blow, I was overtaken by a strong desire to be elsewhere; not, however, at the regimental depot.' Patry's company eventually broke and ran from the battlefield, an experience that he shared without understanding it or remembering much about it, and he ended up with the rest of the army trapped in the siege of Metz.

Patry's account of being besieged at Metz includes a bayonet charge by his own battalion on 31 August, and his increasing contempt for all staff officers. While trapped at Metz he was promoted to captain on 15 September, which gave him great satisfaction, and made battalion adjutant. Two days later Bazaine, a renouned French gneral, proclaimed that the emperor was a prisoner and the republic had been formed, news that Patry says most of the troops received with indifference. On 27 October, when Bazaine, a renowned French General, surrendered at Metz, Patry records that 'the political aspect, which had to some extent passed me by, suddenly appeared to me in all its sordid reality.' He and other officers, rather than become prisoners in Germany, chose to dress in civilian clothes and escape to continue the fight. Travelling by cart with the aid of local people, on 6 November Patry and his friends crossed the border into neutral Luxembourg, where the customs guards willingly let them through, then took a train to Brussels, and by 10 November he was back in France at Lille.

Captain Patry was given command of a company improvised from troops of the 75th Infantry Regiment of the Line. Travelling with his men by train to Albert (near Amiens, later famous in World War I as a British base), he joined his battalion as part of the Army of the North under General Bourbaki, later replaced by General Louis Faidherbe. Campaigning in winter in the Somme region, Patry's chief concerns became how his inexperienced troops would cope in battle, and once more the problems of staffwork and the weather. In late December the Army of the North was reorganized, and Patry's battalion became 2nd Battalion of the 67th Régiment de Marche (made up from two battalions of the 75th and one battalion of the 65th Infantry Regiment of the Line). Patry records that he was offered the post of divisional chief of staff with the rank of major, but that he declined, preferring to command fighting troops.

On 23 December Patry and his men took a minor part in the battle of Pont-Noyelles – 'their morale was very good, and I was optimistic after this first trial' – and they were also under fire in the battle of Bapaume on 3 January 1871. But in the battle of St Quentin on 19 January 'the men lost their heads' and fled from the battlefield. Patry cynically records that he called out, 'So is there no one who will have the courage to die here doing his duty?' and that the utter failure of 'this piece of arch-pomposity' led him to 'profound scepticism on the subject of the effect that the words spoken by a leader can have on thirty or forty thousand men in perilous circumstances.'

After the armistice, Patry's regiment was sent to Dunkirk, where he was surprised to be treated as a hero, then in February by ship to Cherbourg. When peace was announced the regiment moved by train to Paris. With Patry temporarily in command of his battalion, the regiment entered the city centre on 9 March and camped in the Luxembourg Gardens, where he listened to the 'foolish nonsense' of other people's war stories. With the uprising of the Commune on 18 March, the regiment was ordered out of the city to Versailles, and then returned in April to take part in the siege and the Commune's suppression. Understandably, Patry writes that 'this campaign deeply repelled me,' partly because he considered that it was drawn out longer than necessary for political reasons. His own company, now down to 75 men, took seven casualties fighting the Communards.

Patry was decorated for his actions with the Army of the North, but says that he refused a second decoration for helping suppress the Commune. He married in 1872 and rose to lieutenant-colonel by 1884. Three years later, when 46 years old, a financial scandal forced him to leave the army. In 1896, cleared of all debt, he was made chief of staff of a reserve division. A year later he published his memoirs of the Franco-Prussian War, written largely from the conviction that no one understood the war as he had experienced it. He retired from the reserve in 1914 at the age of 72, managed to return to duty for World War I, retired again from ill-health in 1915, and died in 1917.

PIRACY,
RISINGS AND
MUTINY

PIRACY,
RISINGS AND
MUTINY

*A general move was made towards the mountain, to take up
a last position, but it was too late; the Zulus were too quick
and fleet of foot, they caught up with the men on foot before
they could reach the new position, completely overpowering
them by numbers, and assegaing right and left...*

(Captain William Cochrane)

*Dead and wounded soldiers lay all around, and the cries
and groans of agony, and the dreadful sights, haunted
me for many a day, for though I had seen death by
violence of late, there had been nothing to approach
the horrors accumulated here.*

(Deneys Reitz)

COMMODORE STEPHEN DECATUR, US NAVY

The Wars of the Barbary Pirates

Gregory Fremont-Barnes

One of America's greatest naval heroes, Stephen Decatur was born in Sinepuxent, Maryland, on 5 January 1977, to a prominent naval family. Commissioned as a midshipman aboard the 44-gun *United States* on 30 April 1798, the very day the Department of the Navy was established, he served in the Quasi-War against France and rose rapidly to lieutenant, receiving his commission on 21 May 1799. Decatur is best associated with his role in the war against Tripoli, where he initially commanded the 12-gun schooner *Enterprise*, with which he captured the Tripolitan ketch *Mastico* on 23 December 1803. With this prize, renamed *Intrepid*, he daringly led a raid into Tripoli harbour on the night of 16 February 1804, boarding the former American frigate *Philadelphia* and setting her on fire with combustibles without the loss of a single man.

The event served as an inspiration to US Navy personnel ever since. One naval officer, writing in 1942, said of the event: 'To the example of personal gallantry thus set by Decatur before Tripoli, and the chivalrous spirit communicated to his companions in arms, we may ascribe in no small degree the heroic tone which has characterized all the after achievements of our navy.' The deed made him an instant national hero and earned for him a captaincy, making him, at the age of 25, the youngest officer of that rank in the history of the United States Navy. He displayed considerable intrepidity yet again when, during the gunboat action in Tripoli harbour on August 3, he and his men boarded and captured an enemy gunboat, and avenged the death of his brother, James, by seizing another. His life was saved by Quarter Gunner Reuben James, who, though himself badly wounded in both arms, placed himself between Decatur and an assailant poised to deliver a blow to the back of Decatur's head with a scimitar. Decatur wrote to a fellow officer on 9 January 1805, saying of the affair: 'I find hand to hand is not child's play, 'tis kill or be killed.'

After the war with Tripoli, Decatur oversaw the construction of gunboats at Rhode Island and in Virginia, and took command of the frigate *Chesapeake* in June 1807. During the War of 1812, he commanded the frigate *United States*, aboard which, in a bitterly fought action on 25 October 1812, he captured HMS *Macedonian*. In May 1814 he was assigned to the *President* and in July commanded naval forces at New York. Owing to the blockade of the Atlantic coast by the Royal Navy, Decatur was forced to remain in port for many months, but he managed to put to sea in January 1815. Persuaded by a numerically superior British squadron on the 15th, Decatur took a battering and failed to shake off his pursuers. Despite a spirited resistance, he eventually accepted the inevitable, as he explained to the secretary of the navy: 'Then situated, with about one fifth of my crew killed and wounded, my ship crippled, and a more than fourfold force opposed me, without a chance of escape left, I deemed it my duty to surrender.'

No sooner had the war with Britain come to an end than Decatur was dispatched in command of a squadron for the Mediterranean, where he dictated peace terms to Algiers, Tunis and Tripoli, so putting a definitive end to Barbary raids on American shipping. From 20 December 1815, he served as a member of the Board of Naval Commissioners, in which capacity he opposed giving Captain James Barron command of a ship of the line. This resulted in a duel, held at Bladensburg, Maryland, and fought at only eight paces, on 22 March 1820. Both men were wounded in the contest, Decatur mortally. The whole nation mourned his death.

That Decatur was brave there can be no doubt. Apart from his exploits in combat, while aboard the first ship under his command, the *United States*, Decatur had challenged to a duel the mate of a merchantman who had refused to return deserters from Decatur's ship. Decatur wounded his opponent in the hip, with no injury to himself. In another incident, in July 1801 as first lieutenant aboard the *Essex*, he wrote an angry message to the commander of a Spanish guard ship that had fired over one of his ship's shore boats. When Decatur declared that he would come aboard the following morning in search of an explanation, the Spanish officer did not risk being present, prompting Decatur to leave a threatening message: 'Lieutenant Decatur pronounce him a cowardly scoundrel and that, when they met on shore, he will cut his ears off.' No such encounter ever took place, but the Spanish thereafter ceased to annoy the American vessels.

Decatur had also served as a second in duel on 14 February 1830, between 16-year-old Midshipman Joseph Bainbridge (younger brother of William Bainbridge), of the USS *New York*, and James Cochran, secretary to the British governor of Malta, Sir Alexander Ball. After becoming the object of insulting remarks about the US Navy from a group of British officers attending an opera in Valetta, the midshipman knocked down his tormentor. Decatur, as the second, established the rules: to compensate for the fact that Bainsbridge's adversary was a crack shot known to have killed several men in previous duels, Decatur declared that the duelists exchange fire at four, rather than the customary ten, paces, thus leaving no possibility of missing. 'Good Lord, Sir,' replied his opposite number, 'that looks like murder.' 'Not murder,' Decatur replied, 'but surely death.' Thus was the result – with Bainbridge the survivor.

Apart from his naval exploits and duelling prowess, Decatur is remembered for the patriotic toast he made in April 1816: 'Our Country! In her intercourse with foreign nations may she always be in the right; but our country, right or wrong.' Energetic and sociable, he was known to possess a strong sense of humour. In his mid-19th century biography of Decatur, Alexander Slidell Mackenzie observed that he:

… possessed, in an eminent degree, the happy art of governing sailors rather by their affections than their fears. He was averse to punishment, and rarely had occasion to resort to it, being usually able to rely, for the preservation of discipline, on the reluctance of his inferiors to displease him. It was remarked of him … by an officer, that 'he seemed, as if by magic, to hold a boundless sway over the hearts of seamen at first sight.' Such a conquest could only have been gained by a just regard for their rights, a watchful care of their comfort, and a sympathy in their feelings.

BREVET-MAJOR O. H. S. G. ANSON, 9TH LANCERS

The Indian Mutiny

Gregory Fremont-Barnes

At the beginning of the Mutiny, Brevet-Major Anson commanded a squadron of the 9th Lancers, one of the few mounted regiments of the British Army in India, and at various points during the conflict he commanded the regiment as a whole. By 1857 he had already served in India for nearly 20 years, and had fought at Punniar and Sobraon in the First Sikh War, and at Gujerat and Chilianwallah in the Second. His term of service in the Mutiny was in fact short, for though he took part in the siege and recapture of Delhi, his health seriously declined in March 1858, and he died the following January. In the course of his service on and around the Ridge at Delhi, Anson frequently wrote to his wife, who, with many other civilians, had taken refuge at Kussowlee, a hill station much like Simla.

In early June the Delhi Field Force approached the city, passing through country dotted with old buildings, woods, swamps, dry canals and walled villages, which, in combination with the enemy's determined resistance, held up the column's advance. Finally reaching the Ridge, Anson's regiment took up a position near Hindu Rao's house, a derelict mansion of substantial strength. It soon became clear that the space in front of the Ridge had to be cleared of the enemy's skirmishers, for the Anglo-Indian force continued to come under fire from mutineers who used the extensive cover for sniping. Only 1,000 yards (914m) separated the batteries on the Ridge from the ramparts of Delhi, whose towering walls and bastions even Anson recognized as too formidable to breach with the calibre of guns available. He appreciated, too, that time was not on the side of the British, for cholera and other diseases took a constant toll on their numbers.

He often stood to watch British guns fire at the city, as 24lb shot was returned. It was commonplace for both sides to re-fire spent shot at one another.

On 12 June he noted how 'the big guns and mortars were firing fiercely all night on the enemy, who were very slack in returning the fire, and every minute our mortars or 24-pounders are sending them a pill; but we are too far off, and Delhi will never be taken in this way.' At times the enemy's fire was so heavy that Anson had to 'watch and dodge the cannon-balls'; apart from that, he found the heat and glare of the sun to be especially enervating. He made frequent reference in his letters to the many sorties made by the rebels, some of which harassed the picket of his regiment, which performed the vital task of protecting the flanks and rear of the camp.

Conditions on the Ridge were difficult, as Anson observed, but there was no chronic shortage of provisions. He complained of 'no good brandy' and noted the great expense of luxuries, such as tea, an 'extravagant treat,' as well as sugar and beer, but there was soup, meat and onions – though no potatoes – as well as bread and butter 'washed down with sherry and water.' On another occasion he writes of 'goose, rice pudding and stewed guavas for dinner.'

In several respects Anson's attitudes reflected the popular opinion of his comrades on the Ridge, not least a complete confidence in ultimate success. Delhi would be retaken: it was merely a matter of time. His correspondence moreover expressed a widespread confidence derived from faith. As he explained to his wife:

> ... it would be most cruel to think that God was not on our side. We have His own covenant and promise to guide and protect us eventually; but knowing India and our people in India as well as I do, I am not in the least surprised at His sending this severe judgment on us. I look upon the business in the light of a heavy punishment for the ungodly, infidel lives the greater part of us have lived in India.

A few days later he added:

> Yes; the Lord may sacrifice us as a wicked and adulterous generation, but there is nothing more certain than that He is on our side, and that after justly punishing us for our sins, He will grind the heathen to powder.

Through June and July the rebels continued their attacks, particularly on the camp's rear, where Anson was regularly engaged. The rebels approached the Ridge both during the day and night: 'I cannot describe to you the confusion that ensued in the dark, and how grand it was to see the battle raging in the dark, when one could see the flash of every matchlock.' Under these circumstances, the troops were forced to remain ever vigilant, for no one could be sure when the next sortie would come: 'we literally know not what an hour may bring forth.'

The first rains arrived at the end of June, which came in torrents, and while they brought down the temperature – 'the air now is delightfully cool and refreshing' – they also made Anson feel 'out of sorts, heavy about the head, sleepy, and lethargic.' The rains carried on through July, and the casualty lists grew. Anson's picquets, their blue uniforms regularly drenched as they made rounds of the camp, often came under fire. When the sun reappeared, the temperature soared; Anson recorded the temperature at 99 degrees Fahrenheit (37.2 degrees Celsius) at 5.30pm one day. With the heat came clouds of flies, obliging Anson 'to battle for every mouthful.' Whenever men sat down to eat, flying bugs of various descriptions descended on the scene. There were scorpions, too, and hundreds of camels 'blocking up the road and frightening the horses. They are a dreadful bother, all so scabby, diseased, and stinking, too.'

The days passed wearily, with constant alarms at the approach of the enemy, bouts of heavy rain, thunder and lightning, followed by searing heat, and rising cases of cholera, heatstroke, dysentery and exhaustion. 'Every day now,' he wrote on 20 July, 'some thirty or forty Europeans are expended by the enemy, the sun, disease, and fatigue; and as the season advances we may expect more sickness.' At the same time, the rebels continued to harass the camp from cover. 'There the enemy lie, snugly ensconced behind walls, nullah banks, and large stones, and plying you well at from 150 to 300 yards (137 to 274m) with their deadly small arms. We must advance to drive them away, and thus present them with very fair shots.' He described their method of attack thus:

> They steal up in great numbers to within eighty or ninety yards [73–82m] of the picquet, and, firing off their muskets, run away as hard as they can, one of our batteries helping them to do so with a good grace. Our men being safe behind breastworks, their noisy volleys are perfectly innocuous.

During August Anson recorded several instances of the infantry being engaged for over 12 hours continuously, with a regular exchange of artillery fire. He spent many a sleepless night amidst the noise of the guns and shouts to the camp to repel an attack. The area below the Ridge had long since become pockmarked and scarred by artillery fire; trees had either been felled by the exchange of fire or cut down for firewood, until the landscape had become semi-desert. Over this scene of devastation, under a fierce sun, hung the repulsive stench of rotting animal carcasses and rebel corpses that Anson frequently encountered, in one instance 'an enormous mass of putrefaction in the form of a dead camel or bullock.'

Finally, on the morning of 14 August, to cheers from the entire camp, Nicholson's 'Moveable Column' appeared on the Ridge, with the band of the 52nd Foot playing, and two 24-pdrs and three 18-pdrs amongst the new arrivals. The siege train trundled into camp on 4 September, covering 13 miles of road, some of the heavier pieces of ordnance harnessed to elephants. In all, Anson counted six 24-pdrs, eight 18-pdrs, four 8-in. howitzers, and four 10-in. mortars – 22 pieces with hundreds of rounds of ammunition each. Armed with the right material for the job, Anson wrote to his wife:

> large working parties are now very busy preparing the batteries and approaches and
> in three days from this, if not sooner, there will be a flame of devouring fire and a
> tempest of shot all about the place. Two or three days after the fire has once opened
> we shall, like a flood of mighty waters overflowing, storm the walls, and I fervently
> hope and pray [that we] destroy these murderers and burn up their city.

The men, ragged and exhausted, often worked at night in preparing the batteries, for during the day the temperature exceeded 90 degrees Fahrenheit (32.2 degrees Celsius) under cloudless skies.

By 8 September several batteries, situated between 600 and 700 yards (549 to 640m) from the wall, began firing. In his general orders to the troops, Anson records Major-General Wilson's confidence that British pluck and determination will carry everything before them, and that the bloodthirsty mutineers against whom they are fighting will be driven headlong out of their stronghold and be exterminated. But to enable them to do this, he warns the troops of the absolute necessity of their keeping together and not straggling from their columns; by this only can success be secured. Major-General Wilson need hardly remind the troops of the cruel murders committed on their officers and comrades, as well as their wives and children, to move them in their deadly struggle. No quarter should be given to the mutineers; at the same time, for the sake of humanity and the honour of the country they belong to, he calls upon them to spare all women and children that may come in their way.

Oxen gradually brought the heaviest batteries forward, where, with the assistance of many of the 9th Lancers, they began to batter at the walls until a breach was made. During the assault, the Ridge was to be held by the sick and wounded, a few guns and the small body of available cavalry, including Anson and various irregular units, who were to hold the right to prevent any enemy sorties emerging from the Lahore Gate and threatening Wilson's now precariously weakened position on the Ridge. When the assault came, Anson's cavalry followed up the infantry and stood outside the walls amidst heavy fire from infantry high above. When the rebels forced No 4 Column back out of the city and threatened the Ridge, the 9th Lancers and the Bengal Horse Artillery kept the attackers in check, a process which cost Anson's regiment a quarter of its strength and 61 horses.

CAPTAIN WILLIAM COCHRANE, 32ND (DUKE OF CORNWALL'S) LIGHT INFANTRY

The Zulu War

Ian Knight

For many ordinary soldiers in the British ranks, the Anglo-Zulu War meant long periods of discomfort, long marches in baking heat or pouring rain, poor food and bad water, a regimented routine lived briefly in an alien and often frightening environment, and perhaps occasionally the sudden terror and adrenalin rush of combat.

William Francis Dundonald Cochrane's experiences of the campaign were among the most varied – and dramatic. He was born into the rural gentry in the county of Wiltshire in 1847. He joined the 32nd (Duke of Cornwall's) Light Infantry in 1866 as an ensign – the lowest officer's rank. When Lord Chelmsford appealed in late 1878 for reinforcements for the coming Zulu campaign, there was a rush of enthusiastic young officers to volunteer for any special service posts that might be available. Promotion for officers in the peacetime Victorian Army was notoriously slow, and after 12 years' service Cochrane was still languishing in the rank of lieutenant. A war offered not only the possibility of adventure, but also of promotion and distinction, so he volunteered; having previously travelled in Natal, he was accepted, and sailed for Durban on the steamship *Edinburgh Castle*.

On board were a number of young officers in the same position as himself, several of whom were to play a prominent part in the early stages of the war. Among them was Lieutenant Henry Harford, 99th Regiment, who was attached to the staff of the 3rd Natal Native Contingent (NNC), and would leave a graphic description of the Isandlwana campaign. Lieutenant Horace Smith-Dorrien, 95th Regiment, would be destined to escape from Isandlwana, while Lieutenant Charles Williams, 58th Regiment, would be killed in the attack on Hlobane. According to Harford, Cochrane excelled at the sort of pastimes that were then popular among the British officer class:

> Cochrane was simply the life and soul of the ship, always ready to sit down at the piano and sing a good song, or get up concerts, theatricals and other amusements. Scarcely a day went by without something going on under his direction.

On arriving in Natal, Cochrane was appointed transport officer to Colonel Anthony Durnford's No 2 Column. Under Chelmsford's original invasion plan, this column was given a defensive role on the central Thukela border, above Middle Drift.

Durnford's column consisted almost entirely of African auxiliary troops, supported by an artillery rocket battery. Once Chelmsford himself had crossed the border into Zululand, however, Durnford's column was ordered up to Rorke's Drift to support the advance. On the morning of 22 January 1879, Durnford received Chelmsford's order to advance to Isandlwana. Cochrane accompanied Durnford when he entered the camp at about 10.30am, and overheard the conversation in which Colonel Pulleine reported the Zulu presence to the left of the camp. According to Cochrane, Durnford replied that he would 'go out and prevent the one column from joining the [Zulu Army], which was supposed to be at that time engaged with the troops under the General.'

Cochrane again accompanied Durnford, whose party rode about five miles from the camp when they suddenly encountered the Zulu left horn, approaching from the opposite direction. They retired fighting, and took up a position in a *donga* (a ditch caused by the erosion of soil) some distance in front of the camp. After defending this for a while, however, Cochrane recalled that:

A general move was made towards the mountain, to take up a last position, but it was too late; the Zulus were too quick and fleet of foot, they caught up with the men on foot before they could reach the new position, completely overpowering them by numbers, and assegaing right and left... As far as I am personally concerned, when I got back to camp with the mounted men who had been driven out of the 'donga,' I found that the enemy rushed on the camp from the left, and were engaged hand-to-hand with the infantry, who were completely overpowered with overwhelming numbers. I saw that all was over. I made in the direction which I had seen taken by the mounted men, guns, Royal Artillery, and the natives on foot. I was cut off by the enemy, who had now reached the line of retreat; but with a good horse, hard riding, and good luck, I managed to reach the Buffalo River. The Zulus seemed perfectly fearless; they following alongside, having desperate hand-to-hand fighting with those retreating, mostly our natives on foot. Many of the enemy were killed between the camp and the river. On several occasions they were quite close to me, but I was fortunate enough to escape, whilst others dropped at my side. They fired at us the whole way from the camp to the river, but having mounted the bank on the opposite side we were safe.

Years later, Cochrane would recall ruefully that he escaped Isandlwana by 'damn all but the ears of my horse.' He made his way to Helpmekaar, on the hills beyond Rorke's Drift. That night, and for several days thereafter, the garrison at Helpmekaar lived in expectation of a Zulu attack, and even if that attack never came, life was still far from pleasant. Survivors from Isandlwana huddled together with the garrison behind makeshift barricades, often lying in the mud on wet nights. Those who had escaped the battle had lost everything but the uniforms they stood up in – greatcoats, tents, blankets and personal possessions. Many were so traumatised by their experiences that they cried out in their sleep, setting off a series of false alarms. Gradually, however, the terror subsided, and once it became clear that the Zulu were not intending to mount an immediate attack, the British began to secure the border once more. With the death of Colonel Durnford and the destruction of his column, Cochrane's position as transport officer was superfluous. On 20 February he was given the local rank of captain and was appointed to the command of two of the troops of mounted auxiliaries from the centre column – the Edendale Christian contingent and Hlubi's Sotho detachment – which had remained in the field near Rorke's Drift. Lord Chelmsford had by now begun to reorganize his forces in the aftermath of Isandlwana, and Cochrane's command was attached to Colonel Wood's column in the north, riding into Khambula on 1 March.

Ironically, these survivors of Isandlwana now found themselves in the thick of the next wave of fighting. When Colonel Wood decided to attack Hlobane, Cochrane's men were attached to Colonel Russell's column, which was ordered to attack the western end of the mountain. Russell successfully ascended the Ntendeka plateau, but found it impossible to reach the main summit. His men waited at the foot of the pass until the sound of firing could be heard from Buller's party across the summit, and numbers of Zulus began to gather to snipe at Russell's command. Cochrane's men were ordered to dismount and drive them off. With the news that a much larger Zulu Army was approaching, however, Russell decided to abandon the mountain altogether. For a while, he kept his mounted men lined up at the foot of Ntendeka; then, receiving a confusing order from Wood, he retired several miles away, towards Khambula. By this movement he left Buller's men – and some of his own auxiliaries, who had been herding cattle – unsupported.

The incident later caused much bitterness towards Russell, and it may have affected the behaviour of Cochrane's men the following day. When the Zulu Army first deployed to attack Khambula, the mounted auxiliaries were among those who rode out to sting the right horn into action. Most rode back to take refuge in the main waggon *laager* (an improvised camp), but according to one eye-witness:

> The Basutos [the British habitually referred to all their black mounted troops as such], who had stuck like leeches to the cattle on Hlobane the day before and brought them off safely, left the laager and refused to stay. Throughout the fight they hovered round the flank of the Zulus firing continually.

In the aftermath of the victory at Khambula, Cochrane's men were extensively employed in patrolling. Once Lord Chelmsford began to plan the new invasion, this included long-range reconnaissances into Zulu territory in search of a viable road

Only six months after Custer's disaster at Little Bighorn, Frederick Whittaker published a highly romanticized biography of his former Union Army commander that served as the basis for much of the Custer mystique. This illustration from the book was one of the first to depict the so-called 'Last Stand,' but like so many of the era, is totally imaginary. (Charles M. Robinson III)

'Volunteers for Texas,' a scornful depiction of the volunteers who mustered to defend Texas against Mexican invasion in 1848. When news of General Zachary Taylor's initial engagement with Mexican troops near the Rio Grande River first reached Washington on Saturday 9 May, many men flocked to support the popular cause by enlisting in the army. Most had no military experience and the artist shows an ill-equipped group of men mustering before an equally clueless officer who has failed to spot that the most prominent weapon among them is actually an umbrella. (Library of Congress, Prints and Photographs Division LC-USZ62-1272)

Colonel Juan Nepomuceno Almonte, c.1830, by Carlos Paris. Chief of Staff of the Mexican Army of Operations for Santa Anna during the Texas War of Independence, he left a detailed journal that is arguably the single most important primary document from the Mexican perspective. (Alan Huffines' collection; Mexico: su tiempo de nacer, 1750–1821)

This recreated view of the charge of the Light Brigade, 25 October 1854 is the scene from the Fedioukine Hills. Russian troops can be seen near the captured redoubts on the Woronzov Heights, centre, Balaclava is in the distance. The cavalry lines depicted here are too regular. Two regiments (four squadrons) formed the first line, one regiment the second. A further two comprised the third line, but they were separated during the charge. (Hulton Getty)

The last moments of battle in the Cemetery of St Privat during the Franco-Prussian War. The battle of 18 August 1870 is depicted here in a painting by Alphonse de Neuville. (Topfoto)

Bismarck: 'Pardon, Mon Ami, but we really can't allow you to pick up anything here.' Nap (the Chiffonier): 'Pray don't mention it M'sieu. It's not of the slightest consequence.' 'Peace and No Pieces' A cartoon by John Tenniel from *Punch*, 25 August 1866, depicting Napoleon III as a chiffonier (rag-collector), and reflecting France's attempts to make territorial gains from the Austro-Prussian War. (Topfoto)

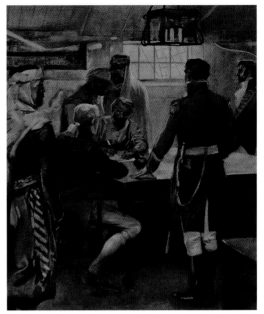

Captain William Cochrane, photographed at the turn of the century. Cochrane was a regular officer in the 32nd Regiment, who volunteered for special service in Zululand. Attached to Durnford's Column, he survived Isandlwana – and went on to take part in the battles of Hlobane, Khambula and Ulundi. (Pietermaritzburg Archives Depot)

The fruits of gunboat diplomacy. A Barbary official signs a treaty of peace with the United States in the captain's cabin of the *Guerrière*. When, barely a century later, Theodore Roosevelt used the fleet for similar purposes, he was merely continuing a tradition begun by his presidential predecessor, James Madison, in 1815. (New York Public Library Picture Collection)

The battle of Isandlwana, 22 January 1879. The conflict with the Zulus opened disastrously when a British force of 1,200 men was wiped out in the opening days of the war. By July, however, Zulu power was broken and their lands were soon incorporated into Natal. (Topfoto)

An Auxiliary member of the RIC and a Black and Tan search an Irish civilian suspect. They were recruited by the British government to cope with the unrest in Ireland. Their reputation caused outcry in Britain and the USA. (Photo by Topical Press Agency/Getty Images)

'They shall not pass.' Republican Civil War poster illustrating the defence of Madrid by young men and women volunteers. The great Communist orator, Dolores Ibárruri (La Pasionaria) made 'They shall not pass' the rallying slogan of Republican Madrid as rebel forces attempted to take it, first from the north, then from the south-west. (Francis Lannon's collection)

Irish Civil War, 28 June 1922 – 24 May 1923. The Irish Free State sought independence from Great Britain. In this image, armed men hide behind a barricade in a street during the fighting in Dublin. (Corbis)

Whit Monday 1917. The Wright brothers meet near Gaza (left to right) Harold, Noel, Cecil. They never met again. Cecil, bound for France on transfer to the King's Shropshire Light Infantry, died of Spanish Influenza in November 1918, two days before the Armistice. (Michael Hickey)

Soldiers of the 2nd Royal Scots Fusiliers in a rudimentary trench near Neuve Chapelle during the winter of 1914–15. (Imperial War Museum)

British Private (later Guardsman) F. E. 'Fen' Noakes, who fought throughout the World War I. (IWM)

Lieutenant Charles Hazlitt Upham, c.1941. Upham served throughout the World War II, and somehow survived his adventures. He twice won a Victoria Cross for his bravery. (Alexander Turnbull Library, National Library of New Zealand F-1993-1/4-DA)

Lieutenant-General Bernard Montgomery, Commander Eighth Army, wearing his famous tank beret, watches the beginning of the German retreat from El Alamein from the turret of his Grant tank on 5 November 1942. (Imperial War Museum)

In the spring of 1981 Iran moved to the offensive and in a series of large-scale operations drove the Iraqi forces from its territory. Here, Iranian troops are on their way to battle during Operation *Jerusalem Way*. (Gamma / Rex Features)

The march of the heavily laden Marines and Paratroopers across East Falkland was an epic of endurance. The most highly trained infantry in the world at that time, the loss of the helicopters was not going to immobilise the Marines and Paras while they still had their legs. (MOD, print from MARS)

This Marine is removing a piece of shrapnel from his armoured flak vest. It is probably exactly the same kind of vest that Corporal Martin Russ wore during his time on the front line in the Korean War. The vest consisted of fibreglass plates woven together. (Department of Defence)

Two US soldiers in the midst of a firefight during a Search and Destroy mission in Vietnam. Such missions and firefights were a common feature of the US strategy of attrition in 1967. (THR Pictures)

Staff Sergeant John Winston Young, aged only 21 and an infantry squad leader in Vietnam during 1967. (John Young)

to oNdini. Skirmishes with Zulu scouts were common, and one irregular officer left a vivid account of such actions, which must have been very familiar to Cochrane:

> We were reconnoitering some six miles over the Zulu border, and were suddenly fired on; the Basutos loosed off in all directions wildly, they were so excited. The scene was characteristic, the Zulus shouting challenges to the Basutos to come up the hill, the Basutos challenging the Zulus to come down; both parties fired at random, and the only damage done was a broken rifle-stock, which a huge bullet from an elephant gun had shivered. The Basutos used to level their guns over their horses' heads with one hand and fire wildly; they are nevertheless capital Irregulars, the best scouts in the world, hardy, active, and enduring, their only faults are their excitability and their random firing.

On 1 June, a patrol from the 2nd Division was attacked in a deserted Zulu homestead on the Tshotshozi River. The survivors fled towards Wood's column, and the following morning a large detachment of mounted men was sent out to search for the bodies. Ironically, Cochrane again found himself present at a historic moment: 'About the same distance lower down in the main donga,' wrote an observer, 'lay another body perfectly nude, with Captain Cochrane standing guard over it. I at once recognised it as the corpse of the ex-Prince Imperial of France.'

For a further month, Chelmsford's columns continued to advance into the heart of Zululand. The irregular cavalry – and with them Cochrane's men – took part in the skirmishes which marked their progress. On 3 July, when Buller's men crossed the White Mfolozi River to scout out positions for the coming battle of Ulundi, the Edendale and Sotho troops accompanied the reconnaissance. When the British were ambushed, these troops found themselves in the rearguard, and at one point were almost cut off. As they broke through the Zulu cordon, the Zulus called out 'tomorrow we will drive you across the river, and we will eat up all the red soldiers.' The following day, however, the auxiliaries had their revenge:

> Cochrane's Basutos distinguished themselves at the battle of Ulundi by their dash. They were ordered by Colonel Buller to draw on the Zulus from the right side of the square. Instead of firing a few shots and falling back, they made a stand and poured volley after volley into the advancing masses of the enemy. When told to retreat they asked their officers what was now to become of them? They were under the impression that they had to remain outside the square, and wait patiently until they were all killed … but when they drew near the glittering line of bayonets and saw the veteran 13th open a way for them to enter the square, they saw that they were not to be aimlessly sacrificed. When they had dismounted they asked the soldiers what they had to do. 'Eat your biscuits, Johnny, and lie down'…

> A few minutes after the Lancers swept out from the left corner of the rear, the Basutos dashed out at the right corner of the front ... they shouted out after the very same [Zulu] regiment that had chased them [earlier] the ironical words, 'Well, are you going to the [river] now?'... During the chase one of the Basutos shot a Zulu in the leg, and then interviewed the man with all the thirst for news which distinguishes a New York reporter... Then he gently asked the Zulu if he had got nothing more to tell, and on being assured that there was no more information to be had, he quietly shot the man, mounted his horse, and joined again in the chase.

The battle of Ulundi marked the end of the Anglo-Zulu War for Cochrane. While the auxiliaries under his command were disbanded and returned to their ordinary lives in colonial Natal, Cochrane, the professional soldier, went on to serve in a number of Queen Victoria's many wars. He fought with colonial forces in South Africa again in the BaSotho 'Gun War' of 1880–81, and the following year served at the other end of the continent, when British troops quelled an anti-European revolt in Egypt. In 1893 he was given a brigade command in the reorganized Anglo-Egyptian army, and he took part in the early stages of the conquest of the Sudan in 1896.

Throughout his career, Cochrane took part in the wide range of combat that in many ways typified the experience of Victorian officers. Nothing, however, would ever compare to the ordeal of his escape from Isandlwana.

He died in London in 1928 with the rank of brigadier-general.

DENEYS REITZ, BOER COMMANDO

The Boer War

Gregory Fremont-Barnes

Several days before the outbreak of the war in 1899, Deneys Reitz (1882–1944), a Boer aged just 17, left 'on commando' (the commando was the basic unit of the Boer militia). He was to remain in the field until the last day of the conflict. Immediately after the war, he committed to paper his adventures, exploits, hardships, combat experiences and harrowing escapes, which would later be published in 1929 as *Commando: A Boer Journal of the Boer War*, a minor military classic. Reitz describes in compelling detail his trials and triumphs with the Pretoria Commando, from the first action of the Natal campaign under Botha at Talana, to the siege of Ladysmith and the bloody affair at Spion Kop, through the guerrilla phase of the war in the western Transvaal under de la Rey, and on to the final stages when he accompanied Jan Smuts on his daring incursion into the Cape Colony in 1901. Reitz was also present with Smuts at the signing of the Treaty of Vereeniging.

Reitz witnessed all the horrors of the war, watching as his comrades were killed in combat or executed for wearing captured British uniforms. He himself suffered the considerable hardships of the conflict, including a shortage of food and exposure to the severe climate. His account of the fighting just prior to the investment of Ladysmith provides an accurate impression of combat conditions during much of the conventional phase of the war.

The son of the Transvaal state secretary, Reitz was well educated, intelligent, keen for the fray and innocent of the true nature of war. Though privileged by the standards of Boer society, he was by no means pampered:

[We] ... learned to ride, shoot, and swim almost as soon as we could walk, and there was a string of hardy Basuto ponies in the stables, on which we were often away for weeks at a time, riding over the game-covered plains by day, and sleeping under the stars at night, hunting, fishing and camping to our heart's content...

Having personally received his Mauser rifle from President Kruger, Reitz and the rest of the Pretoria Commando of about 300 men left by train to the Natal border just before the outbreak of war. At dawn on the morning after the declaration of war, the assembled commandos set out. 'As far as the eye could see,' Reitz recalled, 'the plain was alive with horsemen, guns, and cattle, all steadily going forward to the frontier. The scene was a stirring one, and I shall never forget riding to war with that great host.' Still, in the field, Reitz's commando possessed only five days' ration of biltong (dried meat), and were exposed to the elements. 'It was our first introduction to the real hardships of war, and our martial feelings were considerably damped by the time the downpour ceased at daybreak.'

At Talana, Reitz encountered the British for the first time, amidst a furious exchange of artillery. 'We could see nothing, but heavy fighting had started close by, for the roar of the guns increased and at times we heard the rattle of small arms and Maxims.' As Reitz and the other members of his unit approached the scene, they discovered a party of British soldiers, 'Khakis,' taking refuge in a small farmhouse and manning the stone walls of a cattle kraal. The place was soon surrounded. Reitz made for the dry bed of a stream in front of the British position, which put him in the line of fire:

... now, for the first time in my life, I heard the sharp hiss of rifle-bullets about my ears, and for the first time I experienced the thrill of riding into action. My previous ideas of a battle had been different, for there was almost nothing to see here. The soldiers were hidden, and, except for an occasional helmet and the spurts of dust flicked up around us, there was nothing.

147

A sharp exchange of rifle fire followed, but when the Boers brought up a Creusot gun and opened fire, the British raised a white flag and threw down their arms.

Reitz soon lost his preconceived notions of a glamorous war. He had already discovered that his adversaries remained largely unseen in battle. This added a particularly frightening new element to warfare, the 'empty' battlefield experience so characteristic of World War I memoirs. It was, understandably, the sight of the dead that made the greatest impression:

> These were the first men I had seen killed in anger, and their ashen faces and staring
> eyeballs came as a great shock, for I had pictured the dignity of death in battle, but
> I now saw that it was horrible to look upon.

After Talana, General White ordered a withdrawal towards Ladysmith, which he reached on 26 October, his troops having exhausted themselves during long marches in searing heat, which alternated with bitterly cold nights. The Boers followed, and Reitz took part in the actions around Ladysmith, where his commando established itself on the slopes overlooking the town, building earthworks in case of a British sortie.

White understood that to avoid being bottled up in Ladysmith he must assume the offensive. On 30 October British troops advanced in an attempt to drive the Boers from their makeshift defences on a number of eminences surrounding the town, including Pepworth Hill and Nicholson's Nek, at both of which Reitz was present. At dawn the Boers on Pepworth Hill began to rain down artillery fire on the attackers:

> ... what with the thunder of the British guns and of our own, the crash of bursting
> shells and the din of a thousand rifles, there was a volume of sound unheard in
> South Africa before. I was awed rather than frightened, and, once I had got over
> my first impression, I felt excited by all I saw and keenly joined in the firing.
> We were so successful that by the time the foremost infantrymen came within
> 1,200 yards of us, many fallen dotted the veld, and their advance wavered before
> the hail of bullets.

With the British attack frustrated, Reitz went in search of his brother, making his way to the top of Nicholson's Nek, a broad, flat-topped hill strewn with boulders and brush, occupied by Free State burghers. His enemy was, once again, unseen. In fact, the British were only 30 to 40 yards (27 to 37m) away, posted behind rocks and any other available shelter. Here Reitz began to appreciate that the British were no match for his comrades in a sharpshooting contest:

Time after time I saw [British] soldiers looking over their defences to fire, and time after time I heard the thud of a bullet finding its mark, and could see the unfortunate man fall back out of sight, killed or wounded.

As Reitz and the others moved to occupy the abandoned ground, they surveyed the field, strewn with the large number of casualties they had inflicted. Finally, around noon, the shrill of a bugle, carrying above the sound of rifle fire, signalled, together with a white flag held aloft, the surrender of over a thousand British soldiers. 'Hundreds of khaki-clad figures rose from among the rocks and walked towards us, their rifles at the trail.'

A short time later Reitz watched as many more thousands of British troops that had assembled on the plain in front of Ladysmith that morning were now in full retreat into the town itself, throwing up 'great clouds of dust,' a withdrawal that 'had every appearance of a rout.' The elation Reitz felt about the victory was tempered by the sickening sights of the aftermath of battle:

Dead and wounded soldiers lay all around, and the cries and groans of agony, and the dreadful sights, haunted me for many a day, for though I had seen death by violence of late, there had been nothing to approach the horrors accumulated here.

The day subsequently became known to the British as 'Mournful Monday.' Their defeat in front of, and refuge in, Ladysmith, would leave them trapped for the next 118 days, rendering White's field force of almost 10,000 troops useless. For Reitz, the success at Ladysmith provided only temporary satisfaction. General Joubert refused to exploit the opportunity to rush the town and drive the British out. The Boers could not know that the siege would bring a premature end to the Boer offensive and sow the seeds of ultimate defeat:

There was not a man who did not believe we were heading straight for the coast, and it was as well that the future was hidden from us, and that we did not know how strength and enthusiasm were to be frittered away in a meaningless siege, and in the holding of useless positions, when our only salvation lay in rapid advance.

At the end of the war Reitz refused to sign the oath of allegiance and promptly settled in Madagascar, where he nearly died of malaria. In 1906 he was persuaded by friends to return, and later took part in suppressing the Boer rebellion of 1914. He went on to serve under Jan Smuts during World War I in the campaign in German West Africa and later against the Germans in East Africa. He was promoted to colonel of his mounted regiment and, later in the war, went to France, where – the process of reconciliation having run full course – he enlisted in the British

Army and commanded the 1st Royal Scots Fusiliers. He was wounded twice, the second time severely, in early 1918, but recovered to fight in the closing phases of the war on the Western Front.

After the war Reitz returned to South Africa. He served in the cabinet under Smuts, his former commander, and as deputy Prime Minister in 1939. Shortly before he died in 1944, Reitz, then an extremely popular high commissioner for South Africa in London, received an unexpected visitor. Into his office strolled a man smiling, bearing a long, slender parcel wrapped in brown paper. 'We have actually met before, Colonel,' the mysterious visitor explained, 'but under rather less auspicious circumstances. Perhaps you will recognize this.' He unwrapped the parcel, which contained a Mauser. This was the very rifle that, its magazine emptied, Reitz had abandoned on the battlefield more than 40 years earlier. It was the same weapon with which Reitz had shot the man standing before him, Lord Vivian. Speechless, Reitz looked down to discover his own name carved on the rifle butt.

CIVIL WAR IN THE 20TH CENTURY

Whatever happens, my fellow countrymen won't kill me.

(Michael Collins)

DAVID NELIGAN, IRISH REVOLUTIONARY

The Anglo-Irish War

Peter Cottrell

It is very difficult to know accurately what the experience was like for the ordinary foot soldiers that fought in the Anglo-Irish War. However, some survivors did write down their experiences, and one of the most unusual sets of memoirs is probably that of David Neligan.

Neligan's experience of the violence between 1919 and 1923 was unique, as during this period he served as a Volunteer, G-Man, IRA intelligence officer, British secret service agent, National Army intelligence officer and founder of the Garda Siochána Detective Branch. His book, *The Spy in the Castle*, is highly readable and it is difficult not to like Neligan. Although his narrative appears to be frank and starkly honest in places, it is worth remembering that it is a subjective account of his time as a G-Man and IRA informer.

Considering many of the men killed in his story were known to him personally or were work colleagues, Neligan usually dismisses their deaths in the surprisingly bland factual statement 'he was shot by the IRA' without any emotional exposition. There can be no doubt that Neligan was a ruthless man whose work for Michael Collins led directly to the deaths of several men, and whose conduct of intelligence operations in Kerry during the civil war earned him the hatred of the anti-Treaty IRA.

Neligan was born in 1899, in Templeglantine, Co. Limerick, and was the youngest of eight children. He grew up in a happy, middle-class Catholic household and his book paints a picture of a rural Ireland more interested in labour shortages and foot-and-mouth than the climactic battles on the Western Front. Interestingly, Neligan never indicates that he had any intention of enlisting in the army to fight. In fact, World War I hardly features in his account at all.

Neligan's revelations give some interesting insights into the life of both ordinary policemen and IRA activists at the time. Although two of Neligan's uncles were policemen and so were several of his father's friends, he joined the National Volunteers when he was about 15. His unit was poorly equipped and 'had no arms except wooden guns,' which seems to have been typical of many Volunteer units. Even though he was a Volunteer, Neligan decided to join the police in 1918 and even got a glowing reference from his parish priest.

In 1915 the government had passed the Emergency Provisions (Police) Act, which placed a moratorium on police recruiting in order to keep the army up to strength. Despite his Nationalist sympathies, Neligan seems to have had little difficulty in enrolling in the Dublin Metropolitan Police (DMP). From his account he could have just as easily joined the Royal Irish Constabulary (RIC) but being stuck at some 'strategically placed crossroads' with three or four other 'Peelers' just did not appeal to him, despite the pay being better than the DMP.

Neligan tells us that promotion 'in both forces was as a result of examinations and open to Irish Roman Catholics' but that 'the top brass was reserved for English or Irish Protestants and Freemasons.' There were some Catholic senior officers, like DMP Assistant Commissioner Fergus Quinn, but they were rare. In Neligan's estimation 'religious and racial discrimination were rife.' Overall he paints a sympathetic picture of the police, and despite Sinn Féin's calls for a boycott of the police Neligan tells us that in 1918 the public still had confidence in the police force and joining was seen as a good job with good prospects.

Neligan paints an affectionate picture of the DMP as a force full of decent men doing a thankless task for very little money. Their strength was that they had an intimate knowledge of their 'patch' and stuck together to the extent that 'the police would lie like devils inside and outside court to save a comrade.' Such was the close-knit world that Neligan entered in 1918 and ultimately betrayed. He joined the DMP mostly because, like so many country boys, the lure of the city as 'an unknown entity' was too much for him to resist. When he got to Dublin he discovered that much of it was squalid and overcrowded and in his estimation the DMP depot in Kevin Street was little better.

Neligan's training was fairly uneventful, but his book gives a fascinating insight into life in the DMP and some of its characters, such as the dapper but elderly Constable Denis 'Count' O'Connor who was reputably the best-dressed copper in Dublin. He also explained how the DMP was divided into six uniformed divisions, A to F, and the infamous G Division.

G Division was a cross between the CID and the Special Branch, and dealt with civil as well as criminal investigations. It relied on 18 detectives to keep tabs on Dublin's political and criminal underworld. Its members were known as G-Men long before the name was popularized in American gangster films – they operated in plain clothes and unlike the rest of the DMP they were armed with notoriously unreliable .38 automatics.

After a brief period working out of College Street police station and as a clerk in the G Division archives in Brunswick (now Pearse) Street, Neligan volunteered to become a G-Man at the end of 1919 because he was 'heartily tired of uniform and beat duties.' Before the Troubles Neligan tells us that G Division was difficult to get into, but casualties had made it unpopular.

Whilst in uniform Neligan had been amongst the party who had found the body of DMP Detective Sergeant (DS) Daniel Hoey after Collins' Squad had shot him outside the central police station in Brunswick Street on 13 September 1919. Neligan also knew another victim of the Squad, DMP DS John Barton, killed by Sean Tracey on 29 November 1919. He probably even knew DMP DS Patrick

Smyth, who was killed on 30 July 1919. The men who probably were guilty of these murders were other G-Men: DS Eamonn 'Ned' Broy, Detective Constable (DC) James McNamara and DC Kavanagh, who had worked for Collins since at least 1917. In fact, Broy even smuggled Collins into the G Division archives in Brunswick Street, where Collins was able to assess just how much the authorities knew about his organization. Between them these men were responsible not only for the deaths of a number of British intelligence agents but also for damaging the Castle's efforts to contain the IRA.

Even after joining G Division, Neligan remained acquainted with several Sinn Féin activists, including Éamon de Valera's secretary Paddy Sheehan. How and why Neligan knew Sheehan is never explained, but he does mention that he recognized DS Hoey from a Sinn Féin meeting without explaining why he was there himself. His brother Maurice was a Trade Union activist, and along with Sheehan they convinced Neligan to resign from the police, which he did on 11 May 1920. Before Neligan resigned he did make an offer to Sheehan to work for the rebels, but Sheehan declined to accept. When Collins heard of this he was furious that the opportunity to turn another G-Man had been squandered, and not long after his resignation Neligan was contacted by the IRA and eventually met Collins in Dublin.

It was the beginning of an association that would only come to an end when the IRA shot Collins during the civil war. On Collins' instructions, Neligan made his way back to the Castle and told his old boss, Detective Chief Inspector (DCI) Bruton, that the IRA had threatened to kill him. Neligan always felt that Bruton did not really believe him, but he was reassigned to G Division nonetheless.

Neligan proved to be a valuable asset and was soon passing Collins high-grade intelligence. It was Neligan who told Collins that an ex-RIC district inspector and resident magistrate, Alan Bell, was investigating how the rebels were funding their operations. Neligan betrayed Bell's address, movements and security arrangements and within days he was dead.

By 1921, G Division had been rendered more or less ineffective against the IRA. Five G-Men, including Assistant Commissioner William Redmond, had been murdered and at least four were IRA activists. Both RIC Special Branch and the secret service knew that something was wrong with G Division and consequently placed little reliance upon it. According to Neligan, the division's parlous state was simply a symptom of a 'demoralized state practically finished.' Despite his IRA activities, no one suspected Neligan of 'working for the enemy,' and much to Collins' delight he managed to join the secret service in May 1921.

Neligan was extremely complimentary about the secret service, which he claimed 'sent some of their crack operators here. I must say they were brave men who carried their lives in their hands.' Despite obvious admiration and a degree of empathy for them, he provided much of the information that led to the mass killing of British agents in Dublin on 21 November 1920, which is perhaps a comment in itself about their efficiency.

When the civil war broke out, Neligan became a colonel in military intelligence, where he earned a fearsome reputation in Co. Kerry. He was allegedly involved in the torture and execution of several anti-Treaty IRA men in February 1922.

After the civil war ended, Neligan returned to the DMP as a chief superintendent heading up its post-war G Division, and eventually became the head of the Garda Detective Branch. By the time he retired he was in receipt of a pension from the British government for his time in the DMP and secret service, and from the Irish Government for his time in the Garda. When asked in later life if he would do any of it again his answer was an unequivocal no – 'revolution devours its own children.'

MAJOR-GENERAL JAMES EMMET DALTON MC

Irish Civil War

Peter Cottrell

Considering that Emmet Dalton (1898–1978) was a Secretary to the Senate, played a prominent role in the IRA during the Anglo-Irish War, commanded the artillery that attacked the Four Courts, broke the back of the 'Munster Republic' and was with Collins when he was killed at Béal na mBláth, it is astonishing that so little information about his life seems to have survived. He left no published memoirs and except for a series of interviews for Irish television no biography of Emmet Dalton has yet been written.

Born in the USA on Friday 4 March 1898, Dalton grew up at 8 Upper St Columbus Road, Drumcondra, a solidly middle-class Catholic suburb of Dublin, and was educated by the Christian Brothers at their school in North Richmond Street. The O'Connell School still survives and has an extensive museum commemorating its old boys; however, Dalton does not receive a mention in it.

Dalton's father was a third-generation Irish-American Republican who had returned to Ireland in 1900. His family's political activism probably explains why he joined the Dublin Volunteers at their inaugural meeting in 1913 at the tender age of 15 and was actively involved in smuggling arms by the time he was 16. His younger brother Charlie also joined and went on to become a member of Collins' inner circle. Much to the chagrin of his father, in 1915 Dalton answered Redmond's call to arms, joining the British Army at 17, as a temporary 2nd lieutenant in the 7th (Service) (Dublin Pals) Battalion, Royal Dublin Fusiliers (RDF). By 1916 he was attached to the 9th Battalion, RDF, 48th Infantry Brigade, 16th Irish Division under Major-General W. B. Hickie. Most of the officers and men in this division were Redmondite Home-Rulers and like Dalton were horrified by the news of the Easter Rising.

It was whilst serving with the 9th 'Dubs' that Dalton befriended an old acquaintance of his father, Lieutenant Tom Kettle MP, the 36-year-old Nationalist MP for East Tyrone and professor of economics at University College Dublin. It was Kettle who had famously declared that Irishmen should fight 'not for England, but for small nations,' a sentiment that Dalton seemed fully to endorse. Kettle hoped that, 'with the wisdom which is sown in tears and blood, this tragedy of Europe [World War I] may be and must be the prologue to the two reconciliations of which all statesmen have dreamed, the reconciliation of Protestant Ulster with Ireland, and the reconciliation of Ireland with Great Britain.'

By the summer of 1916, the 16th Irish Division was fully embroiled in the bloody battle of the Somme. Dalton was amongst those recognized for their courage in the fight on 9 September near the village of Kinchy, in which Kettle was killed, and was awarded the Military Cross.

According to his Military Cross citation, he 'led forward to their final objective companies which had lost their officers. Later whilst consolidating his position, he found himself with one sergeant, confronted by 21 of the enemy, including an officer, who surrendered when he attacked them.' Later that year King George V presented him with his medal at Buckingham Palace. In many respects it was typical of the courage he demonstrated throughout his military career and such was his pride in the award that on occasion he even wore the ribbon on his NA uniform.

By 1917 Dalton had returned to his old battalion, 7 RDF, 30 Brigade, 10th Irish Division in Palestine, where he first commanded a rifle company and then became OC of a sniping school. By 1918 what was left of 7 RDF, along with A/Major Emmet Dalton MC, redeployed to the Western Front. Speculation that he once served on the staff of Sir Henry Wilson is unfounded, as is the unsubstantiated innuendo that he was a British spy and shot Collins.

Like thousands of other Irish soldiers he returned to Ireland after the war. Whilst Dalton was 'away at the wars,' his brother Charlie was an active Volunteer who became a member of Collins' 'Squad,' his hand-picked team of assassins, and was one of the participants in the Bloody Sunday killings of 21 November 1920. It is unclear whether he used the German pistol his brother had given him as a souvenir.

It was probably inevitable, given Charlie's connections and his military experience, that Dalton rejoined the Volunteers on leaving the army. As a disillusioned Redmondite he probably felt that after the 1918 General Election the Dáil and the IRA best represented the will of the Irish people. He had fought for Ireland during World War I and once said that he had no difficulty fighting for Ireland with the British or fighting for Ireland against the British.

Regardless of his personal beliefs, Dalton developed a close friendship with Collins and in an interview screened by RTE on the day he died in 1978 said,

'I loved him. I use no other word. I loved him as a man loves another man, with pure love.'

When Seán MacÈoin was captured in March 1921, it was Dalton who led the attempt to rescue him from Mountjoy Gaol. Dressed in his old uniform and leading members of Collins' 'Squad,' he had devised a plan that was typically daring and involved a stolen armoured car, British Army uniforms and a lot of luck. Dalton and Joe Leonard, dressed as British officers, managed to bluff their way into the governor's office on the pretence of moving MacÈoin to another prison before they were rumbled and shooting broke out near the prison gate. Although the rescue attempt failed, Dalton managed to extract his raiding party intact.

His raw courage as well as his wealth of military experience won him the admiration and trust of both Collins and Mulcahy. His membership of Collins' inner circle was also unusual, as he does not appear to have been a member of the Irish Republican Brotherhood. His loyalty to Collins was purely personal rather than doctrinal, and despite his pedigree as an ex-British officer he rose rapidly through the IRA's ranks to command the active service units during the failed attack on the Customs House in May 1921. In addition he became the first director of munitions and, by the time the Truce was agreed in July 1921, the director of training for the IRA.

When Collins was nominated to go to London as part of the Irish peace delegation, Dalton was dismayed that the 'Big Fella' would be negotiating with the British but accompanied him nonetheless as his military advisor and head of security. He felt that the Treaty was the best deal that Ireland could get and true to his loyalty to Collins he came out in support of it.

In January 1922 Dalton became a brigadier in the new NA when his unit was absorbed into the Dublin Guards. Along with J. J. 'Ginger' O'Connell and John Prout, who had both served in the US Army, Dalton was one of the few senior officers in the NA with formal military training. When Dalton's troops began shelling the Four Courts on 28 June 1922, he even helped aim and fire the borrowed British guns for their inexperienced crews.

Dalton's real *coup de main*, however, was his amphibious attack on Cork on 8 August 1922. Michael Hayes told Mulcahy that the attack broke 'all the rules of common sense and navigation and military science.' Without charts and at one point holding a gun to the head of the captain of his ship, the *Arvonia*, Dalton put ashore 456 men, an armoured car and an 18lb gun outside Cork. According to Tom Crofts 'there was panic' and, after fighting at Rochestown and Douglas, Cork fell to Dalton on the 9th, making a Saorstát victory almost inevitable. In fact Dalton complained bitterly that the war could have been brought to a close in September 1922 if troops had also attacked overland from Dublin at the same time.

On 12 August the now Major-General Dalton was appointed General Officer Commanding, Southern Command. He announced that it was his avowed aim to restore normality to the city and helped establish a temporary police force until the Garda arrived on 16 September. In late August Collins was in Co Cork, ostensibly on an inspection tour but also attempting to make contact with leading Republicans to end the war; according to Coogan's biography of Collins, Dalton had been central to this 'peace' process and acted as an intermediary.

When Collins was warned that it was not safe for him to drive around the county he told local NA commander Joe Sweeney that, 'whatever happens, my fellow countrymen won't kill me.' When the IRA ambushed Collins' convoy on 22 August Dalton had shouted, 'Drive like hell' but Collins contradicted him. Dalton attributed Collins' death to his lack of combat experience: 'If Mick had ever been in a scrap he would have learned to stay down.'

To this day no one really knows what happened at Béal na mBláth, but it was obvious that Collins' death affected Dalton. When he returned from his honeymoon in September 1922 his heart was no longer in the fight. He objected to the execution of captured Irregulars and resigned his commission in December to work briefly as the secretary to the Senate. In a military career that had spanned eight years he had become a retired major-general at 24 on a pension of £117 per annum.

Despite being an accomplished soldier, Dalton had always been interested in the cinema and by the late 1920s was working as a film producer who gained some trans-Atlantic success. In the late 1950s he helped establish the Irish Ardmore Studios where the films *The Blue Max*, *The Spy who Came in from the Cold* and *The Lion in Winter* were filmed in the 1960s.

After 1922 Dalton never held a military appointment again, even though Lord Mountbatten offered him the command of an Irish special operations unit in World War II. Dalton declined, preferring to follow the 'sport of kings' – horseracing – and produce his movies. On his 80th birthday, 4 March 1978, Emmet Dalton died in Dublin, barely commemorated by the state he did so much to create.

JOSÉ DURÁN, ANTONIO IZU, SATURNINO CAROD AND JASON GURNEY

The Spanish Civil War

Frances Lannon

In the early stages of the Spanish Civil War, both sides were poorly organized, with a confusing mixture of regular soldiers, armed security forces and militias with limited or no military training. Regular soldiers wore the standard-issue greenish-khaki tunic, cap, trousers and brown boots of the prewar Spanish Army, whichever side they ended up on so that it was easy to mistake the regular soldiers on both sides.

JOSÉ DURÁN, NATIONALIST

A sense of the chaos and the territorial extension of the war is given in the account of his war experiences by José Durán, of Jerez de la Frontera, in Cádiz province, where his father was a doctor. Immediately after the rising of 18 July 1936, he joined the rebels, even though he was underage. He chose first the town Guards, but got bored with security duties that he was assigned. He enlisted with the Falange, and took part in the Nationalist attack on Málaga. He then decided to leave the front, trusting in the fact that he was still underage to save him from any repercussions, because he simply did not like the officers of his unit. Next, he headed for Cádiz, enlisted in the Nationalist army and went through a brief training course, from which he emerged a sergeant. His war itinerary then took him to Córdoba and Talavera de la Reina. He transferred to a Navarrese unit because he heard that its arrangement for leave was generous, and was sent to the front at Guadalajara, after the Nationalist and Italian defeat. He eventually participated in the Ebro campaign, where he was in command of 500 men. He entered Barcelona with the triumphant Nationalists. His final posting was back in the south, in Murcia, where – now a lieutenant – he was instructed to take the Republican military command centre. Colonels of the Republican army surrendered to him, and he arrested them. In three years the war had taken him across half of Spain, and changed his status from that of a boy-volunteer to an experienced military officer. However, his ability to leave the front and change units is a useful reminder of the confusion and lack of ordinary army discipline in the first months of the war.

ANTONIO IZU, CARLIST

There were many who had been waiting for the day to dawn when they could fight for the Spain of their desires. One example in Ronald Fraser's oral history of the Civil War, *Blood of Spain*, was Antonio Izu, from a Carlist village near Pamplona. His family of modestly prosperous peasant farmers had been Carlist for generations. On hearing of the military rising, he was happy. 'I didn't sleep all that night, thinking what a hell of a shindy we were going to kick up.' He immediately grabbed a rifle and joined the Carlist militia, the *requetés*. He and his companions were directed to march on Madrid, and headed for the Somosierra Pass, north of the city, in the Guadarrama Mountains. They wore *alpargatas* (espadrilles), and made do for several days with a cold diet of bread and sardines.

For them, the war was above all a religious crusade. Many Nationalists, but especially Carlists, wore badges of the Sacred Heart of Jesus stitched on to their uniforms over their hearts as a symbolic protection against enemy fire. These were called *detentes* because the soldiers said this prayer: 'Stop, bullet, the heart of Jesus is here.' But Antonio was appalled when he heard about the repression of leftists back in Pamplona, and sickened when his company commander, a Falangist officer, seized 13 poor peasants from a village near them at the front who had supported the Popular Front, and shot them.

They took the poorly defended pass fairly easily, then fought their way to control of several villages. Antonio was shocked at the near-destitution he encountered in these villages. It was eye-opening to see the poverty from which so much support for the Republic's policies had sprung. Once they reached a point where enemy lines were strongly defended by artillery, they settled down and became part of the siege of Madrid. The enthusiasm with which Antonio had greeted the war did not last. He hated the amalgamation of the Carlists with the Falange in April 1937, and thought that Carlism's commitment to local liberties was betrayed by Franco's dictatorship.

SATURNINO CAROD, REPUBLICAN

Saturnino Carod began the war as convinced of the importance of defending the Republic as Antonio Izu was about destroying it. He was the son of a poor agricultural labourer in Aragón, and had begun working at the age of six. As an adult, he joined the CNT (Confederación Nacional del Trabajo) and learned to read. Before the war Saturnino had become CNT regional propaganda secretary in Saragossa, preaching anarchism in the local villages. He escaped from Saragossa during the rising, and joined an Anarchist militia column fighting its way through Aragón back to the provincial capital. The column was poorly armed with whatever had been to hand – hunting rifles, shotguns, pistols and knives. It was undisciplined, but when he began to reorganize and militarize it, the peasants simply abandoned it. He eventually persuaded them to return, and to accept a fortnight's military instruction from loyal Civil Guards. He found it hard to persuade his column to dig trenches opposite the Nationalists' position at Belchite. His men wanted – suicidally – to advance, not dig in.

Saturnino was out of sympathy with the wave of collectivizations that swept over Aragón because he knew how attached to their own small plots of land many peasants were. He nonetheless worked hard to make the collectivization experiment a success. He understood the rage of many CNT members against the Spanish Communist party and its agrarian policies in 1937, and had to struggle to prevent his column from leaving the front to fight against the Communists in the rear. More and more he felt that the Communist forces at the front were being better equipped and armed than the Anarchists, and he recalled that at Teruel he was offered further arms supplies only on condition that he joined the party, which he refused.

At the end of the war, Saturnino was one of the thousands at the port in Alicante, waiting for ships that never came. He watched people round him committing suicide rather than be rounded up by the Nationalists. Yet by this stage he himself had decided that a Republican victory would have been fruitless because of the savage political conflicts between Republicans. He remained, however, a fervent anti-Francoist. After escaping from a prison camp in Spain, making his way to France and being held in a camp there, he embarked on clandestine CNT activity in postwar Spain. For this he was condemned to death, and served 18 years of a commuted sentence before being released in 1960. His extraordinary brand of idealism was one of the factors that kept the Republic fighting, yet in the end he was not convinced that the Republic represented him any more.

JASON GURNEY, INTERNATIONAL BRIGADE

Among the approximately 35,000 volunteers in the International Brigades were about 2,000 from Britain. Jason Gurney's detailed memoir, *Crusade in Spain*, was published in 1974. He was a 26-year-old sculptor in Chelsea when he volunteered in December 1936. Like all International Brigaders, he was taken to the brigades' centre at Albacete, where the men were issued with brownish shirts, trousers and jackets, some boots and a khaki beret. They were harangued by the chief political commissar of the Brigades, André Marty, and eventually sent on to the British battalion's training centre at the village of Madrigueras.

Coping with cold, winter rain and a poor diet was not easy, and the lack of tobacco made it worse. They had no rifles, and training was perfunctory. When eventually automatic weapons appeared, they were old, and with the exception of the reliable Maxims, did not work, or got jammed. Only the night before they left Madrigueras for the front south of Madrid were they issued with poor quality Soviet rifles. They were paid 10 pesetas a day. Of the 600 men with Jason Gurney, over half would be dead within weeks.

In February 1937 the British battalion went into action as part of the XV International Brigade in the battle of Jarama, with the aim of preventing the Nationalists moving east and cutting the Madrid–Valencia road. The XV was a mixed brigade of infantry, artillery ('two old French 75s and one even more ancient English 5.2 Howitzer') and nine Soviet tanks. Different types of light automatics and rifles needed different ammunition. There was a babel of languages in the brigade, making communication difficult at the best of times, and perilous in battle. They had no maps. They found themselves attempting to hold an exposed position against heavy artillery fire and a swift advance by experienced Moorish Regulars, whose speed and prowess were terrifying. They were overwhelmed. In the end Jarama was a success for the Republic because the Nationalists never got to the Madrid–Valencia road, and were driven back some way in a counter-offensive. But in 21 days, there were about 45,000 casualties. It was a soldier–intensive war.

THE WORLD WARS

I would give you my word, I would rather have come to dear old Blighty and as cold as it is to stand in the food queues all day just to get amongst a little bit of civilisation.

(Harold Wright)

We were only told what we were going to do at the last moment, or sometimes not at all, and the command we mostly heard from our officers was just 'follow me.'

(Russian soldier on the Eastern Front in World War II)

My boys are back there, I must be with them.

(Thomas Currie Derrick)

PRIVATE FREDERICK 'FEN' NOAKES, 3RD COLDSTREAM GUARDS

World War I: The Western Front

Peter Simkins

Private (later Guardsman) Frederick Elias 'Fen' Noakes, a draper from Tunbridge Wells in Kent, was born on 27 January 1896 and made several attempts to join the British Army between 1914 and 1917, always being rejected on medical grounds. As a youth he suffered badly from asthma and was, by his own admission, thin and 'weakly' with 'little physical strength.' When turned down yet again in 1916, a mixture of patriotism and fear of being thought a 'shirker' drove him to improve his fitness by using chest-expanders and taking long walks and cycle rides. He finally passed a medical board in May 1917 and was soon called up for military service in June, being posted to Windsor for training in a reserve formation of the Household Battalion. From then until 1919 he wrote regularly to his family. He saw action during both the German March offensive and the victorious Allied advance in 1918 and was wounded twice. Even allowing for wartime censorship, his articulate letters provide an interesting commentary on the war, containing not only reports on his own daily activities but also forthright views on wider political issues. In 1934 he collated and typed these letters and then, in 1952, used them as the basis for a privately printed memoir, *The Distant Drum*, in which he added many of the previously missing military and geographical details and included some mature reflections on his opinions as a young man. Together the letters and book offer a valuable glimpse into the last 18 months of the war and can be seen as an accurate barometer of the attitudes and morale of British soldiers on the Western Front in 1918.

Noakes crossed to France in November 1917, joining the Household Battalion – a unit of the 4th Division – in the Arras area. At this stage he still retained a 'credulous idealism,' counting it 'an honour to take part in the most righteous war England ever waged, the Last Crusade… Victory is in our grasp, and we should be utterly unworthy of the trust reposed in us if we turn back now. No peace until Prussian militarism is in pieces.' After a few weeks his views began to change. On 8 January 1918 he complained about the 'spirit of savagery' in the British press. 'Could the fighting men … of both sides come together there can be no doubt that complete unanimity would result,' he remarked. Noakes now felt that 'national pride,' or obstinacy, 'will prove a great obstacle in the way of a reasonable settlement.' He called for a 'much greater openness of mind and humanity' lest Britain become infected with 'the very spirit of Prussianism we set out to crush.' By 12 February he was asking when 'all this indiscriminate murder' would cease. 'Everyone, except the people in power is heartily sick of it… There is not a man out here who would not make peace in a moment…' In later life, however, he declared that this was 'a temporary wave of disillusionment' which represented 'no more than the normal habit of grousing for which the British soldier is notorious.'

From the end of January until early March, Noakes suffered from a poisoned finger and leg sores and was hospitalized in February at Le Tréport, near Dieppe. During this period the Household Battalion was disbanded as part of the reorganization of the BEF (British Expeditionary Force) and, on recovery, Noakes was sent to the 3rd Coldstream Guards, then serving in the 4th Guards Brigade attached to the 31st Division. Between 23 and 25 March the battalion was in action near Ervillers, north of Bapaume, on the Third Army's front. Noakes recalled how tired he was following three days and nights without sleep. Eventually, as the German attacks grew heavier and more intense – and with the battalion in danger of being outflanked or surrounded – the order was given to retreat. Noakes, by then, had sunk into a mood of weary fatalism. 'I ran for some distance with the rest,' he told his mother, 'and then, with a feeling of disgust for the whole job, I slowed down to a walk. I really didn't care which way things went.' He was, in fact, knocked unconscious and wounded in the forearm by a shell.

'Fen' Noakes spent over four months convalescing near Boulogne. The March crisis and the threat of defeat revived some of his former 'enthusiasm for the national cause,' although 'my "patriotism" was never afterwards so unqualified and my devotion was more critical, than they had been in the past.' By 5 May he was again optimistic and commented with remarkable insight that:

> I think we have got Fritz on the toasting-fork all right. He has made progress, but it has cost him far more casualties than he expected, and all the result has been is to put him in an impossible position. He is weakened out of all proportion to his gain, but he cannot stay where he is…

He returned to his unit in August but, towards the end of that month, was transferred to the 1st Battalion of the Coldstream Guards in the prestigious Guards Division. The Allied offensive had now been in progress for three weeks and Noakes was 'fairly certain that the war will be definitely decided, if not ended, before the winter.' In September, as the Guards Division advanced towards the Canal du Nord and Hindenburg Line, Noakes was struck, more than once, by the absence of Germans on his immediate front. On 13 September he recorded that men coming back from the forward positions were saying 'We can't find the enemy' or 'We've lost Fritz.' Noakes also noted that he had seen only three dead bodies and no wounded all day. 'I wish all battles were like that,' he added. Noakes was profoundly impressed by the scale of the supporting barrage during the attack on the Canal du Nord on 27 September and, although he felt 'stark naked' when required to cross open ground under heavy fire, he also experienced 'an extraordinary sensation – curiously like relief – that I was no longer personally responsible for my own safety.' The attack was successful but Noakes and his comrades were too exhausted to care about their achievement: 'Our mouths and throats were dry as lime-kilns. Nerves were on edge and tempers frayed as always after the intense strain of "going over the top."' On 9 October, in another attack at Wambaix, near Cambrai, Noakes was wounded in the left leg. 'That was the end of the war, so far as my insignificant personal part in it went,' he recalled.

As the war drew to a close, Noakes was convalescing at a camp at Cayeux, near the mouth of the Somme. Attracted by the ideas of President Woodrow Wilson of the United States, Noakes was worried that Britain and France, in the elation of victory, would impose a vengeful settlement upon Germany. 'A lasting peace it must be,' he told his father, 'but it must also be an absolutely clean peace. Otherwise, the war has been in vain.' The announcement, on 11 November, that the Armistice had been signed was, however, 'a moment of such undiluted happiness and emotion as I had never known and probably shall never know again.'

Rejoicing in his new rank of Guardsman, Noakes served briefly with the British occupation forces in Cologne before coming home to England in March 1919. Demobilized in October that year, he returned to work in his family's drapery business. This sensitive and perceptive former soldier died at the relatively young age of 57 on 12 April 1953.

CECIL, HAROLD AND NOEL WRIGHT, BROTHERS IN ARMS

World War I: The Mediterranean Front

Michael Hickey

The Great World War of 1914–18 affected entire populations. Few families were spared the impact of the casualty lists publishing the dead, wounded and missing. One family in Christleton, a Cheshire village far from the battlefields, was typical. Frederick Wright, a joiner, married Frances Tushingham in the 1880s, and they moved into a cottage in Quarry Lane. A large family duly arrived. Fred, the eldest, was followed by Marshall (Marsh), Harold, Hylton, Cecil, Noel, and finally three daughters: Effie, Amy and Eva. All the children attended the village school until their 14th year, when the boys sought work. The Wright boys found employment in Chester, three miles' walk away.

In 1907 a major overhaul of the British Army and its reserve forces created the Territorial Force, which included the Earl of Chester's Yeomanry, originally raised in the 18th century for home defence. By the summer of 1914 Cecil was riding as a trumpeter with the regiment for its summer camp at Llangollen. Weeks later, on mobilization, the yeomanry went to Northumberland to defend the coastline. They were still there a year later. Cecil wrote to his sister Eva from Morpeth Common camp in October 1915 describing the primitive conditions and appalling weather (spelling throughout the letters remains uncorrected):

> It has rained for 28 hours without a stop, things are in a fine mess if it is only catching hold of the dirty wet headropes, it is rotten. I have finished transport driving and gone to the troop again. We do very little drill here, it is all road work, every other day we go between 40 and 50 miles we are seeing the countryside and a very nice country it is… on Thursday we started at 6.30 am and landed back at 7.15 pm just before dark, it was a lovely day and the Cheviot Hills looked fine… PS the Scotchish Horse that was here before us went to the Front some at home may have been in the papers where they have been cut up. [The Scottish Horse had been sent via Egypt to Gallipoli where they had to fight as infantry.]

On one postcard dated 15 October 1915 Cecil added a message telling her that he had been promoted to corporal:'I believe we are going to the first line in a month or two. We have had a big week. The ground was covered with frost at 11 am so you can see what it is like sleeping in the open…'

Cecil's subsequent letters are all from Egypt and Palestine. Three of the Wright brothers served in that theatre. Noel transferred to the Royal Flying Corps as ground crew, and Harold served in the Royal Garrison Artillery (RGA). By May 1917 General Murray's Egyptian Expeditionary Force had slowly advanced up the Mediterranean coast into Palestine, but had been repulsed in two attempts to take the town of Gaza. Harold wrote to his sister shortly after the second battle:

> … don't think we are having a bad time here although there is a war on, for speaking the truth we are having a jolly good time at present… I hope they forget us and leave us here for the duration. We get nothing else but sunshine from morning till night, we have blue glasses and short pants. The lanes are 3 inches deep in dust so when we were marching we got smothered and choked and we were not allowed to have a drink out of our water bottles and when we halted we dared not drink for it is a bad practice to drink water out here we just rinced our mouths out. We rise in the morning and go on parade at 6 and have an hour on Swedish drill, then we have breakfast, oatmeal porridge, bacon and bread and good stuff it is and we wash it down with a pint of tea with plenty of sugar – the only thing we go short of is milk for cows are very scarce here. We go on parade again at 9 until 11.30 on the guns, a bit tiring owing to the heat. Then we go to the guns again from 3 to 4.30, getting cooler than, and we have finished the day.

Shortly after this, by a happy coincidence, the three brothers managed to meet on Whit Sunday 1917 on the battlefield, an event celebrated with a photograph. It was the last time they would all be together. Meanwhile, Cecil continued fighting and marching with the dismounted yeomanry. On the eve of the third battle of Gaza he sent a card to Eva:

> Well, I have not got much time as we are on the move tonight. All the movements are done at night, it's a lot better for marching in the cool. We are looking forward to the rainy season starting. You can take this for granted an infantryman out here never as a good time. We are starting tonight on this mobile stunt that means iron rations…

In a letter dated 22 November 1917 Harold described the recent battle of Gaza, although he also took the opportunity to complain that none of his sisters had written to him for weeks – 'how would you like it all my pals receiving letters from home and me having none you don't seem to realise what a letter means on a shell-riddled desert…' He then goes on to describe the battle:

> Now before the great advance I had a letter from Cecil to say he was ready, that meant to meet the Turkish Army so you could tell what my feelings were when the great guns roaring and the Turkish shells flying not far from me, then to see the lights going up and lighting the earth for miles. Our artillery forming the barrage to clear the way for our infantry that were firing their rifles and charging with there bayonets. You at home don't seem to realise what a horrible clash it all is and me thinking how poor Cecil was going on. I knew he was in front but what part I did not know but I afterward found out that he was in the attack on Beersheba, that is where the Cheshire Yeo made there debut and they were received with a strong force of the Turkish Army but they did not fail to do so for they put him on the run with there bayonets … we have had some very hard strugles and our infantry must have had very hard times for we have had very hot weather considering it is well on in November and we have had some very wet days, marching in this country with a full pack is above all jokes but the scarcest thing of all is water but in spite of all these drawbacks we have chased him for miles, we are well past Jerusalem and Bethlehem…

After the third battle of Gaza the campaign slowed down. While Cecil was in a Cairo hospital with fever in April 1918, Harold met Noel in Alexandria where they lived in luxury for a couple of days:

> Fancy me and Noel in Alex with bags of cash and Cecil stony in Cairo, me and Noel had a royal time, we did live, he only had two half days off but was out by 5.30 every night and we had supper together every day, it's a true saying that there's corn

in Egypt but not only corn. To give you some idea, for breakfast, 4 eggs, bread, butter, and tea as much as I wanted for one shilling, for dinner which I had at the finest café in Alex, Chip potatoes, beef steak, two vegetables, and tea... After tea we went for a stroll or the pictures, then for Supper we went to a Posh café for coffee ... then I sent Noel home like some Lord going from his club in our open carriage and if that's not going the swank I don't know what is...

However, despite this luxury, Harold was still homesick:

... but Eva, a leave here seeing all these sights is nothing, I would give you my word, I would rather have come to dear old Blighty and as cold as it is to stand in the food queues all day just to get amongst a little bit of civilisation and to here the Old English language spoken once more...

Back in the desert conditions were harsh again:

Today there is a terrible sand storm so when we go out we have to wear sand goggles to protect our eyes or otherwise we would get nearly blinded and the flies are terrible while I am writing these lines they are in bunches on my hands and face I believe they are watching what I am writing about...

When General Edmund Allenby resumed the offensive, Harold's battery was in constant action. His letters increasingly reflect his homesickness and the soldier's eternal complaint about mail from home. In July, from 'Somewhere in Judaea' he writes at length:

You never wrote me a single line telling how you enjoyed yourself at 'Whit' Monday. I was wondering Eva when I shall have that great pleasure of rowing on the Dee and listening to the band ... it's Saturday night 9 pm and I am on duty till Monday night on the telephone at the guns and we have just finished firing for Johnny [Turk] as given us a very rough time in our section today. He has done a deal of damage the shrapnel as been falling like rain and flashing like lightning but I am pleased to say they were falling 1/2 mile short of me. It's a fine sight watching them but not very pleasant stopping it according to what I could see Harry Culham and Frank Rowlands were having their full share I am anxiously waiting to hear all they have to say about it for we go visiting each other when things are quiet. (PS Harry as been over tonight, Monday, he's alright.)

Cecil had been posted from the Yeomanry to the Kings Shropshire Light Infantry on the Western Front. After home leave he saw much action until October 1918, when he fell sick with the virulent Spanish influenza sweeping Europe. Taken to a military hospital at Etaples near Le Havre, he died on 9 November, two days before the Armistice. The telegram notifying his death was delivered to the family cottage at Christleton on the 11th, casting the Wrights into deep mourning as the rest of the village rejoiced.

In August Harold, his long epistles failing to draw a response, wrote to Eva calling her an 'ungrateful hussy' but as the Egyptian Expeditionary Force's campaign ended he wrote in mellower mood on 5 November:

> Just a few lines to tell you I am still in Ismailia Egypt but returning to Palestine in a few days but I am pleased to say as you know I am not returning to fight. That is one great consolation for the scrapping finished last week so it only means going back to Ludd to rejoin my battery... I don't think I will ever see any more fighting and a good thing too...

Two days later Harold wrote again:

> Dear Eva, a few lines to let you know whilst I was commencing to write in the 'Chester Hut' Ismailia, YMCA, it has been announced that Germany has signed an Armistice. With Loud Cheers and everybody sang (praise God from whom all blessings flow) ... and I am now longing for the day when I embark on the boat to sail for Good Old Blighty and be with you all at home and to remain ... get plenty of music ready for that happy day.

A week later, from Palestine, and unaware of Cecil's death, he described the celebrations of the previous week:

> How did you all receive the news. I hope you are not all suffering from shell shock. We got the great news at 5.30 pm on the 11th you see how quickly good news travels and it is approaching 4000 miles from home. It was received here as you can guess with loud cheers we nearly all went mad, they all sang songs, beat tins, and made bon-fires. The big guns fired blank cartridges and gun cotton but the anti-aircraft fired shrapnel so you can imagine what a time we had that night. But Eva that will be the night when we get safely home, we will have a jubilee, what do you say. The next time we meet will be in Good Old Chester. So keep smiling Eva, you will have a good time running to the station to meet us all in our turns. That will be great sport, what do you think ...

For the Wrights of Christleton at least, the war was over.

A TROOPER, AN ENSIGN AND A SERGEANT

World War I: The Eastern Front

Geoffrey Jukes

ALEXANDER GORBATOV, ALEXANDER VASILEVSKY AND GEORGIY ZHUKOV

German Eastern Front soldiers were regularly required to beat numerically superior Russian forces, and almost invariably did. Their leaders seldom exposed them to pointless risk, and normally fed, equipped and rested them adequately. The infantryman could see that his artillery, machine gun and air support was vastly superior to the Russian, and his feeling of having the edge seldom left him. There was no breakdown of morale in 1918 comparable to that on the Western Front; it was historical irony that, after the failure of a strategy explicitly devised to avoid a two-front war, Germany fought one for three and a half years successfully enough to eliminate one of the fronts, then conceded defeat on the single front in only eight more months.

The Russian view of military service was expressed in a four-line verse: 'clever to the artillery, drinker to the navy, rich to the cavalry, stupid to the infantry.' It was meant for newly commissioned officers, but the 20–25 per cent of literate conscripts tended to be sent to the artillery or cavalry, and the rest to the infantry. The average soldier could keep no diary or journal, and in the turmoil that followed the 1917 collapse, almost nothing was published about the ordinary soldier's experiences. However, enough military censorship reports survived to give a general picture, and significant accounts were written later by a cavalry trooper, a sergeant, and an infantry junior officer (ensign). The sergeant was Georgiy Zhukov, of the 10th Novgorod Dragoons. The ensign, later staff-captain, was Alexander Vasilevsky of the 409th Infantry Regiment, and the trooper Alexander Gorbatov of the Chernigov Hussars. All three rose high in the Red Army. In World War II, Zhukov and Vasilevsky, both marshals, held its two top posts, respectively deputy supreme commander and chief of general staff, and masterminded the victories that eluded their tsarist predecessors. Gorbatov became a full general and commanded an army.

The three soldiers served on the same front (South-West) in different units; their accounts are generally consistent with each other and with the censors' reports. All three were villagers; Gorbatov, the trooper, and Zhukov, the sergeant, were born into peasant families, Vasilevsky being the son of a village priest. They were typical in that their families subsisted only by their fathers taking on extra work, and their mothers and sisters making gloves and mittens for sale during winter. They were atypical in receiving education – Vasilevsky (intended for the priesthood) to the age of 19, the others to the age of ten – and in 'escaping' their rural background early, Vasilevsky to a theological seminary, the others apprenticed to a shoemaker and a furrier. Gorbatov was conscripted in 1912, the others in 1915 – Vasilevsky in January, Zhukov in August.

Vasilevsky underwent officer training from February to May 1915. The programme paid much attention to drill, but taught nothing about surviving on battlefields dominated by 'field obstacles' (trenches, barbed wire, machine guns), or about the possible roles of motor vehicles and aircraft, and next to nothing about co-operation between the different arms of service. He joined an infantry regiment as an ensign in autumn 1915, and noted that the Russian trenches were primitive, uncomfortable and badly laid out compared to those of the opposing Austrian Seventh Army (Gorbatov made the same point after inspecting abandoned Russian and German trenches in 1916). The soldiers had no blankets and slept in their greatcoats.

The regiment was entirely equipped with captured Austrian rifles, and had only two machine guns per battalion; the artillery was short of howitzers, heavy guns and ammunition of all calibres. After rest and training during the winter, the regiment returned to the line for General Alexei Brusilov's 1916 offensive. The men, and most of the officers, welcomed facing Austrians, instead of Germans, and heaved collective sighs of relief when shell bursts showed the pink smoke of Austrian high explosive, an indication of the moral ascendancy that the Germans had established over the Russian soldier by mid-1916.

Gorbatov was at war from the outset. Like Zhukov, he noted the lack of contact between officers and men, and that soldiers were frequently beaten for minor infractions. Vasilevsky was told to impose discipline by the 'Prussian rule,' that 'the soldier must fear the Corporal's stick more than the enemy's bullet.' Zhukov noted 'One aim was pursued, the soldier was to be an obedient automaton... The regulations did not provide for corporal punishment, but it was rather widely employed.'

Career officers came from the richer families, and few attempted to adapt to wartime circumstances, in which officer casualties could only be replaced by commissioning the less privileged, such as Vasilevsky, or promoting warrant officers and sergeants. For example, two sergeants in Gorbatov's regiment, decorated for bravery and promoted to ensign, 'were suddenly posted to another regiment; our regiment's officers and gentlemen were unwilling to shake hands with ex-rankers.' He went on to say:

> when the general withdrawal [from Galicia in 1915] began ... depression became more and more marked, and derogatory comments about the High Command became frequent... Reinforcements reaching us from the rear depressed us even more with their talk of imminent famine and our rulers' incompetence. The troops also found it hard to tolerate our officers' disregard for their most basic needs.

Zhukov said that during training he saw his company commander only twice, and that both times the officer was drunk. He described lack of rapport and unity between officers and men as the most characteristic feature of the tsarist army, though, contradictorily, he also gave instances of considerate and understanding officer behaviour. He also noted that the influx of officers from less privileged backgrounds improved relations up to battalion level, but that the higher commands remained dominated by officers 'alien' to the soldiers.

The typical Russian soldier with whom these three men served was a peasant who, unlike them, had not 'escaped' his background. He lived in a village with no electricity, gas, piped water or sewers, served by unsurfaced roads that were impassable for several weeks at a time during the autumn rains and spring thaw. He was used to hardship and a monotonous diet, described in another popular epigram as 'cabbage soup and buckwheat porridge,' and to ill-treatment by 'gentry,' whether landlords, factory owners or his military superiors. He was also, however, unused to handling and maintaining even the simplest machinery. Only the literate minority could do the paperwork of administration, and if they became battle casualties, a unit could soon find itself short of food, fodder or ammunition, or unable to operate the primitive radios used for communicating with higher formations.

Another junior officer, Alexander Zhiglinsky, serving on the West Front in February 1916, summed up his men optimistically in a letter home:

> Whomever you ask 'well, brother, fed up with sitting around?' replies, '…we'd like to go forward now. We've got shells, we can push on…' And in our brigade they've all been under fire, they're experienced soldiers … they survived the painful time when we had no shells … people here don't weep or grieve, they're just full of energy and faith in the future, they can even joke happily in their own circle, here you don't meet mournful, sad faces, calm and confidence are written on them … about the war, in the sense of assessing results, betrayals or horrors, they don't talk; rest is devoted to laughter and gossip.

His assessment was made before the allies' unsuccessful offensives on the Russian West Front of March and July 1916, and his subsequent letters made no reference to his men's morale. Gorbatov, Zhukov and Vasilevsky, and the military censors' reports, point to its deterioration during 1916, particularly in its last few months. Zhukov, en route to the front in August 1916, mentioned conversations with wounded, from which he learned that 'our armies were very poorly armed, the senior commanders had a bad reputation, it was widely held among the soldiers that traitors, bought by the Germans, sat in the High Command, and the troops were poorly fed.' He went on to say that in September 1916 disaffection among the troops mounted, 'especially after letters from home told them of hunger and dreadful disorganisation.' In October he was seriously wounded, and he returned to the front only in December, where 'talking with the men I realised they were not burning with a desire to "sniff gunpowder," and didn't want the war. They already had different thoughts, about land and peace.'

Estimates of Russia's losses differ considerably, but on the latest available assessment 1.45 million were killed, 3.41 million captured, 3.22 million wounded and over 1 million missing. The ratio of 251 captured or missing to every 100 dead was far the highest for any of the belligerents. In the first two years, the captures resulted mostly from inept generalship, but in 1916–17 they were accompanied by high rates of desertion, indicating erosion of the will to fight. The signs of decay began to accumulate in the last months of 1916.

Unrest was not exceptional, as military censors' reports showed, and the commanders knew it was fragile. However, optimists, such as Brusilov's general quartermaster, Dukhonin, expected the winter lull to provide relief, and morale to be much improved by the spring of 1917.

That this view was unrealistic soon became apparent. On 1 and 2 October 1916, in the Eastern Carpathians, two Siberian regiments of the Seventh Army refused orders to attack. On 9 October a regiment of the Special (ex-Guard) Army was forced at gunpoint by the two adjacent regiments to cease working on defences. Another threatened to fire on its neighbours if they obeyed orders to attack. Two more regiments were found to have been distributing peace propaganda for several months, including an anti-war manifesto written by the commanding officer of one of them; this in an 'elite' army raised in 1915, with specially selected officers and men.

In April 1916 the head of the Petrograd Okhrana (Security) could write: 'The Petrograd Garrison does not believe Russian arms can succeed, and finds prolongation of the war useless, but soldiers in fighting units express confidence that victory is possible.' By the end of 1916, this distinction was disappearing. Military censors' reports referred both to the depressive effect of letters from home ('Almost every letter … expresses a wish for the war to end as soon as possible'), and to the disgruntled tone of many soldiers' letters.

Food and fuel shortages and escalating prices affected morale. The Petrograd Military Censorship Commission on 27 November quoted soldiers' complaints of shortages of food, warm clothing and equipment, and added, 'in letters from the army, just as mostly in letters to the army, dissatisfaction begins showing itself more and more acutely about the country's internal political situation… Rumours reach the army about disorders, strikes in factories, and mutinies in rear units, and cause morale to decline.'

To free Russian troops for the front line, the tsar on 25 June 1916 had ordered conscription for non-combatant duties from populations hitherto exempt, including the Muslims of Turkestan (to provide 250,000), and Steppe (243,000) Governorates. This sparked risings throughout central Asia, which continued until December;

barely had they been put down, and about half the desired numbers conscripted, when the regime collapsed.

However, the success of anti-war propaganda among troops in the rear was not yet matched in the front line. There the shared purpose of self-preservation, unit pride, comradeship among men who had been under fire together, and measures taken to keep out anti-war propaganda, defeated Bolshevik efforts. The party then infiltrated members into the military zone, but on 26 May 1915, the Grand Duke prohibited front-line visits by persons of 'dubious political reliability,' and had some leaflet distributors exiled to Siberia.

As the 1916 campaigning season approached, revolutionary propaganda intensified, including spreading false rumours that soldiers on both sides were already refusing orders to attack. Henceforth claims that German troops were mutinous and Germany ripe for revolution became increasingly prominent in Bolshevik propaganda. The front-line soldiers knew they were false, but troops in the rear and civilians were more credulous.

One reason for the impact of anti-war propaganda was military reliance solely on repression to maintain discipline. Stavka (the command element of the army) never attempted persuasion, or even telling the troops why Russia was at war – the trooper said that only by talking to officers' orderlies did the men learn that Russia was about to go to war. To explain the autocrat's decisions implicitly undermined the principle that they must be obeyed unquestioningly; but eschewing counter-indoctrination meant taking the troops' docility for granted, an ever less realistic attitude as time passed.

In the circumstances, it was surprising not that Russian troops sometimes performed badly, but that they often performed well. Defeatist revolutionary activities constantly worried the High Command, but the examples cited above suggest that reliability was the norm, not the exception, among front-line units until the last quarter of 1916. And in March 1917 it was not the front-line troops but the Petrograd Garrison that mutinied and brought down the regime.

PRIVATE DONALD EDGAR, EAST SURREY REGIMENT AND PRISONER OF WAR

World War II: Europe

Robin Havers

In 1940 Donald Edgar joined the reserve element of the British Army, the Territorial Army. As a barely trained private soldier in the East Surrey Regiment, he was sent to France along with rest of the British Expeditionary Force (BEF) in much the same fashion as the original BEF in 1914. Unlike the BEF of 20 or so years previously, however, the BEF of 1940 was not to halt the German advance. Edgar himself was captured by the Germans and spent the next five years as a prisoner of war.

Donald Edgar, along with many thousands of young men, responded to a government appeal in March 1939 to join the Territorial Army. Adolf Hitler had occupied Czechoslovakia and it was apparent to many that the war was highly likely, if not inevitable. Edgar was in many ways an atypical private soldier, having attended Dulwich School, where he served with the Officer Training Corps, and Oxford University, from where he went to work as a stockbroker in the City of London. Edgar wrote of his enlistment that 'I was patriotic and there was a general feeling around in the City … that it was time for us young men "to do something."' Edgar was also keen to volunteer, rather than await what he considered to be the inevitable conscription, declaring that 'No one in my family had ever been conscripted. They had always been volunteers.'

Edgar's unit was part of the British 12th Division, one of three 'second-line' formations that Edgar considered to have been 'denied equipment and arms' and left to perform 'humdrum, menial tasks that left no time for training.' Edgar believed that the War Office thought these units were little more than a 'bloody nuisance.' This was an especial injustice for Donald Edgar and one that he felt all the more keenly because, as he put it, 'the ranks of these battalions contained a large proportion of the men who had patriotically responded to the Government's call in the spring. They were the real volunteers of the war.'

Edgar was called up in August 1939 and reported to his unit at the Richmond Drill Hall. He was fortunate to be made a number of financial guarantees by his employers in the City and he noted also that they gave him a 'handsome gift' to help him on his way, following a 'glass or two of champagne' at his farewell luncheon. This rather pleasant farewell was followed by a rude introduction to the realities of army life. Edgar's unit moved to a camp near Chatham, a naval dockyard on the south coast of England, where they were each issued with five rounds of live ammunition and told, 'This is real guard duty, see?' Edgar's experiences of the regular British Army were not positive: the conditions of their initial camp and the reception granted him by two regular warrant officers were described as 'lazy inefficiency' and 'only the first example we were to experience of the Regular Army's appalling state of slackness.'

At 11.15am on 3 September, Edgar and his comrades listened to Prime Minister Neville Chamberlain's speech announcing Britain's declaration of war on Germany. On this momentous occasion, according to Edgar, Chamberlain gave his speech 'as though he were giving one of his budget talks on the radio when he were Chancellor.'

After a month or so at Chatham, Edgar's unit moved back to Richmond, where they were employed guarding 'vulnerable points' – the railway bridge over the Thames being Edgar's own duty. He recalled the mood that seemed to pervade the country during the 'phony war,' a mood that seemed to suggest that Britain was doing all it could to honour her promise to Poland – even though that country had already been dismembered by Germany and the Soviet Union. Edgar thought the British had 'convinced ourselves that by mobilising the fleet and sending a few divisions to France we had done just about all that was necessary for the war against Germany.'

Despite Edgar's many complaints about the wider conduct of Britain's war effort, he himself was successively promoted through lance-corporal, corporal, and lance-sergeant, working in the unit's intelligence section. Edgar's unit spent a long and cold winter in England, relocating to Richmond Park and undergoing occasional training forays in the wide expanse of parkland on offer.

In March 1940, Edgar's unit was told that it was to proceed to France where its members would at last 'train hard and receive all our equipment from supplies already there.' They embarked for France and landed at Le Havre, before moving to a large château in the Normandy countryside. Edgar's bilingual capability led to his being appointed as a translator and he participated in a number of meetings between his battalion commander and the local French military authorities. These meetings Edgar termed 'predictably uncomfortable,' but 'no more so than those held at the highest level between French and British generals.' Given the lack of adequate co-ordination between the French and British forces in France, it is interesting to see these considerations replicated at the battalion level.

Because of his evident language capabilities, Edgar was tasked with translating a number of documents that the French had passed on to their British counterparts. These documents concerned the French arrangements to defend the important dock areas of Le Havre, but they had wider implications for the forthcoming fighting – implications and conclusions that had Edgar concerned: 'When I came to translate the French documents I was shaken out of my complacency. The analysis envisaged a war of movement as a distinct possibility with the breakthrough of German armoured columns deep into the rear areas.' These conclusions, as we have seen, were to prove extremely accurate. As Edgar also noted, however, the officers now leading his and many other battalions of the British and French armies had seen service on the Western Front during 1914–18 and this was not the type of war they were accustomed to.

Donald Edgar obviously had many criticisms of the British Army. Many of these may be dismissed as the typical grumbling of any soldier; some are more valid, however. Edgar informs us that many units were short of machine guns and anti-tank weapons, what they did possess being far less than the official complement.

What Edgar considered to be the worst omission was one of the areas in which the Germans had both a marked superiority and, perhaps even more crucially, a greater understanding of its importance: communications. While Edgar conceded that the regular BEF units were provided with wireless and telephone communications, the men of the three 'labour' battalions had neither and 'went forward blind.' This was an unsatisfactory state of affairs at any time, but given the manner in which the Germans utilized new technology in combination with rather less original tactics, these shortcomings were particularly damaging to the effective conduct of the war on the Allied side.

Despite all the problems identified by Donald Edgar, writing on the eve of battle, he was not totally pessimistic about the future. Edgar believed that 'the spirit of the men was still high – in spite of everything.' Although Edgar's reminiscences at this point perhaps border on the sentimental, he comments that 'it is with a bitter smile that those English Territorial battalions [went] to battle in May 1940 with a raucous laugh, singing a silly song: "Roll out the barrel."'

Edgar's experiences of the fighting are interesting. He noted that his:

> Intelligence section travelled in three handy 15 cwt trucks and were just about self contained. We had ample ammunition for our rifles and brens and reserve supplies of petrol… I made sure … that we had plenty of cigarettes and bottles of whisky and brandy.

Edgar thought that these preparations were:

> to prove vital in the following days. It gave us a certain confidence, and an army marches – even in trucks – on its stomach. A swig or two of spirits and a cigarette also help to keep up morale. Other units in the area were reduced to begging for food and water.

While Edgar's unit waited for further orders he noticed a 'tall figure in khaki standing on some rising ground … wearing one of those beautifully-tailored near ankle-length great-coats favoured by senior officers. I looked again and saw the red tabs and realized he was probably a Brigadier or General.' Edgar was shocked to see that the officer was 'unshaven and bore marks of dishevelment,' which Edgar considered unforgivable, observing: 'I am shaved. So are my men. That's discipline… Generals should never appear unshaven or unkempt. They must always be immaculately turned-out. It is part of an army's morale!'

In all probability, however, it would have taken more than morale alone to save the British (and indeed French) position in France in May 1940. While awaiting further instructions, Edgar ran into a column of refugees who included in their number a former British soldier of the 1914–18 war. This man, now in his 40s, had met a French girl during that war and returned after leaving the army to marry her and set up a business renting holiday cottages. The man quizzed Edgar about the development of the fighting and after Edgar informed him that he expected the French to counter-attack, the former British soldier, Edgar observed, 'sniffed disbelievingly.'

The evident disbelief was to prove reasonably well founded, as the counter-attacks that were planned, notably the initially successful BEF attack at Arras, soon ran out of steam. Edgar found himself and his men surrounded by the fast-moving German forces. After retreating toward the small French port of Veules, Edgar was given instructions to take a message to his battalion commanding officer at St Valery. When he made the obvious point that 'it won't be easy, Sir, the French tell me that the Germans have cut just about all the roads,' Edgar was told that 'this message must get through.' Edgar and two other men set off, and while they were gone, the officer who had ordered Edgar to St Valery evacuated the rest of the unit.

Edgar managed to rejoin his unit and with men from other units began the march towards the sea. Reaching St Valery, they were told that 'evacuation was now impossible' due to the deteriorating situation, and tentative plans were made to attempt to break through the German lines in small groups. These plans, too, came to nothing with the announcement on 12 June of a ceasefire. Edgar and some 8,000 BEF soldiers went into captivity. Edgar himself survived five years in a German prisoner-of-war camp, but had not fired a single shot in anger during the whole duration of the battle for France.

SOLDIERS OF THE GERMAN AND RUSSIAN EASTERN FRONTS

World War II: The Eastern Front

Geoffrey Jukes

THE GERMAN EASTERN FRONT SOLDIER

Few German soldiers were committed Nazis, but all took into the invasion a faith in Hitler and his generals created by two years of victories, and the younger ones several years of indoctrination in school and the Hitler Youth about German racial superiority. The welcome they received, particularly in Ukraine and the Baltic States, and the enormous early captures of Soviet troops boosted that euphoria, but it faded somewhat after weeks of tramping over seemingly endless plains, and finding that however many of the enemy they killed or captured, more came at them the next day. Panzer crews were shocked to find the newest Soviet tank, the T-34, superior to their hitherto unstoppable Panzer Marks III and IV, but in 1941 there were few of them.

The defeat at Moscow affected morale little; they attributed it more to the weather than to the enemy, and expected to reassert their superiority when summer came. This they duly did, only to suffer another winter disaster at Stalingrad. This depressed them more, but Manstein's successful counter-offensive in February 1943 somewhat restored morale.

The crunch came at Kursk. The Prokhorovka tank battle was the swan song of the Panzers as attack spearheads, until the abortive Ardennes and Balaton offensives of 1945; the infantry for the first time experienced failure in summer, decisive Soviet air superiority and the start of a series of Soviet offensives that dwarfed even that of Stalingrad. Most German soldiers remained disciplined and skillful to the end, but after Kursk they fought in fear of the consequences of defeat rather than in expectation of victory.

A typical German soldier from a tank destroyer unit, who fought in the east from the very first day, summed up his experiences as follows. First encounters with the Red Army suggested they would not be much trouble, but 'things were different later.' Many felt they should not have invaded, but it was not safe to say so. His belief that the war was lost came with the retreat from the Volga in 1942, but he and his comrades expected to be shot if captured, so they fought hard and nobody deserted or defected.

He had a month's home leave in mid-1942; before going on leave soldiers were sent to a transit camp for two weeks, and fed better than usual, so as to make a better impression at home. On leave they were privileged to wear civilian clothes and received extra rations of food and chocolate. He found home front propaganda so untruthful that he listened mostly to the BBC; this was punishable by imprisonment or death, but soldiers sent back to the Soviet Union thought they would probably be killed anyway, so were not deterred. He was shocked by the poor standard of replacements for casualties, and his friends envied him when a leg wound finally removed him from the front. He 'would not wish his worst enemy' to have to fight the Russians.

In the Third Reich's last throes desertions increased, despite the activities of SS execution squads. So many units retreated, to surrender to the Anglo-Americans rather than the Red Army, that General Eisenhower had to threaten to close the Elbe crossings against them. Their fears were not baseless; the Anglo-Americans released most of their prisoners within two years, whereas those taken by the Soviets were kept as forced labour from four to ten years.

THE RUSSIAN EASTERN FRONT SOLDIER

The Red Army had a draconian disciplinary code together with Stalin's 1941 Order 270, which defined 'voluntary surrender' (i.e. if neither wounded nor unconscious) as treason. Yet the first six months saw mass surrenders on an unprecedented scale.

Since only a little over half the Soviet population was Russian, soldiers' attitudes to the war covered as wide a spectrum as the civilian populations from which they came. The instinct for self-preservation kept most in the ranks, but surrender at the first opportunity was rife in 1941, particularly among conscripts from the recently annexed Baltic States and former eastern Poland.

The backbone of the Red Army was the ethnic Russian, mostly a peasant or first-generation urban worker. He retained the hardiness and self-sacrificing qualities of his forebears, but added basic literacy and familiarity with machinery that they lacked. His training and tactics were generally primitive – right until the end of the war, infantry attacked frontally in successive waves, with little regard for casualties; outflanking manoeuvers were usually left to the tanks and motorized infantry. The heavy casualties affected morale less than they might have; they were frequent enough to become regarded as normal, and the soldiers had no basis for comparison with other armies. In the later campaigns, material superiority and experience substantially reduced them, though they remained high compared to what allies and enemies alike regarded as acceptable.

Apart from the first weeks, when some units fled in panic, there was nothing resembling the breakdown of discipline that disrupted the Russian Army in 1917, though there were numerous instances in 1941–42 when NKVD troops were stationed behind the front-line soldiers, to shoot any who ran away. Unlike in World War I, no cases were recorded of collective refusal to obey orders. This owed something to the regime's greater ruthlessness, but probably more to indoctrination. Unlike its predecessor, the Red Army, through its political officers, took much trouble to tell the troops why they were at war, and to inculcate hatred of the invader.

Communist values were not particularly emphasized; membership of the Communist Party was not easily granted, and most troops were below the minimum age for membership. However, Communist Party members in the armed forces were expected to set an example to the rest, and many set one good enough for soldiers' applications to join the Party to rise, especially on the eve of major campaigns.

The cult of Stalin was all-pervading, but it was only in films that soldiers went into battle shouting 'For the Motherland! For Stalin!' Many would, much later, admit putting more trust in God, others that they went into the assault shouting obscenities. One who ended the war in Berlin recollected that:

> … luxuries such as leave seldom came our way. Food was monotonous but usually adequate, clothing, especially for winter, much better than the Germans had, but small amenities such as playing cards, dominoes, writing materials or musical instruments were scarce, and usually the first things we looted when we took a German position. Correspondence was censored, and we learned not to criticize our leaders, especially Stalin, because such criticisms attracted heavier punishment

than disclosure of military secrets. We knew few of those anyway, because we were only told what we were going to do at the last moment, or sometimes not at all, and the command we mostly heard from our officers was just 'follow me.' Most of our officers earned our respect for their readiness to lead, but we wished they had been trained to do more than just take us to attack the Germans head on. We respected the Germans as soldiers, and to begin with many of us doubted our own propaganda about German atrocities. But when we began recapturing territory and seeing what they had done there, we came to hate them, and when we reached German soil some of us vented our hatred on German civilians, even on some who claimed to be Communists, in ways I still shudder to think of. As the war ended, Stalin ordered us to change our attitude to the German people, and even to start feeding them. That did cut down the amount of murder and rape, but it didn't stop us looting, or beating up any Germans who didn't accept that they were the losers.

LIEUTENANT THOMAS CURRIE DERRICK VC, AUSTRALIAN SOLDIER

World War II: The Pacific

David Horner

Like most American and Australian soldiers in the Pacific War, Thomas Currie Derrick was a child of the Great Depression. With his limited education, army service gave him opportunities that would never have been available in civilian life. Although he was to become one of the Australian Army's most courageous and accomplished soldiers, the story of his life is otherwise representative of the thousands of young men who volunteered 'for the duration.'

Born in Adelaide, South Australia, in 1914, Tom Derrick left school at 14, but could only find odd jobs. As the Depression deepened, aged 16, he rode with some mates on their bikes about 140 miles to the Murray River irrigation area, seeking itinerant work in the vineyards and orchards. Cheerful and hardworking, he was often up to mischief, but enjoyed football, boxing, gambling and the company of his mates, who gave him the nickname 'Diver.' By 1939 he had gained steady employment in a vineyard and was able to marry his long-time sweetheart, Beryl. Newly married, Derrick hesitated to volunteer for the army when war was declared in September 1939, but, loyal to his country, and also to his mates who had joined, he persuaded Beryl, who eventually relented. Like others, he was influenced by Germany's invasion of France in May 1940, and next month he enlisted in the 2/48th Battalion, then being raised in Adelaide.

Used to hard living, Derrick thrived on army life, but he found discipline difficult to accept. The battalion sailed for the Middle East in November, but stopped for a week at Perth. Confined to ship after going absent for sightseeing, he was taunted by another soldier, who punched him. In a letter home Derrick wrote, 'Got clocked last night, broke teeth and cut lip. I then got stuck into him, made a real job of him. On another [charge] now for fighting.' Although only 5ft 7in. tall, Derrick was strong and wiry, with plenty of fighting experience. The commanding officer fined him 30 shillings.

Between April and October 1941 the battalion – part of the 9th Australian Division – helped defend the besieged port of Tobruk, in Libya. Derrick was soon leading his section and was promoted to corporal. He was recommended for a Military Medal. It was richly deserved but was not awarded.

Back in action in July 1942, the battalion attacked a German–Italian position near El Alamein. Derrick's leadership was inspirational. Hurling grenades, he personally destroyed three machine gun posts and captured more than a hundred prisoners. When the Germans counter-attacked, he destroyed two enemy tanks and restored the position. He was awarded the Distinguished Conduct Medal and promoted to sergeant. Derrick was also in the thick of the fighting at El Alamein in late October. Those present thought that he should have earned the Victoria Cross. In a week of savage combat the battalion lost more than 400 men. Derrick had been slightly wounded.

The 9th Division returned to Australia, and Derrick enjoyed his leave with Beryl in Adelaide in February 1943. Then the battalion took the long train journey to the Atherton Tableland in north Queensland, where it began intensive jungle training in preparation for operations against the Japanese. Valuable lessons from the 1942 Papuan campaign were incorporated into the training, and platoons learned to patrol silently in the jungle.

The battalion also practised amphibious operations with the US 532nd Engineer Shore and Boat Battalion. Derrick wrote, 'Spent morning embarking and debarking – find there is little to it and should not take many attempts to become really efficient.'

Lieutenant Murray Farquar, an officer in Derrick's battalion, recalled that Derrick met a young American soldier from Wisconsin, still in his teens, from the Shore and Boat Battalion. They adjourned to a hotel, where civilians and soldiers were:

> elbowing their way forward to replenish their glasses. In turn this young Yank pressed forward. He became the target of what was, at first, only good-humoured banter. One or two louts soon became vicious. Finally, backed up by a team of six or seven, one spat out, 'If you think you'll get out of here, Yank, without a few teeth smashed in, you've got another thing coming.' This aggressor was a real lump of a man. Quickly Diver sized things up. Stepping in front of his new mate, he stated: 'Well, you'll have to go through me first.' No histrionics, just a quiet statement of intent.

Staring this mob out, he held his ground… There were a few rumbles, they shrugged shoulders, and turned back to their drinking … finishing his beer, Diver exclaimed, 'Well, come on Yank. We'll try another pub.' The confrontation was over; Diver had won yet another ardent admirer.

Derrick merely wrote in his diary, 'Nought to do today … Murray Farquar and myself went into Cairns, teamed up with a Yank and had a most enjoyable day.'

In August 1943 the battalion sailed for Milne Bay in New Guinea. After arriving, Derrick wrote in his diary:

Slept on some very wet ground and was surprised to find I had a very comfortable and dry sleep. Seen my first glimpse of the Fuzzy Wuzzy's [sic] who appear very friendly. The camp is situated midst a huge coconut plantation, my first effort to climb a palm ended at 30 feet. But I think I can master it. The average height seems to be almost 45 feet.

The battalion landed near Lae in September, and by November was attacking the heights of Sattelberg, overlooking Finschhafen. The Allied advance hinged on clearing both sides of the Vitiaz Strait. Sattelberg dominated the mainland side. On 17 November the battalion led the brigade attack, but by 24 November the attack was grinding to a halt, the battalion suffering casualties. Late that day Derrick was leading the advance platoon when the battalion commander ordered a withdrawal. Derrick appealed to his company commander, 'Bugger the CO. Just give me twenty minutes and we'll have this place.'

It was a one-man front up an almost vertical incline covered in jungle. Covered by his platoon members, Derrick alone clambered up the cliff, holding on with one hand, throwing grenades with another, pausing to fire his rifle. He cleared ten machine gun posts before, at dusk, he reached an open patch, just short of the crest. Fifteen Japanese dead remained on the spur. Derrick's platoon occupied the area. That night the remaining Japanese withdrew. Awarded the Victoria Cross, Derrick said that the achievement was due mainly to his mates.

When the battalion returned to Australia for leave and more training, Derrick attended an officer training course. Although lacking formal education, he had a great thirst for knowledge. In November 1944 he returned as a lieutenant to his battalion on the Atherton Tableland. Friends thought that he should not have returned; after three campaigns he had 'done his bit.' But he merely replied, 'My boys are back there, I must be with them.'

On 1 May 1945 the 2/48th Battalion was part of the Australian landing on Tarakan, Borneo. The Japanese fiercely resisted attempts to clear the island. On 23 May Derrick's platoon led the assault on a position known as Freda. One soldier recalled: 'At Diver's signal, we smashed forward. Grenades burst among us. Diver was everywhere, encouraging, shouting orders, pressing us on.' Those present thought that his actions were worthy of a bar to his Victoria Cross. The Australians took the knoll but expected a Japanese counter-attack that night. At about 3.00am Japanese machine guns fired down a track where Derrick was sleeping. He sat up to assess the direction of the fire. Another burst of fire struck him in the abdomen. 'I've been hit. I think it's curtains,' he said. 'I've copped it in the fruit and nuts' (rhyming slang for 'the guts'). He insisted that the other wounded be evacuated first, and died the next day.

Apart from his extraordinary feats on the battlefield, Derrick was typical of the Australian soldier who enlisted in the early years of the war. He learned his trade of soldiering against the Germans and Italians in the Middle East and then returned to deal with the Japanese. With few advantages in life, he had come to rely on his mates and applied himself to any task. His ever-present grin and outgoing leadership masked a sensitive and reflective side. He collected butterflies, composed poetry, kept a diary and wrote regularly and frequently to his wife. After the war he would have happily returned to the Murray River fruit blocks.

Raised as a Salvationist, Derrick was not overtly religious. In the Middle East, in February 1942, he wrote, 'Changed my church today, went to Catholic parade – doubt if I'm improved any.' During his evacuation on Tarakan, he asked a friend to get the padre so that he could 'bring on the hocus pocus.' Cheerful to the end, he had done his duty as he saw it. It was men like him who made the Australian Army a formidable force in the south-west Pacific.

CAPTAIN CHARLES HAZLITT UPHAM VC AND BAR, NEW ZEALAND SOLDIER

World War II: The Mediterranean

Paul Collier

Charles Hazlitt Upham is the only combat soldier, and one of only three men ever, to have twice been awarded the Victoria Cross for outstanding gallantry and leadership, in Crete in May 1941 and at Ruweisat Ridge, Egypt in July 1942. Upham was born on 21 September 1908 in Christchurch, New Zealand, and was educated at Christ's College and Canterbury Agricultural College. From an early age he was quiet, unusually determined, and developed a spirit of independence that bordered on belligerence towards authority, which he would only accept when shown that it was right. Above all Upham abhorred injustice, a characteristic that grew in intensity and indicated the force of his personality.

Upham aspired to a simple life on the land. He spent six years as a shepherd, musterer and farm manager, on high-country sheep stations, and prior to the war was a government farm valuer. In 1938 he became engaged to Mary (Molly) Eileen McTamney, a nurse he had met at the races, but they had only a few happy months together before she left New Zealand for Singapore and then London, where she remained throughout the war. While living in the harsh conditions of the rugged high country, Upham honed his natural skills of survival, observation and understanding the lie of the land and acquired the physical toughness, strong stamina and cool temperament – as well as a large vocabulary of expletives – that would serve him so well during his war in the Mediterranean.

When World War II broke out in September 1939 Upham, aged 30, immediately enlisted out of a conviction that he wanted to fight for justice and stop the Nazis. His first task as a soldier, however, was more mundane. Because of his agricultural training, he was ordered to lay down a lawn around Burnham Camp Headquarters in Christchurch, which he saw as futile to the war and completed under great protest because he missed bayonet training. But from the beginning of his military service he displayed leadership, a tactical flair and an intense desire to master the practical skills of the soldier's craft, inherent qualities that would be nourished by warfare. Promoted to corporal, Upham led his men in training exercises that he made extremely realistic and rapidly became noticed as a committed commander by both his men and his superior officers. Nevertheless, he rejected a place in an officer cadet training unit (OCTU), preferring instead to embark for Egypt with the advance party of the 2nd New Zealand Expeditionary Force in December 1939 as a sergeant in the 20th Canterbury–Otago Battalion.

Upham was intent on learning the essentials of fighting and becoming skilled in using the bayonet, machine gun and grenade. He showed no inclination for the parade ground, where he was well known for making a bungle of any drill, or respect for army conventions or rank. His intolerance of anything not directly of benefit to the war and his forthright, outspoken nature often led him to disagree bluntly with superior officers. Despite his insubordination and impatience to fight, in July 1940 Upham was persuaded to join an OCTU. Due to his outspoken opinions and his tendency to question almost everything, however, he was highly unpopular with the British officers. Upham was particularly critical of the lack of consideration that was given to the problems caused by tanks and aircraft, and felt that the tactics being used relied too much on the methods that had been successful in World War I. As a result he was placed last in his course, but was commissioned as a second lieutenant on 2 November 1940.

Upham was posted to 15 Platoon, C Company, 20th Battalion, tough men from the rugged west coast of the South Island of New Zealand, but he quickly won their respect as a capable officer who made them train hard but was equally concerned for their safety and comfort.

In March 1941 the New Zealand Division was sent to Greece. While the campaign rapidly developed into a withdrawal, Upham was seriously ill with dysentery. He was unable to eat anything but condensed milk, which his men scrounged for him from every source, and he became very weak as his weight diminished. He was soon unable to walk, but his battalion became accustomed to seeing him astride a donkey, which he insisted on using to ride along the hillsides between his section posts and headquarters.

Upham and his men were successfully evacuated to Crete and when the German airborne invasion began on 20 May they were positioned around Maleme Airfield, the centre of the assault. Upham was in the thick of the fighting from the beginning and soon became celebrated among his comrades not only for his daring but also for his skill at out-thinking the enemy at close quarters. He was renowned for combining controlled courage with quick-thinking resourcefulness, and for his implacable determination to kill as many German soldiers as he could. While most medals for bravery are awarded for a single act, Upham's citation for his first Victoria Cross was for a sustained series of remarkable exploits and conspicuous heroism, showing outstanding leadership, tactical skill and indifference to danger over nine days between 22 and 30 May.

After four of his men were shot on 22 May, Upham was possessed by 'an icy fury' and personally dealt with several machine gun posts at close quarters using his favourite attacking weapon, the hand grenade. When his platoon withdrew, Upham helped to carry a wounded man out under fire, rallied more men together to carry other wounded men out, and then went back through over 600 yards (550m) of enemy territory to bring out another company that had become isolated and would have been completely cut off but for his action.

During the following two days, his platoon was continuously under fire. Upham was blown over by one mortar shell, painfully wounded behind his left shoulder by a piece of shrapnel from another and was shot, receiving a bullet in the ankle that was removed two weeks later in Egypt. Although he was also still suffering from dysentery, Upham disregarded his wounds and remained on duty, refusing to go to hospital.

One incident, in particular, during this action typified Upham's deeds. At Galatas on 25 May his platoon was heavily engaged and came under severe mortar and machine gun fire. They killed over 40 Germans, but when ordered to retire Upham went forward to warn other troops that they were being cut off. Two German soldiers trapped him alone on the fringes of an olive grove and his platoon watched a helpless distance away on the other side of the clearing as they fired on him. With any movement potentially fatal, he feigned death and with calculated coolness waited for the enemy soldiers to approach. With one arm now lame in a sling, he used the crook of a tree to support his rifle and shot the first assailant, reloaded with one hand, and shot the second who was so close as to fall against the barrel of his rifle.

During the whole course of the operations, Upham showed great skill, complete disregard of danger and superb coolness even though he was wounded, battered and very weak, still suffering from dysentery and able to eat only very little. He looked like a 'walking skeleton,' exhausted and with his wounds festering, but his determination never faltered and he had to be literally dragged on to an evacuation ship. His outstanding courage, conduct and leadership inspired his whole platoon to fight magnificently throughout, and in fact was an inspiration to the battalion. Nevertheless, Upham was genuinely distressed to be singled out for a Victoria Cross. He believed that many others deserved the honour more than he did, and could only cope with the award and the unwelcome fame that went with it by seeing it as recognition of the bravery and service of the men of his unit. He even refused to wear his medal ribbon until directly ordered to do so. But Upham did keep a promise he made to his men in the heat of the battle, and took the only five who survived death, capture or injury to a slap-up meal at Shepherd's, the top hotel in Cairo.

In November 1941 Upham was promoted to lieutenant but was mortified when his commanding officer, Lieutenant-Colonel Kippenberger, decided to leave him out of Operation *Crusader* because he believed that Upham was fretting for more action and would get himself killed too quickly. Experienced men like Upham were required to rebuild his battalion after its heavy losses, and in May 1942 he was promoted to captain and made company commander. After suffering bouts of pneumonia and jaundice, Upham went with the New Zealanders to Syria, where they prepared positions to resist a possible German advance through Turkey and continued their battle training.

Following Rommel's assault at Gazala, the New Zealand Division was rushed to the Western Desert, where it joined the Eighth Army to stop his advance in the first battle of El Alamein. In these operations Upham performed five acts of conspicuous gallantry that would have earned two VCs in their own right, but three awards to one man was unheralded.

On 27 June, the New Zealand Division attempted to halt the German advance at Minqar Qaim Ridge. Although the air was thick with tank, artillery, mortar and machine gun fire, Upham ran across the open ground from one section post to another, rousing his men to stand firm. Wearing only a soft cap, since he rarely ever wore a tin helmet because they would not fit the size of his head, to the bewilderment of his men at one point he even climbed on top of a truck so he could identify the enemy positions that were decimating his company. The New Zealanders held off the sustained attacks but became encircled by the Germans, cutting off their line of retreat. During the night they broke out, with Upham leading from the front, inspiring his men in savage hand-to-hand fighting. His encouraging voice was heard above the noise of battle as he rushed numerous enemy vehicles, heedless of the fire pouring at him, destroying them all with grenades and regardless of wounding himself in the explosions.

During the New Zealander's attack on Ruweisat Ridge on 14–15 July Upham was instructed to send up an officer to report progress of the attack. Typically he went himself and, after several sharp encounters with enemy machine gun posts, succeeded in bringing back the required information. Just before dawn 20th Battalion was ordered forward, but it encountered very heavy fire from a strongly defended enemy locality. Upham, without hesitation, led his company in a determined bayonet charge. A machine gun bullet shattered his arm but he personally destroyed several machine gun posts, a tank and several guns and vehicles with grenades. Exhausted by pain and weak from loss of blood, Upham was then removed to the regimental aid post, but immediately his wound had been dressed he returned to his men. He held his position under heavy artillery and mortar fire until he was again severely wounded in the leg by shrapnel. Unable to move, Upham fell into the hands of the enemy when his position was finally overrun, his gallant company having been reduced to only six survivors despite his outstanding gallantry and magnificent leadership.

In abhorrent conditions Italian doctors attempted to amputate his arm without anaesthetic, but Upham stubbornly refused and probably saved his own life. He recuperated from his wounds in an Italian hospital and was then sent to a prisoner of war camp but, typifying his character and nickname, 'Pug,' he soon began a private war with his captors by making increasingly daring efforts to escape. In his first attempt he leapt from a truck, with German SS guards firing at him. He was transferred to Germany in September 1943 and was involved in several escape plots, including an audacious solo attempt to scale the barbed wire fences in broad daylight in which he was lucky not to be shot. The Germans eventually branded Upham as dangerous and in October 1944 he was incarcerated in the infamous prison fortress Colditz Castle. But even during his journey there he made another risky escape attempt that involved leaping from the toilet window of a moving train in the middle of the night.

When Upham was liberated in April 1945, he was keen to see action again. Instead, he was sent to Britain, where he was reunited with and married Molly McTamney, who was then serving as a nurse, and on 11 May King George VI presented Upham with an official Victoria Cross. In September 1945 he returned to New Zealand to resume life as a sheep farmer.

Shortly after returning home, Upham learned that he was to receive a bar to his Victoria Cross. The award caused much attention to be showered on him, but he modestly said only: 'Naturally I feel some pride in this distinction, but hundreds of others have done more than I did. They could have given it to one of them.' Upham always insisted that the military honours were the property of the men of his unit and claimed that he would have been happier not to have been awarded the Victoria Cross because it made people expect too much of him, saying: 'I don't want to be treated any differently from any other bastard.' He hated the popularity and remained a tough and forthright Kiwi in spite of his fame.

A modest and reluctant hero, who evoked fierce loyalty and friendship from everyone who knew him, Upham never saw himself as anything other than a New Zealander doing his duty. He was genuinely embarrassed by the publicity and accolades he received and attempted to avoid international media attention. Upham turned down a knighthood and refused to accept land offered to returning servicemen after the war. The people of Canterbury raised £10,000 by public donation to buy him a farm but he declined the offer, requesting instead that the money be placed into an educational trust that would help the sons of servicemen attend university. Upham bought land at the mouth of the River Conway, North Canterbury, with a rehabilitation loan and, although hampered by the injuries to his arm, turned it into a successful farm through his own hard work. He and Molly had three daughters and lived on their farm for the remainder of his years, avoiding the spotlight of fame that the media occasionally tried to shine on him. Even at the end of his life, when a state funeral was mentioned, Upham was said to remark: 'A bugle will do.'

Charles Upham died on 22 November 1994 in Christchurch, New Zealand. He was a formidable soldier and a natural leader who was able to shrewdly assess situations, weigh up risks and quickly decide on a course of action. He was utterly fearless and tenaciously single-minded, but his implacable hatred of Nazi Germany and its allies certainly played a part in his success. When asked how he had become the only person in living memory to receive two Victoria Crosses, he just said: 'I hated Germans.' It was a sentiment that mellowed only slightly with the passing of years, as his obituary noted: 'It was said that no German-made car was ever driven onto Charlie Upham's farm.'

DONALD BURGETT, 506TH PIR

World War II: Northwest Europe

Russell and Stephen Hart

Sprinting low to the ground, his feet surrounded by bursts of machine gun fire, Donald Burgett glanced over his shoulder to glimpse a German Tiger tank lurching toward him. It was 19 December 1944, in a field on the north-eastern outskirts of Noville, near Bastogne in the Belgian Ardennes. Intense enemy fire had just set alight the haystack in which Burgett had sought cover, and now the raging flames forced him to dash across the open, snow-covered fields back toward the shelter of nearby houses – a dash that would expose him to deadly enemy fire.

Luckily making it unscathed to a nearby house, Burgett rushed into a room to find two of his squad buddies already hiding there. Looking back through the glassless window frame, however, the paratroopers saw the Tiger approaching the house, and so dashed out of the back door. Within seconds the tank had advanced so that its gun barrel actually pointed through what used to be the front window of the house; then it fired its lethal 88mm cannon. Burgett scarcely avoided the tons of ruined brick that came crashing down on his nearby hiding place as the building's back wall disintegrated. He had survived this close shave, he mused, but for how long could he avoid that lethal enemy bullet 'that had his name marked on it?'

By now a campaign veteran – he had dropped from the skies on D-Day, 6 June 1944 – Burgett realized that the battle at Noville had been his most terrifying combat experience to date. However, luckily for historians, Burgett not only survived the campaign, but also wrote down his recollections not long after VE-Day and then published them in a poignant memoir, *Seven Roads to Hell*, during the 1990s.

During the campaign, Burgett served as a private in the 2nd Platoon, A Company, 506th Parachute Infantry Regiment, part of the elite 101st US Airborne Division – the 'Screaming Eagles.' Born in Detroit, Michigan, in April 1926, he volunteered for the paratroopers in April 1943, on the day of his 18th birthday, having been previously turned down for being too young. On the night of 5/6 June 1944, he dropped with the rest of the 'Screaming Eagles' behind German lines in the Cotentin peninsula to aid the imminent American D-Day landings on 'Utah' beach. On 13 June he was wounded twice in bitter fighting near Carentan, first by a grenade detonation that left him temporarily deaf, and then by a shell fragment that tore open his left side. After three weeks in hospital, he returned to his division, which soon came out of the front line for much-needed replenishment.

Burgett then dropped with his division around Zon in Holland on 17 September 1944, as part of Montgomery's ambitious *Market Garden* offensive. After fighting its way north through Nijmegen, Burgett's company held the front near Arnhem for nine weeks of mostly static actions amid sodden low-lying terrain. Eventually, on 28 November, after 72 days' continuous action, the 'Screaming Eagles' redeployed to northern France for rest and recuperation. On 17 December 1944, as news filtered through about the success achieved by the surprise German Ardennes counter-offensive, Burgett's division rushed north to help defend the vital road junction at Bastogne. During 19 and 20 December, Burgett's company resolutely defended Noville against the determined attacks launched by the 2nd Panzer Division. The next day, the Germans outflanked the 506th Regiment, forcing the Americans to conduct a costly withdrawal south through the village of Foy. Over the next week, however, in a series of bitter engagements, Burgett's company helped drive the

Germans back to the start lines they had held prior to the commencement of their counter-strike.

Burgett's recollections vividly captured the brutal realities of combat in the north-west Europe campaign – the diseases that afflicted soldiers, the terrible wounds suffered in battle, the awful food on which they had to subsist and the intense emotions generated by these experiences. For example, he recalled with horror the diseases that lengthy exposure to Holland's wet conditions caused among the front-line troops. Burgett himself suffered from trench mouth, an ailment that made his gums ooze with pus and left his teeth so loose that he could easily move them with his tongue. Although penicillin eventually cured him, he then succumbed to trench foot after his boots disintegrated due to the length of his continuous front-line service in sodden terrain.

Scabies was another problem from which Burgett's company suffered in Holland, an unpleasant condition where microscopic parasites develop under the skin, causing insatiable itching. Such a disease flourished in the unhygienic conditions in which the paratroopers often served. Indeed, while in the front line near Arnhem, Burgett's comrades only occasionally managed to take what they termed a 'whore's bath' – a quick scrub of the head, armpits and crotch with icy cold water collected in their helmets. It was only when the division went on leave in France during late October 1944 that Burgett managed to take his first hot shower in ten weeks!

Sanitary arrangements, too, were often rudimentary. During the 101st Division's dash north to Bastogne on a bitterly cold 17 December, for example, the 380 open-topped cattle trucks that carried the paratroopers did not halt at all during the 24-hour journey, not even for a quick toilet stop. This meant that those unfortunate soldiers who could not wait any longer had to perform their bodily functions over the back of the truck's tail gate.

Such lack of hygiene, of course, proved a particularly serious problem for those paratroopers unlucky enough to be wounded in battle. Burgett recalled the moment during the savage 19 December battle for Noville when a new replacement soldier suddenly ran into view around the corner of a building, screaming in agony. Enemy fire had caught him in the stomach, and in his arms he carried most of his intestines, the remainder dragging along the ground through the dirt.

It took Burgett and two of his squad to hold down the sobbing soldier so that they could carry out emergency first aid. Laying a tattered raincoat down on the ground, the paratroopers placed the injured man on it and proceeded to wash his entrails, picking out the larger bits of dirt as best they could, before shoving his guts back inside his wide-open abdomen. They then tore the raincoat into strips, bound the man's midriff with this filthy makeshift bandage, and gave him the vital shot of morphine that each soldier carried. Finally, they dragged the wounded private into the relative safety of a nearby ditch while another trooper dashed off in search of a medic – all this being undertaken while enemy artillery rained down on their location. While such desperate measures undoubtedly saved many wounded soldiers' lives, the filthy conditions in which the wounds were either inflicted or initially treated often subsequently led soldiers to succumb to virulent infections.

Apart from the ever-present fear of death or serious injury, the other concern that dominated the paratroopers' lives, Burgett recalled, was food. A soldier's aluminum mess kit – bowl, knife and fork – was his most important possession next to his weapon. If a soldier lost his mess kit in action, there were seldom any replacements, and the luckless individual had to use his helmet to take his ration from the regimental field kitchen. In tactical situations that allowed soldiers to draw food from the field kitchen, Burgett would always sprint to the front of the queue, then wolf down his food – just on the off-chance that if he rushed to the back of the queue, there might just be enough left over for some meager seconds.

For much of the time at the front, however, the fighting prevented hot food from reaching the troops, and then the soldiers had to subsist on boiling up their dehydrated K-Rations and 'consuming' their D-Bars. The unpopular K-Rations were stodgy, lumpy and tasteless substances but – as Burgett recollected – if you had not eaten for several days, even K-Rations could taste tolerable. Even more unpopular, however, was the D-Bar, a mouldy-tasting so-called chocolate bar. These were so hard, Burgett maintained, that you could not smash one with your rifle butt, or melt it by boiling! Burgett insisted that he never successfully managed to consume a single bar throughout the campaign.

Apart from fear, disease, discomfort and hunger, many of the other emotions that Burgett experienced during the campaign stayed with him. He vividly remembered, for instance, the odd little superstitions that some soldiers held. Many paratroopers from America's southern states would never take the first sip out of a liquid container that had a closed lid: as you opened the lid, so the old wives' tale went, the devil lurking inside would get you. Burgett also recollected that when a veteran 'old sweat' experienced a premonition of his own impending death, very often that individual would be killed by enemy fire in the following days.

Although Burgett himself did not experience any such frightening premonitions, he was well acquainted with the phenomenon of abject terror. He recalled, for example, the sense of mind-numbing fear that overwhelmed him during one phase of the battle for Noville. He lay, heart pounding and sick with nausea, in the bottom of a slit trench just outside the town, while German Panther tanks moved round the American positions, systematically spraying the frozen ground with their machine guns. With no bazookas or satchel charges available, Burgett and his comrades had no choice but to press their bodies into the mud at the bottom of their trenches and pray that the tanks did not come close enough to collapse the trench on top of them. The fear of a horrible death by crushing or suffocation effectively paralyzed him and left him almost unable to breathe. Burgett even remembered that at one point the enemy tanks were so close that he could feel the heat of their engines warming the bitter winter air.

Perhaps surprisingly, even when the enemy came as close to Burgett as they had at Noville, he merely regarded them as abstract objects – either you killed them first, or else they killed you. Rarely did the enemy individuals whom he faced in close quarter combat register as human beings in his mind for more than a few hours. Usually, the immediate requirements of staying alive and accomplishing the mission took priority over any sense of compassion for his opponents.

One particular German soldier, however, stayed in Burgett's mind long after the war had ended. The incident occurred in late December 1944, as the paratroopers drove the Germans back to the positions that they had held before the Ardennes counter-offensive commenced. In a dense wood, Burgett came across a wounded, and obviously helpless, enemy soldier. As Burgett contemplated what to do, one of his comrades stepped up and shot the German dead. Burgett exploded in anger, grabbed his comrade and threatened to blow his brains out if he ever again shot a German who was attempting to surrender. For the rest of the campaign, in quiet moments between engagements, the imploring face of this anonymous enemy soldier would return to haunt Burgett's thoughts.

Few sources reveal the often unpleasant realities that ordinary soldiers faced in war better than a soldier's memoirs written close to the events. This certainly remains true of Donald Burgett's recollections. Whether it be the strange superstitions, the unpleasant rations or the heroism of emergency first aid dispensed to a wounded comrade while under enemy fire, any study of the north-west Europe campaign is enriched by drawing on such vivid memories of those individuals who participated in its events.

MODERN
WARFARE

There is no training that prepares a soldier for all of this.
The shocking violence and visual horrors of infantry
fighting are far beyond anything imaginable...
When we lost men, we lost brothers.

(John Young)

But anything is better than dying. If I have a son
I will never let him go to war until he is old enough to
understand and make up his own mind. I was too young
to fight. I was a little boy who wanted to play with guns.
When they gave me a real one I'd never been happier.
But when I went to fight and shoot people, I was petrified.

(Samir, boy soldier)

CORPORAL MARTIN RUSS, US MARINES

The Korean War 1950–53

Carter Malkasian

After November 1951, operations on the front settled into static warfare. Corporal Martin Russ served in the 1st US Marine Division in the last year of the war. Russ joined the Marines after completing his undergraduate education at St Laurence College. He was a member of Able Company, 1st Marine Regiment. During his time in Korea, he kept a daily journal of his experiences. It was later published as a book, *The Last Parallel*.

As a corporal, Russ was a non-commissioned officer. He carried a Browning automatic rifle (BAR), a 20lb light machine gun that provided rapid and long-range fire. Most infantry carried the semi-automatic M1 Garand Rifle. Another valuable item in Russ' kit was his armoured flak vest. The flak vest made its first appearance in Korea. It contained fibreglass or nylon padding that reduced the impact of shell fragments but could not stop a bullet. By 1953, the vest had become a standard piece of personal equipment.

As static warfare set in, the Eighth Army front line began to resemble the Western Front of World War I. The front line consisted of a Main Line of Resistance (MLR) and a line of outposts. The MLR was a string of mutually supporting strong points, constructed to absorb and stop any enemy blow. Outposts were forward of the MLR within no man's land. They served to detect and slow an enemy advance. Bunkers, several aprons of barbed wire and minefields protected most defensive positions. Bunkers were largely underground, with a roof of thick logs and sandbags to protect against artillery and mortar hits. Underground passageways often connected several bunkers. Each outpost and various points in no man's land were pinpointed so that mortars and artillery could deliver quick and accurate fire. Generally around half a mile (0.8km) wide, no man's land became familiar territory for both sides. In Russ' sector, it was littered with empty ration cans, discarded weapons, minefields, patrol paths, a burnt-out tank, downed Corsairs and dead men.

Russ' platoon occupied an outpost, New Bunker Hill, for 16 days in March 1953. He defended a listening post within the front-line trench with one other man. There was a bunker directly behind his position and barbed wire in front of it. Further to the rear, there was another bunker for sleeping. During the night, Chinese snipers observed and intermittently fired on New Bunker Hill. Russ always had to keep his head down and sleep curled up.

Patrols into no man's land were conducted both day and night. The object of a patrol was generally reconnaissance or combat. A reconnaissance patrol observed and kept contact with the enemy, reporting on unit identification, headquarters, locations and the layout of his forward defences. Combat patrols sought to fight the enemy, usually through staging an ambush or probing a Communist outpost. Patrols varied in size from a mere fire team to an entire platoon. Most front-line UNC companies conducted one patrol per night. Raids were conducted in platoon to battalion strength. They were mounted in order to seize a small outpost, capture prisoners or simply harass the enemy.

Russ became adept at patrolling. He learned how to move stealthily and guide a patrol as a point man. The Chinese frequently fired upon these patrols with mortars and machine guns and, on a number of occasions, Russ engaged in actual firefights. In the dark, the enemy was rarely seen and aiming consisted of firing as much ammunition as possible in the general direction of the enemy's muzzle flashes. In April 1953, Russ became an acting squad leader and began leading more patrols.

For many UNC units, patrolling and raids proved burdensome. Raiding enemy outposts and capturing prisoners resulted in hard-fought battles and heavy casualties. Russ recorded that one proposed raid to capture a prisoner required 50 men, all of the regimental artillery and mortars, three tanks, two flame-throwing tanks and a flight of Corsairs. Russ was very sceptical about American estimates of Chinese casualties from raids and patrols. He wrote of one particular estimate:

> We scoffed at the estimate of Chinese casualties. From the little experience I've had in raids and from the stories I've heard of other raids, I'll bet the Chinese suffered half the number of casualties that we had. When we raid the Chinese, we get clobbered. When the Chinese raid the marines, they get clobbered worse. But they are a bit more intelligent about it; they don't make raids very often.

Nevertheless, formations that did not control no man's land, unlike the Marine or the Commonwealth divisions, suffered heavy casualties and lost terrain to Communist surprise attacks.

Shortly before the end of the war, Russ was temporarily sent to Fox Company. Able Company was about to relieve them and Russ was to familiarize himself with Fox' position and no man's land in that area. On his second night with Fox Company, Russ joined a 30-man combat patrol sent out to assault an enemy outpost. As the column approached the objective, the point man discovered a trip wire across the path. The lieutenant followed the trip wire into a clump of bushes. Then, a burst of fire brought him down. The patrol had walked into a Chinese ambush. Russ described the following moments:

> A tremendous volume of fire, coming from our right front, at a distance varying from twenty to fifty yards. These were the first muzzle blasts I noticed... Fire of

equal intensity came from our left but at a greater distance. The ambush had been deployed in an inverted V formation and the fire from its apex was obviously the most deadly.

Nine of the first ten Marines in the column were hit. A staff sergeant died in hand-to-hand combat trying to rescue the lieutenant, who was captured. Further back, after overcoming his surprise, Russ began to return fire with the BAR, along with the remaining members of the patrol. The firefight lasted for less than five minutes. Once the Marines had suppressed the Chinese fire, they aggressively began to withdraw.

The Chinese were still trying to surround the patrol and the Marines had to fight their way out. Moving back down the path, Russ spotted two Chinese approaching two prone Marines in a ditch less than 50ft away. Later, Russ wrote what happened as the Chinese tried to drag one of the Marines away:

I was mesmerized… It's taken me a month to even think about writing a description… The BAR was not in firing position; it was necessary to bring it up from my side. I did this quickly, planting both elbows on the ground with an audible thud. I squeezed off an unnecessarily long burst before the Chinese could react. The muzzle blast was blinding… When my eyes became again accustomed to the dark, I saw that one of the Chinese lay crumpled up near the edge of the paddy. The other was nowhere in sight. The Marine had been dragged only a few feet and ankles protruded from the first level or step of the paddy. At this moment – as I took notice of these things – I was fired upon from that area in which the two Chinese had appeared… I heaved grenades in that direction. After the explosions I could still hear people moving around in the paddy. Someone fell noisily into a puddle off to the left.

Of the two prone Marines, one was a corpsman (medic) playing dead and the other was unconscious. Russ and the corpsman lifted the unconscious Marine and withdrew to friendly lines. Six Marines were killed, 14 were wounded and one was captured in the ambush. Chinese casualties were impossible to estimate in the confusion and uncertainty of night fighting.

Russ safely returned to the USA at the end of the war. In his last month in Korea, he was promoted to sergeant, a job whose duties he had been performing for some time as acting squad leader. He also earned a Purple Heart. Tiny splinters from a grenade and barbed wire had injured him during a combat patrol in May. He went on to write several books on Marines in combat in World War II, Korea and Vietnam.

JOHN YOUNG, INFANTRY SQUAD LEADER, 9TH INFANTRY

The Vietnam War 1956–1975

Andy Wiest

John Young served as Squad Leader in the 9th Infantry in the Mobile Riverine Force in the Mekong Delta in 1967. He holds the Combat Infantryman's Badge, three Bronze Stars for valour, a Purple Heart, two Air Medals and the Vietnamese Cross for Gallantry.

In mid-May 1966 I was near the end of my third year of college at the University of Minnesota. Exactly one year later I was an infantry squad leader in Vietnam. The year in between was the last year that I was young. Of course it was a different world then. Certainly it was a different United States. The Cold War put an edge on life, but we were a confident people, with no reason to doubt that we could deal with whatever the world might send us.

Looking back, it is hard to believe that we were once so innocent. For 190 years the United States had built on an almost unbroken record of success, and the little war in south-east Asia that we seemed to have stumbled into was surely no cause to fear for our future. Quite the contrary: my father and all his brothers, and all of my mother's brothers, had served in World War II, and Vietnam was simply my generation's call to duty. I honestly wanted to serve. There was not the least doubt in my mind that what the US was doing in Vietnam was right. The US was always right, and this was a challenge that John Kennedy might have had in mind when he spoke of 'supporting any friend,' 'opposing any foe,' and 'bearing any burden' in defence of liberty.

It was all so simple, and so generous. South Vietnam was a small country that wanted to stay free, and its Communist northern neighbour was trying to conquer it. The South Vietnamese had asked the US for help, and we were helping. It was a little like the Peace Corps with rifles. The enemy, in any event, was often portrayed as little more than bandits, and if I wanted to fight there, I had better go soon or it would be over.

So I went. A lot of us did. More than one might think today. It was not a matter of any threat to this country. We all knew that. It was not a matter of any wartime-induced hatred of an enemy. It was something a male citizen of military age did, and nothing more.

The 9th Infantry Division that the army was building just then holds the record for the quickest activation and deployment to combat in American history. That record probably will never be broken. Fort Riley, Kansas, was empty since the 1st Infantry Division had already gone to Vietnam. The army made a skeleton unit with NCOs and officers drawn from all over the world, then filled up the ranks with trainees. We were C Company, 4th Battalion, 47th Infantry from the first day forward. We trained hard that spring, summer and fall of 1966. The training was over in December. Nearly everybody got leave time to go home for Christmas. On 4 January 1967 the main body of our brigade left Fort Riley railhead bound for Oakland, California. A lot of soldiers' families had come to see them off. It must have been terribly hard for them to say goodbye there. Still, there was something reassuringly familiar in it: flatcars loaded with jeeps and deuce-and-a-halfs (trucks), and armoured personnel carriers, and GIs with duffel bags getting aboard the troop cars − it was little different from what our fathers had done in the big war.

A couple of days later those of us in the 'advance party' (company and battalion commanders, and a lot of platoon leader lieutenants and NCOs) got on board Air Force C-141 cargo jets, the big hump-shouldered four-engine jobs, to make the flight to Vietnam by way of Alaska and Japan. The main body would board troop ships and spend nearly two weeks at sea.

You cannot put your finger on *esprit-de-corps*, but it is real. Without being aware of it, we had acquired it during the months of training together. There had not been a single AWOL (absent without leave) after the Christmas leaves, and we believed that we were ready and our morale was very high. It was Kansas winter when we loaded the C-141s, and after about 24 hours of flight time, we got off into the heavy tropical air of Vietnam. It was like walking into a warm, damp blanket. It was a bit past midnight, and the first breaths of Vietnam were a mix of jet exhaust, jungle and honest-to-God live artillery fire. We could see occasional tracers like red meteors on the horizon in any direction. We were in the war zone.

For three weeks or so we ran short operations out of an established base camp called Bear Cat. This was dry forest country that might have been Missouri, except for the heat and the size of some of the trees. We did not know it at the time, but it was also in a province where there were almost no enemy units. The time we spent here was time allotted for getting used to the climate and for learning the basics of navigating the terrain.

One day in February we left for Dong Tam in the Mekong Delta. This was the 9th Division's new base camp near My Tho, built by dredging the Mekong mud and pumping it into rice paddies to make dry ground. When we got there, we carried our duffel bags to the edge of the piled up mud, tossed them down and that was the perimeter defence. Within a few months, Dong Tam would be more than 600 acres, and General Westmoreland called it the place where you could be up to your knees in mud, and have dust blow in your eyes.

Down in the Delta is where the dying began. We had lost some men up to this time, a few to booby traps, some to accidents and a few more to gunshot wounds, but we were intact, really. We were the same battalion that had left Kansas. Now we met real enemy units, in company and battalion size, got into day-long fights and lost people in serious numbers. By late spring more than two-thirds of our original men were gone, either killed or wounded badly enough for evacuation.

There is no training that prepares a soldier for all of this. The shocking violence and visual horrors of infantry fighting are far beyond anything imaginable. Now we learned the cost, not just the known cost of casualties, but the cost of having trained together and become buddies. When we lost men, we lost brothers. Week after week, until the weeks were months, we lost friends, much of the time in ways too ugly to describe. The losses get to you sooner or later.

Sooner or later you realize that the real objective is simply survival. I was a squad leader and I keenly felt the responsibility for the lives of my men. The military mission did not matter much by this time. I would do what they told me to do, but no more, and that I would do as safely as possible.

But it was impossible to keep everybody safe. I lost men anyway. One of the terrible things about war is that it consumes the soul. When a close friend is killed or maybe has a leg blown off only feet away, it makes you sick with fear, and you rage inside at the waste and tragedy, and yet … and yet … from somewhere inside you hear a tiny voice saying, 'Better him than me,' and you know that it is true, and you know that you will do anything, anything at all, to stay alive. War burns away the veneer of what we call civilization, and shows you that the last 10,000 years really had not made much difference in what we are.

Losing men to wounds is one thing. Killing is quite another. The killing is the worst part of war. The memory of it never goes away. There is little to say about this, because it is utterly removed from any other human experience, and there are no comparisons to make. It is the killing that haunts me the most.

More than three decades since I fought there, Vietnam is still close to the surface for me. I remember the men and the battles and the horror and the ugliness and the fear. I see much of it every night before I sleep, and still have nightmares about it. Much of my life stopped in 1967. Perhaps it might have been different. Maybe it did not have to turn out so miserably. All such thoughts are idle, of course. The only thing that matters, after all, is that we learned from our experience. I think we did.

You cannot put your finger on post-traumatic stress disorder (PTSD) either, but it is real too. I had not heard the term until an army psychiatrist told me that I had it. Knowing there was a name for it did not do much good, but at least it was a start.

The army discharged me because of PTSD, but when I turned to the Veterans Administration for some kind of help, I was told that the VA did not recognize it. It was a sad and frustrating time.

Today I understand myself a lot better. I would rather live than die, and that is an improvement. I have always been secretly proud of my service in Vietnam, and I am glad that I went. Americans learned a hell of a lot during the Vietnam years, and I had the privilege of being a part of it. I am not sorry.

AHMED AND SAMIR, IRANIAN BOY SOLDIERS

The Iran-Iraq War 1980–88

Efraim Karsh

Of the many battlefield spectacles of the Iran-Iraq War, none has struck and confounded foreign observers more than the blind devotion of the Basij (an Iranian paramilitary force made up of volunteers) and their relentless quest for martyrdom. Coming mainly from rural areas or from the most devout Shi'ite families, these poorly trained and ill-equipped youths, some as young as 12, were little more than cannon fodder or human minesweepers sent in advance of Iran's other military forces to clear the fields, desert scrubland and marshes. With their red and yellow head bands proclaiming Allah's or Khomeini's greatness, a piece of white cloth pinned to their uniforms as symbol of a shroud, each one carrying his death with him, and a plastic key around their necks, issued personally by Khomeini as a symbol of their assured entry into paradise upon martyrdom, they charged towards the Iraqi positions in total disregard of the danger to their lives, and to the shocked disbelief of their enemies. 'They come on in their hundreds, often walking straight across the minefields, triggering them with their feet as they are supposed to do.' An Iraqi officer described the effect of these assaults on him and his men:

> They chant 'Allahu Akbar' and they keep coming, and we keep shooting, sweeping our 50 millimetre machine guns around like sickles. My men are eighteen, nineteen, just a few years older than these kids. I've seen them crying, and at times the officers have had to kick them back to their guns. Once we had Iranian kids on bikes cycling towards us, and my men all started laughing, and then these kids started lobbing their hand grenades and we stopped laughing and started shooting.

What was the source of this unqualified readiness for self-sacrifice? Were these child-warriors brainwashed by the authorities? Were they coerced? Not according to Ahmed, who was 14 when he volunteered to defend his homeland against the

Iraqi invasion. 'When Khorramshahr was recaptured by our troops in 1982, I made up my mind to go to the front,' he told a Western humanitarian aid worker who spent some time trying to help captured Basij boys in Iraqi prisoner camps. 'I wanted to defend my country, that's all.'

What about the concept of martyrdom? Did he join the forces with the explicit desire to martyr himself?

> I am not very religious so I don't know much about the subject. It's true that martyrdom is important to Shi'ites – we all learn about the Imams and how they died – but I didn't go to war to die for Islam. I went to defend Iran and I think most of my friends went for the same reason.

Was Ahmed, or anyone he knew, forced in any way to join up? The answer was an unequivocal no:

> In my case, my father and mother never wanted me to go to the front. Neither did my teacher. But I was determined to go. I've never heard any stories of mothers forcing their sons to join the basij. It was the opposite case with all my friends and I can't believe that a mother went on television to say that about her own child. My mother loves me and writes to me here to say how much she misses me and that she wants to see me again.
>
> I was so determined to go to war that I ran away from home. The first time I was sent back home because the officer said I was too young – I was thirteen at the time. The second time I tried was a year later when I was fourteen. I went to the local HQ of the basij. The officer told me that I had to be fifteen to join up, so I told him I was. He wanted to see my identity card, so I gave it to him, and he saw I was only fourteen. Then he asked what my parents had said, because he needed their permission if I joined before I was fifteen. I said they agreed and he allowed me to join up. There were hundreds of young boys pushing to get into the office that morning. All were very young, so the officer had no choice but to let us in.

Did he consider himself a victim of the regime? An innocent bystander lured into the whirlpool of war by the sheer weight of propaganda? Absolutely not, protested Ahmed:

> Of course there was a campaign to recruit men into the army. Our country was threatened by invasion. It's normal to want to defend it. So mullahs would come to the schools to talk to us and we watched military programmes on the television which told us what was going on in the war. But no one influenced my decision. At fourteen I could decide things for myself and I wanted to go to war, so I went. It was as simple as that.

Not all Basij fighters had such unquestioning patriotic zeal. Ahmed's fellow prisoner of war, Samir, had a far more disillusioned view of the Basij phenomenon and its motivation. 'It was a game for us,' he said:

> On the television they would show a young boy dressed as a soldier, carrying a gun and wearing the red headband of the basij. He would say how wonderful it was to be a soldier for Islam, fighting for freedom against the Iraqis. Then he would curse the Iraqis and all Arabs, saying they were not good Muslims. Next he would tell us to join him and come to war. We didn't understand the words 'patriotism' or 'martyrdom,' or at least I didn't. It was just an exciting game and a chance to prove to your friends that you'd grown up and were no longer a child. But we were really only children.
>
> At school there were always mullahs coming to speak to us and interrupting our lessons. The teacher didn't like them coming, but he was too afraid to say anything in case he lost his job. They talked about the glorious Islamic Revolution and the Ayatollah who had rescued us from the hands of the Americans. Then we would chant, 'death to America, death to Israel, death to Saddam' for a long time. The mullahs said it was an honour to go and fight for Islam and to be martyred for Islam, just like Imam Hussein [son of Ali, the Shia's patron imam]. I didn't want to die for anyone, but wanted to stay at school. My mother and father wanted me to stay at school, too. When I left for the war, my mother was crying. My father didn't say anything, but I could see he was very sad. My mother begged me not to go, holding and kissing me on the head, screaming for me not to go. My father had to pull her away to let me leave the house. I should have stayed, but all my friends were leaving, too, and I was excited about going. I had already done some training in the camp and I knew how to use a gun and throw hand grenades.

What did he think of the impact of the regime's wider propaganda effort, such as the screening of mass demonstrations by Basij warriors on television? Though not giving a definite answer, Samir's own experience would seem to vindicate the powerful pull of 'mob mentality' on the undecided individual:

> I took part in those demonstrations. They gave us red head bands to wear and we all stood in the square in the middle of Tehran… Twice there were TV cameras to film us. The mullahs were at the front, directing us. We would shout various slogans against Israel, America, France and, of course, Saddam, the President of Iraq. He was worse than the rest put together. After the slogans, the mullahs would address the crowds, telling us what an honour it was for us to be going to fight and die for Islam. I have no idea why I was shouting, since I don't have any bad feelings against America. Many Iranians live in America and Europe, so it can't be all that bad.

Looking back at the whole experience, did Samir deem it worthwhile? And should young boys be recruited for front-line fighting in the first place?

I am not sure, but it was difficult to stop them. And anyway, the boys who attacked the Iraqis were a very important weapon for the army, because they had no fear. We captured many positions from the Iraqis because they became afraid when they saw young boys running towards them shouting and screaming. Imagine how you would feel. Lots of boys were killed, but by that stage you were running and couldn't stop, so you just carried on until you were shot yourself or reached the lines.

I'm glad I was captured, even though it's very hard to live in the prisoner of war camps. But anything is better than dying. If I have a son I will never let him go to war until he is old enough to understand and make up his own mind. I was too young to fight. I was a little boy who wanted to play with guns. When they gave me a real one I'd never been happier. But when I went to fight and shoot people, I was petrified.

COMRADES AND CONSCRIPTS

The Falklands War 1982

Duncan Anderson

The soldiers who fought in the Falklands, Argentine and British, were literate and many kept diaries and subsequently wrote memoirs. There are several hundred such accounts, in Spanish and in English. Because the vast majority of the veterans are still relatively young (average age for an Argentine is 39, and for a British serviceman is 43) it would be invidious to single out any particular individual as typical. Rather, it is better to present their experiences as a compendium. Much was made of the fact that the Argentine Army was composed of nineteen-year-old conscripts but most Royal Marines and Paras were only a year or two older. This is not to suggest there was any equivalence in training, fitness or fighting effectiveness – there wasn't. But they were essentially young men fighting a long way from their homes in an alien environment.

Many Argentine troops came from the semi-tropical Correntias province in the far north. The conscripts of the 5th Infantry Regiment had only eight days of military service left when the Junta launched the invasion. When they received orders to fly to the Malvinas soldiers recalled 'a sort of party atmosphere – all your friends were going so you had to go too.' Another remembered that 'only our mothers were really worried and they were crying.' The 5th Regiment began flying into Puerto Argentino on 11 April. Very quickly the conscripts realised that despite the hastily imposed Spanish names they were in a foreign country. One was struck by 'how English it all looked. There was nothing Argentine there. I even remember picking up a box of nails which had "Made in England" on them.' The biggest surprise was the attitude of the people. Many were afraid and virtually all were unfriendly. The greatest success one Argentine had was 'to establish some communication with one of the locals in my broken English. We communicated like red-skins in the Westerns. "How You?"; "You buy"; "Is good". And he more or less understood me.'

Except for Tierra del Fuego, no part of Argentina is as cold, as windy and as wet as the Falklands. The Argentines were well equipped. They had excellent boots, and warm and generally waterproof parkas bought from the Israeli Defence Force. Those who stayed in Port Stanley – perhaps as many as 5,000 – had a reasonably comfortable time. But from about 1 May the majority had dug into static defence positions. An Argentine private recalled that 'we lived in foxholes and water kept filtering through the peat, so you would find yourself living in the water and ice with no dry clothing. You had to keep as dry as possible and try to eat as much as possible.' At first there was no difficulty but soon British air and naval interdiction began to interfere seriously with attempts to sustain the outlying garrisons, and it was not surprising that they ran short of food. Much more surprising was that many troops in the hills only seven miles from Stanley harbour should have existed for weeks at a time on cold composite rations. Argentine senior officers did hear their men's complaints, but dismissed them as the grumbling of 19-year-olds who were used to eating steak three times a day. There was some truth in this, but the fact remained that body-weight of many Argentine troops in front-line positions declined precipitously, something which should not have happened given that they were in static defensive positions.

Argentine front-line units spent an average of six weeks living in foxholes, during which a fatal torpor seems to have gripped many. On cold wet mornings they stayed in their sleeping bags inside their tents, and paid little or no attention to personal administration. It was up to the officers and NCOs to set and maintain a standard of efficiency, but they were sometimes amongst the worst offenders. The conscripts knew that they should be cleaning their equipment, shaving, washing and patrolling but they lacked the will to do these things. It was not part of their military culture. Many experienced sustained bombing and shelling, which should have shaken them out of their lassitude, but in many cases seemed to reinforce it.

> They would bomb us every night. They would start working their way down, and when they reached the end of our sector they would go back to the front and start all over again. The whole world would seem to be coming on top of you. There was a feeling of impotence, as if you were just waiting for death.

When they did try to counter-attack, it was clear their training was woefully deficient:

Then the order arrived for us to go down into the valley. We knew that we would be going into direct combat. Everybody was very agitated and we all talked at the same time. One talked about his sister, another about his college. Someone else talked about football, anything to evade the issue.

The contrast with the British troops could not have been greater. Unlike the Argentines, the Paras (The Parachute Regiment) and Royal Marines had a six-week voyage to get to the Falklands. The *Canberra* was a floating luxury hotel and the *Norland*, though not quite to the same standard, was comfortable. Six weeks on these ships should have destroyed the fighting efficiency of the Paras and Marines, but it turned out very differently. At the beginning of the voyage, the commanders and their physical training instructors did a computer analysis of every square foot of deck space and instituted a rigorous training programme. Two weeks out of Portsmouth, Lieutenant-Colonel Hew Pike, commander of 3 Para, recorded in his diary that the promenade deck of *Canberra*, solid teak two and a half feet thick, was beginning to crack under the impact of the regime. When the Marines and Paras landed at San Carlos they were fitter than they had been in Portsmouth.

At the same time as 3 Para was setting off on its 'tab' (march), 45 Commando was on its 'yomp' across East Falkland. The 'tab-yomp' was a feat of astonishing endurance. The ground underfoot was often peat bog, soft and springy, so that the heavily laden men sometimes sank up to their ankles. Their boots were soon soaked through. The soldiers' feet slid around inside their boots, rubbing the skin until it was raw and creating blisters. The weather alternated between brilliant sunshine and sudden drenching rain squalls, with the wind never dropping below about 15 knots. After dark the temperature dropped to below freezing and the rain fell as sleet, driven into the faces of the exhausted men.

Most British soldiers spent about two weeks in positions to the west of Stanley, during which time weather became steadily colder. Logisticians had dispatched thousands of arctic tents to the South Atlantic, but had placed most aboard the *Atlantic Conveyor* which had not yet arrived. With no prospect of tents for some weeks (the first actually arrived on 15 June), the troops improvised. While in transit to the Falklands, each man had been issued with a survival guide to the islands prepared by Major Ewan Southby-Tailyour, whose paper showed how many aspects of the apparently forbidding environment could be turned to advantage. The islands abounded with stones and peat, and soon some of the troops investing Stanley had built themselves a variety of shelters, many of which looked like Celtic roundhouses, and which were suprisingly effective. Lieutenant Tony Martin of the Royal Artillery recorded in his diary for 6 June: 'It rained through the night and all this morning. Still, I managed to keep dry in my little house.'

Food, too, proved to be less of a problem than at first feared. The islands have over 600,000 sheep, and all the settlements had potato patches, so that diaries were soon recording dinners of mutton and baked potatoes. The coast was a veritable supermarket, with unpolluted mussels and limpets on virtually every rock, and lobsters and crabs in the shallows. The major deficiency was in fresh vegetables and fruit, though scurvy grass, which grew all over the islands and is rich in Vitamin C, was eaten by the handful.

Unlike the Argentines, British morale remained high. Whenever they could, they attended to their personal administration, strip washing and shaving. They kept their weapons cleaned and oiled, patrolled aggressively and dominated the ground up to the Argentine positions. The single most important thing in sustaining British morale was the regular arrival of mail. Soldiers received letters not just from families, but from well-wishers all over Britain who wrote to express their appreciation and their pride. It was the first intimation many had that the eyes of the world were literally upon them.

As the time for the final assault drew near, the mood of the various regiments was very different. The Scots Guards and Gurkhas were eager to do battle, and the Welsh Guards, the victims of sinkings caused by Argentine aerial attacks at Bluff Cove, were positively thirsting for revenge. It was different with the Royal Marines and Paras, for they had now been in action. The mood, as distinct from the morale, of 2 Para, was instructive. On 13 June, as they moved towards the start line for the attack on Wireless Ridge, they were different from the men they had been only three weeks earlier. Then they had been anxious for action, as only professional soldiers who have spent their lives training for this eventuality can be. Since then they had been in a bloody battle and had helped treat the wounded of the Bluff Cove attack. Now there was to be none of the heroics of the attacks on Darwin and Goose Green. This battle was to be one of the most ruthlessly professional battles fought by the British Army in the 20th century. The chattering Argentine conscripts moving to meet them on the other side of Wireless Ridge didn't stand a chance.

LIEUTENANT ALEX VERNON, 24TH INFANTRY DIVISION (MECHANIZED)

The Gulf War 1991

Alastair Finlan

The Eyes of Orion (Kent, Ohio 1999) with permission of the Kent State University Press.

DESERT SHIELD

Lieutenant Alex Vernon was a typical example of a young officer who found himself (almost overnight) in the hot deserts of Saudi Arabia. His unit, the 24th Infantry

Division (Mechanized), was a core formation of CENTCOM (United States Central Command) whose role was to swiftly deploy to the Middle East in the event of a crisis. Like many competent but inexperienced junior officers (he had not yet faced the test of combat), Alex discovered, on hearing that he was going to deploy to Saudi Arabia, that many of his personal fears bubbled to the surface. The routine preparations for deployment brought with them the sense of the inevitable, as soldiers stood in line for inoculations and medical examinations, in other words being 'processed' for war – a deeply depersonalizing experience in which the individual becomes merely a military asset, to be cleaned, polished and used like a rifle. For a young lieutenant just a few years out of the elite West Point Military Academy, the prospect of going to war was an immensely challenging notion: would he perform well? would men under his command die because of him? All these thoughts loomed large in his mind prior to deployment. The 24th Infantry Division (Mechanized) prepared and loaded its tanks (literally stuffing the turrets with bags full of kit), putting them on ships lying in the Savannah River for the long trip to the Middle East. The troops themselves would then fly on to Saudi Arabia and await the arrival of their equipment. Just before boarding the plane, each soldier was offered a small Bible (Alex took one), a plastic bag containing water, sun cream with other small toiletries and a miniature American flag.

The heat in Saudi Arabia, 105 degrees Fahrenheit (40 degrees Celsius) in the late afternoon, was the first thing that hit the soldiers when walking off the plane at Dammam Airport. Their home for the next few days would be a tent city in the port itself while they waited for the fast merchant ships to arrive with their equipment. On 28 August, just over two weeks after sailing from the United States, the first ships arrived and the 24th Infantry Division (Mechanized) eventually deployed to a place called Assembly Area Hinesville, south of An Nu'ayriyah, on huge heavy-equipment transport systems (vehicles that carried tanks), 225 miles (362km) west of Dammam. Conditions were very difficult in the desert. Everyone was constantly sweating, the sand was too hot to touch and sleeping was often uncomfortable in the heat. The enemy was not so much the Iraqis but dehydration. It made the smallest task an effort, suppressed the desire to eat, made soldiers weaker and had the potential to kill if not constantly fended off by drinking huge amounts of bottled water. Then sandstorms (which often lasted for hours) would force the soldiers to take refuge as well as bake in their tanks (Abrams M1s) and afterwards have to clean the external weapons that were clogged with sand. The notion of having a quiet night's sleep outside the tanks was also dispelled by the threat of snakes and insects, which would get too close for comfort. From these very primitive conditions, tents, latrines and rudimentary showers would be slowly added to make life more bearable and, as the season changed to winter, one of the major problems would be the freezing nights as well as the odd rain shower. Food poisoning from local food was another environmental hazard, and at one stage 40 per cent of the troops in Saudi Arabia suffered from severe bouts of diarrhoea, caused by local bacteria and fortunately treatable with ciprofloxacin.

In his memoirs, Alex Vernon spends a great deal of time talking about the various methods of staying in touch with his girlfriend Maria and the family back in the United States. Telephones were initially rare, just a single phone by a gas station, until AT&T set up a 48-unit telephone bank in the nearby town of As Sarrar. He recalls one conversation:

> From the gas station the morning of 30 October I woke her, catching her completely by surprise: 'Al? ... Al? ... I love you ... I love you' – her first words to me. I still feel them, I wrote to her the next day. I still feel them as I write this sentence today. Outside the store an Arab civilian sat against the corner of the building with an automatic rifle, magazine inserted, and a magazine belt slung over his shoulder. Some American GIs drove by in a Mazda 626.

AT&T also provided a fax service that was used so much by Maria that she was dubbed 'the Desert Faxtress.' Soldiers tried all sorts of methods to make communication with 'back home' more real, and some experimented with voice recordings. But for many, it was just too painful to listen to their loved ones this way. Such was the fascination with receiving the mail that Vernon wrote his only poem about it:

A Desert Shield soldier, to his mistress

> Arabia offers a paucity of pulchritudinous pleasures:
> No bikinied bunnies on beaches,
> No glossy 2-D festal virgins.
> I receive a Playboy in a Pringles can:
> Americans cannot live without America,
> So my friends send this piece of her.
> Peace – her peace, her salaciously splayed solitude:
> Packages pour from her;
> She delivers.
> Only she slakes me:
> My odalisque, my Madonna;
> America, the beautiful.

OPERATION *DESERT STORM*

Alex Vernon's fears grew, naturally, as the likelihood of the ground offensive of Operation *Desert Storm* became more and more real. In an extract from a letter to Maria on 10 January 1991, he reveals the effect of the mounting pressure:

We are, it seems, bound for war. Greg says he is 'resolute.' Bob at least can smile. Matt has not changed. I am terrified.

I had three letters from Mom, all from Christmas time. I read them, in my tent, and started crying. I left the tent and ran into Lt Novak, who had come to visit. I chased her off, 'too busy packing.'

I am terrified. We are packing our gear. Most stuff the army will take from us in the next few days; it leaves us with our 'go to war' gear. All the latrines in the company but one, and all the showers and heaters but one, disappeared today. Tomorrow we begin wearing our chemical suits, flak vests, and steel pots as our regular uniform.

I cannot handle this. I am not cut out for it. All I want to do is cry. Nothing makes sense. I think I wrote earlier that knowing the plan set me somewhat at ease, because I knew something. Well I was wrong. Now I see that I know nothing of the future. Nothing. It is the most terrifying vision, this black hole of a future. It's sucking me close, and I cannot see through it, or behind it. I see pure blackness; that is my future.

Clearly, the strain of uncertainty about the future had come to the fore, and few soldiers in history can boast that they did not have such doubts on the eve of battle nor felt the helplessness of the individual in the face of powerful impersonal forces like armies. Despite his understandable worries, Vernon carried out his duty as an officer in the US Army and, on 24 February 1991, he rolled across the Iraqi border as part of 24th Infantry Division (Mechanized). In contrast to earlier letters, his account of an incident in the battle for Jalibah Airfield on 27 February reveals how professionalism replaced sensitivity while fighting:

I didn't see the sandbag-covered bunker directly in the tank's path until we were too close to fire it up with a HEAT round, and the coax machine gun would have been ineffective against such a deep and fortified position. I could try and dodge it, potentially screwing the formation behind us and allowing Iraqi infantry to pop out of the bunker after we passed, with easy shots at our rear; I could attempt to straddle the bunker, exposing the tank's thin underbelly to whoever inhabited the bunker; or I could order my driver to aim one tread at the bunker and squash it. 'Hit the bunker, Reynolds. Crush it.' We hardly noticed the bump.

Vernon passed the test of combat and during this battle was fired upon, hearing bullets bouncing off the hull of his tank. His 70-ton Abrams M1A1 tank was a powerful vehicle of war that fired 120 mm armour-piercing rounds (made from depleted uranium) that were called 'magic bullets' because they had such a devastating effect on enemy tanks.

The 24th Infantry Division saw a great deal of action in the Gulf War, led by their dynamic commander, Major-General Barry McCaffrey, and found itself not far from Basra by the ceasefire. A few weeks later, Vernon was on a plane back to America and the life that he had missed so much in the deserts of Arabia. For his service, he was awarded the Army Commendation Medal with V-Device (valour in combat) and left the army just a few months later. His own commentary about the effect of the war is revealing, yet familiar to many veterans:

> I returned from the war selfish. The world had robbed me, and now it owed me. I bought the convertible, gave Maria up, chased skirts, then spent the three months after my resignation unemployed, making and breaking and making and breaking an engagement to another woman. The next three years, finally in graduate school at the University of North Carolina at Chapel Hill, were very much a recovery from the war and postwar period of my life.

Dr Alex Vernon is now an Assistant Professor of English at Hendrix College in Arkansas.

LIEUTENANT-COLONEL BOB STEWART, UN WARRIOR

The Collapse of Yugoslavia 1991–99

Alastair Finlan

Lieutenant-Colonel Robert 'Bob' Stewart was the commanding officer of 1st Battalion, the Cheshire Regiment – one of the first British units deployed into Bosnia–Hercegovina in 1992. During his six-month tour of duty, Bob Stewart became synonymous in the international media with the ongoing conflict in the Balkans, and was often filmed negotiating with the various warring factions at checkpoints to ensure that humanitarian aid got through to the people who desperately needed it. The British Army selects commanders of battalions with great care, and Bob Stewart was a typical example of the sort of competent and highly confident officer chosen for such commands, with the additional bonus of a degree in international politics.

In September 1992, Lt-Col Stewart was summoned to the famous Main Building of the Ministry of Defence at the heart of the British political establishment in London. A wide range of officers had been gathered to discuss the parameters of the British Army deployment in the former Yugoslavia. During the course of the operations, a senior officer passed a note to Bob that read, 'It looks like a bag of nails.

Best of luck.' This meeting basically determined the likely base of the British operations, which was pencilled in as Tuzla (later changed to Vitez) and emphasised the need for a reconnaissance party to be sent in order to get first-hand knowledge of the terrain and the local conditions. Lt-Col Stewart noted with interest the level of vagueness concerning command and control of British units in relation to other UN forces, and also with regard to the all-important rules of engagement (ROE). Clearly a great deal would be left to 'the man on the spot,' and this fact merely heightened the importance of the reconnaissance mission that Bob would be part of the following week.

The 1st Battalion, the Cheshire Regiment, was actually based in Germany rather than the United Kingdom, in line with the former Cold War posture of placing sizeable amounts of NATO forces in West Germany to defend against a mass attack by the Warsaw Pact. A considerable amount of preparation had taken place in the light of the orders to redeploy to Bosnia-Hercegovina, in particular, spraying the normally camouflaged Warriors (armoured tracked fighting vehicles) with bright white paint, and issuing blue helmet covers for the troops. Setting up the main base at Vitez was not without problems and, inauspiciously, a huge storm blew up on the night that the bulk of the battalion arrived, destroying many of the carefully constructed tents that would house the troops until more substantial accommodation could be built. In addition, the impact of the severe weather on the local power grid resulted in the electricity being cut off from the base for nearly a week, forcing soldiers to resort to 'Tilley' lamps to work at night. Finally adding to these woes, the toilet system collapsed, which meant that the soldiers had to use buckets for nearly two months until a reliable sewage system was in place. It was not the best of starts to conducting operations in the Balkans at the height of a bitter winter.

Despite these teething problems, Bob Stewart's day-to-day routine consisted of ensuring the smooth running of his area of operations, which effectively required him to base several of his companies in outlying towns around Vitez. This in turn placed great responsibility on his subordinates, especially the more junior captains and lieutenants, who would be at the forefront of responses to incidents and emergencies in those outlying bases. As CO (commanding officer) of the battalion, Bob's responsibilities were very much centred on man-management and ensuring that the morale of his soldiers – from the most junior private soldier upwards – remained high. He did this by visiting his companies as much as possible, and was a familiar figure in his helmet and flak jacket on the front lines between the warring sides. A typical example of Bob's care for his men was illustrated by his actions on Christmas Day, which is probably one of the worst times for soldiers in a war zone, far from friends and family. Bob Stewart eased the burden by taking hot drinks laced with festive alcohol (toddies) to his men in their tents on the morning of that special day.

One of Bob's major technical problems that had enormous implications for operations, as well as morale when deployed in theatre, was that of communications. The British high-frequency radios did not work at night in Bosnia-Hercegovina, and consequently the troops were forced to use satellite telephones. However, this was not the most satisfactory of arrangements as most phones operated from fixed locations, normally base areas, and not moving vehicles. Consequently, if a platoon was engaged in an incident at a distance, then Lt-Col Stewart's ability to communicate with the platoon on a real-time basis was very limited and not the ideal command and communications arrangement for a CO in the field. Bob recalls his frustrations with the communications gear:

> … the high-frequency radio rarely worked and when it did we were never able to get through to the right staff officers, and the INMARSAT (satellite communications) was permanently 'clogged out' with fax messages. The result was that it sometimes took me over an hour and a half to get through to HQ BHC. And even when I did I was often unable to speak to the person I wanted. Command and control in such circumstances is obviously very difficult indeed.
>
> Furthermore, British soldiers needed to contact home on a regular basis to keep their spirits up. Fortunately, British Telecom donated 10 satellite telephone lines for the main base at Vitez, which allowed the soldiers a 10-minute phone call whenever they had access to the system.

The sorts of task facing the British soldiers were immensely demanding and varied in nature. Escorting humanitarian convoys could be a very slow process, with regular stops at checkpoints on all sides before eventually reaching the required destination. 'Crossing lines' (as it was called) was always a slightly tense situation. Occasionally convoys would be fired on and in return the Warriors would either return fire with their 30mm cannons or 7.62mm chain guns. Generally, such accurate fire tended to suppress whoever had taken a speculative shot at the convoy. Generating local ceasefires was an art form in itself and required the soldiers to get to know all commanders, regardless of affiliation. In the former Yugoslavia, such negotiations were usually accompanied by a local custom of drinking a powerful alcoholic drink called slivovitz, which could be dangerously potent in its 'home brew' variety. All sides, including the Bosniacs, drank it.

Occasionally, the Cheshires would recover bodies located in no man's land between the warring sides, and this was highly dangerous as well as distasteful work. Often the bodies had been rotting for days, particularly in the summer, and the soldiers would have to try to fit the contents into a body bag for ease of transport. In winter, such corpses would be frozen stiff. Minefields would have to be avoided, and snipers occasionally fired shots in the distance. Artillery in the form of mortars was one of the biggest concerns. Wounded civilians trapped in the fighting would also need medical care and again, soldiers proved very adept at offering simple first aid that could save a life, or at least stabilize a patient until they reached a hospital.

For Stewart, the death of one of his soldiers, Lance-Corporal Wayne Edwards, was probably one of the hardest moments of his tour of duty. At the time of the shooting, Bob was actually quite close to the incident, so he witnessed the soldiers frantically trying to get Edwards out of the driving position of the Warrior while under fire from snipers. He stood by them as they tried hard to resuscitate the wounded man. His memoirs record his impressions of seeing the body of Edwards in the medical room:

> Standing beside him I felt overwhelmed with guilt. I had brought him down here this morning from Vitez with the Standby Platoon. I had agreed to escort the ambulance through Gornji Vakuf. But, most of all, I was the Commanding Officer responsible for the safety of all members of the Battalion. I had failed completely. Utterly wretched and upset, I felt ill. I wept a little as I stayed with Lance-Corporal Edwards' body for what must have been a few minutes before Tracy came back.

Any commander with experience in the field knows that the death of a soldier obeying his orders is probably one of the heaviest burdens to carry – not for a day or a week, but forever. Stewart, however, was not given much time to dwell on the issue, as his unit was quickly involved in equally difficult circumstances when the Bosniac-Croat civil war blew up in the British zone. On hearing news about a suspected massacre in the village of Ahmici, Bob personally took a patrol of Warriors and discovered the grisly remains of the villagers and their animals. He recalls the ghastly scenes:

> The human remains on the floor probably did not look as disgusting to me as to others. To me they seemed a blackened, sometimes reddish mess. Here and there the outline of a body was recognizable. Two small bodies appeared to be lying on their stomachs, but their heads were bent backwards over their arched backs at an impossible angle. In one the eyes were not completely burnt. At first I was too shocked to notice the smell but then it hit me. God, I felt sick. I went outside and leant against a wall. The soldiers and I exchanged glances, saying nothing. There was nothing we could say to each other.

Holding together a unit that had witnessed these horrors was by no means an easy task for any commander, and to Bob's credit he managed to get the Cheshires through an immensely disturbing incident. In fact, one of his other patrols actually intercepted by accident a group of 150 Bosnians being taken to an area to be shot by Croatian soldiers. The British soldiers (without an interpreter) insisted on the people being escorted to another location, where they were saved. One of the key lessons that emerged from all these experiences was that if an incident arose, then deploying a peacekeeping unit quickly between the warring sides often helped to diffuse the situation.

The Cheshire battalion's tour of duty was over on 11 May 1993, and Bob Stewart took his men back home to Germany. It had been an immensely challenging operation that posed both physical and psychological risks for all those involved. The Cheshires gained valuable experience in what was arguably one of the most complex, and certainly the largest, UN peacekeeping mission in the history of the United Nations. This institutional knowledge was not wasted, and these lessons were passed on to other British units serving in the Balkans. Bob Stewart was awarded the DSO (Distinguished Service Order) after his tour of duty in the former Yugoslavia, and promoted to full colonel before retiring from the British Army a few years later. Today he is often seen on international news networks as a consultant offering advice on humanitarian missions and sharing his hard-won knowledge and expertise with a global audience.

INDEX